LIVING MAGIC

"I included nothing that failed to pass the test of gut reaction. 'The sound of the ax when it enters living wood,' as one poet put it; the feeling, in another's words, 'as if the top of one's head were being taken off.' Call it what you will, there is no other test of poetry," writes Selden Rodman, in explaining the principle of selection which went into the creation of this memorable anthology.

Here are poems of the past and of the present, of every variety of style and mood, tone and temper. But two factors unite them. All touch emotions as old as the human heart. And all shine forth on these pages forever new.

ABOUT THE AUTHOR: Selden Rodman's first book of poetry was published in 1932, and since has been followed by five other volumes. Mr. Rodman is also author of a number of books on art, history, travel, and music, while his notable anthologies of poetry have won him international acclaim. His *100 American Poems* and *100 Modern Poems* are also available in Mentor editions.

Other MENTOR Poetry Books

100
BRITISH
POETS

EDITED BY
Selden Rodman

A MENTOR BOOK
NEW AMERICAN LIBRARY
TIMES MIRROR
NEW YORK AND SCARBOROUGH, ONTARIO
THE NEW ENGLISH LIBRARY LIMITED, LONDON

FOR
Stanley Kunitz
Poet, Mentor, Friend

ACKNOWLEDGMENTS

ANONYMOUS: "A Woman's Message." Modern English version by Burton Raffel. From *Poems from the Old English*. Published by The University of Nebraska Press. Reprinted by permission of Burton Raffel.

AUDEN, W. H.: "Consider" and Number V of "Five Songs," beginning, "O where are you going?". From *Collected Shorter Poems 1927–1957* by W. H. Auden. Copyright 1934 and renewed 1962 by W. H. Auden. "Musée des Beaux Arts." From *Collected Shorter Poems 1927–1957* by W. H. Auden. Copyright 1940 and renewed 1968 by W. H. Auden. Reprinted by permission of Random House, Inc. and Faber and Faber Limited.

BELLOC, HILAIRE: "Lord Lundy." From *Cautionary Verses* by Hilaire Belloc. Published 1941 by Alfred A. Knopf, Inc. Reprinted by permission of Alfred A. Knopf, Inc. and Gerald Duckworth & Co., Ltd.

BRIDGES, ROBERT: "The Philosopher to His Mistress" and "Johannes Milton, Senex." From *The Poetical Works of Robert Bridges*. Reprinted by permission of The Clarendon Press.

(The following pages constitute an extension of the copyright page.)

MENTOR TRADEMARK REG. U.S. PAT. OFF. AND FOREIGN COUNTRIES
REGISTERED TRADEMARK—MARCA REGISTRADA
HECHO EN CHICAGO, U.S.A.

SIGNET, SIGNET CLASSICS, MENTOR,
PLUME AND MERIDIAN BOOKS
are published *in the United States* by
The New American Library, Inc.,
1301 Avenue of the Americas, New York, New York 10019,
in Canada by The New American Library of Canada Limited,
81 Mack Avenue, Scarborough, 704, Ontario,
in the United Kingdom by The New English Library Limited,
Barnard's Inn, Holborn, London, E.C. 1, England

FIRST PRINTING, JULY, 1974

1 2 3 4 5 6 7 8 9

PRINTED IN THE UNITED STATES OF AMERICA

Contents

Foreword

The last word in the title of this anthology was dictated by its contents. The intention had been to offer a companion to my *100 American Poems*,[1] a collection that made no compromise with the merely familiar or beloved yet tried to give the significant poets from Edward Taylor (1644–1729) to Bob Dylan (1940–   ) a fair sampling.

I should have known better. To do the same for verse composed in the British Isles from "Beowulf" (c.750) to "The Beatles" (c.1960) proved impossible. And not merely because of the longer time span. The fact was that until the 1920s American poetry was a country cousin of British poetry, at best an apprentice to the firm in which both the Scotch and Irish were junior partners. Barring Emerson, Whitman and Dickinson, the premodern Americans were more remarkable for frontier charm than consistent originality.

British poetry, in contrast, was incomparably rich. Of western literatures, only the Ancient Greek could compare with it, and only there within the strict canons of the lyric, epic and dramatic modes. Writing in the French, Italian, Spanish, German and Russian languages, there were outstanding *poets*, but they could be numbered in each case on the fingers of one hand. Shakespeare, by almost universal consent, towered over any of them. But would it be linguistic chauvinism to contend that Langland, Chaucer, Marlowe, Milton, Donne, Keats, Blake, Burns, Hopkins, Yeats, Hardy and Lawrence constituted a galaxy of major poets unmatched in any other literature?

True or false, there was no way of revealing British poetry through a mere hundred poems. I began to sense it one night, rereading a Shakespeare play that is not the most poetic. In *Macbeth* alone (and skipping the famous soliloquies) I found myself marking a dozen passages with which the very best

[1] Published in 1947 by The New American Library; revised 1972.

among the poets of the second rank (Spenser, Jonson, Dryden, Gray, Tennyson, Graves, for instance) could not stand comparison. For example:

> Come, seeling night,
> Scarf up the tender eye of pitiful day,
> And with thy bloody and invisible hand
> Cancel and tear to pieces that great bond
> Which keeps me pale! Light thickens, and the crow
> Makes wing to the rooky wood;
> Good things of day begin to droop and drowse,
> Whiles night's black agents to their preys do rouse . . .

> This guest of summer,
> The temple-haunting martlet, does approve
> By his lov'd mansionry that the heaven's breath
> Smells wooingly here: no jutty, frieze,
> Buttress, nor coign of vantage, but this bird
> Hath made his pendant bed and procreant cradle:
> Where they most breed and haunt, I have observ'd
> The air is delicate.

It followed that if only a hundred passages of such pure poetry were selected with a strictly qualitative measuring rod, a very large percentage would be rightfully usurped by this one poet, leaving space for only a handful of equally charged poems by Donne, Milton, Blake, Keats and Yeats. Clearly, it wouldn't be an anthology, nor would it convey any sense of the magnificent variety of British verse.

Without abandoning entirely the arbitrary round number—with its advantage of imposing some concentration within workable bounds—I therefore shifted my compass from poems to *poets*. There would be drawbacks. A certain amount of diffusion would be inevitable; many "minor poets" would have to be included. But this would be outweighed by the advantages. There would not be the lax usage of referring to passages from epics, plays or narratives as "poems." Shakespeare, moreover, could now be represented by almost all of his finest songs and sonnets, and by a sufficient sampling of speeches from one play (I chose the less-quoted *King Lear* because familiarity tends to deaden the shock of recognition) to give a cumulative unity of sorts. Milton's *Paradise Lost* could be excerpted in such a way as to display both the poet's awesome technique and the poem's content. There would be no difficulty in including the best of Keats, though I would have liked to have had the space to include

The Eve of St. Agnes, which proved unextractable. Nothing quintessential of Blake or Hardy need now be omitted. Langland, Burns, Wordsworth, Coleridge, Byron, Shelley, Browning, Hopkins, Yeats, Owen and Lawrence could be at least adequately represented. Moreover I would be able to include a dozen or two poets who wrote at least one poem, in some cases only one, of major quality. And I could even include a very few poets, like Spenser, Dryden, Swinburne, whose poems I have never responded to but whose styles were enormously influential in their time.

With this last exception, I included nothing that failed to pass the test of gut reaction. "The sound of the ax when it enters living wood," one poet put it; the feeling, in another's words, "as if the top of one's head were being taken off." Call it what you will, there is no other test of poetry. And the experience is as personal, and inexplicable, as the writing of the poem.

But though verbal magic is the *ne plus ultra* of poetry, to have this *only* (as with Lewis Carroll and Edith Sitwell, for instance) makes for a diet as spectacularly tiresome as Baked Alaska. The major poet is always at least as interesting for what he has to say as for how he says it. *Not* for what he has to say in terms of information, philosophy, social criticism, psychology—though he may be adept in one or all of these—but for his capacity to make us believe what he believes, see what he sees, feel what he feels, love what he loves, hate what he hates, *in terms of his art.*

This editor's choice is made as poet, not critic; and criticism, noble calling though it sometimes is, has no place here. Even in the Notes to the poems which come at the end, where they may be easily ignored, I have included mainly biographical information, random insights from such of the truly learned as had an ear for poetry, and such exclamations of surprise, wonder or joy as my own voyage of discovery-and-rediscovery elicited.

Anonymous (c.750)

From BEOWULF

MODERN ENGLISH VERSION BY BURTON RAFFEL

Introductory

That towering place, gabled and huge,
Stood waiting for time to pass, for war
To begin, for flames to leap as high
As the feud that would light them, and for Herot to burn.
  A powerful monster, living down
In the darkness, growled in pain, impatient
As day after day the music rang
Loud in that hall, the harp's rejoicing
Call and the poet's clear songs, sung
Of the ancient beginnings of us all, recalling
The Almighty making the earth, shaping
These beautiful plains marked off by oceans,
Then proudly setting the sun and moon
To glow across the land and light it;
The corners of the earth were made lovely with trees
And leaves, made quick with life, with each
Of the nations who now move on its face. And then
As now warriors sang of their pleasure:
So Hrothgar's men lived happy in his hall
Till the monster stirred, that demon, that fiend,
Grendel, who haunted the moors, the wild
Marshes, and made his home in a hell
Not hell but earth. He was spawned in that slime,
Conceived by a pair of those monsters born
Of Cain, murderous creatures banished
By God, punished forever for the crime
Of Abel's death. The Almighty drove
Those demons out, and their exile was bitter,
Shut away from men; they split

[1]

Into a thousand forms of evil—spirits
And fiends, goblins, monsters, giants,
A brood forever opposing the Lord's
Will, and again and again defeated. . . .

Grendel

. . . They named the huge one Grendel:
If he had a father no one knew him,
Or whether there'd been others before these two,
Hidden evil before hidden evil.
They live in secret places, windy
Cliffs, wolf-dens where water pours
From the rocks, then runs underground, where mist
Steams like black clouds, and the groves of trees
Growing out over their lake are all covered
With frozen spray, and wind down snakelike
Roots that reach as far as the water
And help keep it dark. At night that lake
Burns like a torch. No one knows its bottom,
No wisdom reaches such depths. A deer,
Hunted through the woods by packs of hounds,
A stag with great horns, though driven through the forest
From faraway places, prefers to die
On those shores, refuses to save its life
In that water. It isn't far, nor is it
A pleasant spot! When the wind stirs
And storms, waves splash toward the sky,
As dark as the air, as black as the rain
That the heavens weep. . . .

To the Sea

Then the band of Geats, young and brave,
Marching in their ring-locked armor, reached
The shore. The coast-guard saw them coming
And about to go, as he'd seen them before;
He hurried down the hillside, whipping
His horse, but this time shouted no challenge,
Told them only how the Geats would be watching
Too, and would welcome such warriors in shining
Mail. Their broad-beamed ship lay bobbing
At the edge of the sand: they loaded it high
With armor and horses and all the rich treasure
It could hold. The mast stood high and straight
Over heaped-up wealth—Hrothgar's, and now theirs.

[2]

Beowulf rewarded the boat's watchman,
Who had stayed behind, with a sword that had hammered
Gold wound on its handle: the weapon
Brought him honor. Then the ship left shore, left Denmark,
Traveled through deep water. Deck timbers creaked,
And the wind billowing through the sail stretched
From the mast, tied tight with ropes, did not hold them
Back, did not keep the ring-prowed ship
From foaming swiftly through the waves, the sea
Currents, across the wide ocean until
They could see familiar headlands, cliffs
That sprang out of Geatish soil. Driven
By the wind the ship rammed high on the shore.
Harbor guards came running to greet them,
Men who for days had waited and watched
For their belovèd comrades to come crossing the waves;
They anchored the high-bowed ship, moored it
Close to the shore, where the booming sea
Could not pull it loose and lead it away.
Then they carried up the golden armor,
The ancient swords, the jewels, brought them
To Higlac's home, their ring-giver's hall
Near the sea, where he lived surrounded
By his followers. . . .

Beowulf's Last Speech

   The battle-brave king rested on the shore,
While his soldiers wished him well, urged him
On. But Beowulf's heart was heavy:
His soul sensed how close fate
Had come, felt something, not fear but knowledge
Of old age. His armor was strong, but his arm
Hung like his heart. Body and soul
Might part, here; his blood might be spilled,
His spirit torn from his flesh. Then he spoke:
   "My early days were full of war,
And I survived it all; I can remember everything.
I was seven years old when Hrethel opened
His home and his heart to me, when my king and lord
Took me from my father and kept me, taught me,
Gave me gold and pleasure, glad that I sat
At his knee. And he never loved me less
Than any of his sons—Herbald, the oldest
Of all, or Hatheyn, or Higlac, my lord.
Herbald died a horrible death,

Killed while hunting: Hatheyn, his brother,
Stretched his horn-tipped bow, sent
An arrow flying, but missed his mark
And hit Herbald instead, found him
With a bloody point and pierced him through.
The crime was great, the guilt was plain,
But nothing could be done, no vengeance, no death
To repay that death, no punishment, nothing.
   "So with the greybeard whose son sins
Against the king, and is hanged: he stands
Watching his child swing on the gallows,
Lamenting, helpless, while his flesh and blood
Hangs for the raven to pluck. He can raise
His voice in sorrow, but revenge is impossible.
And every morning he remembers how his son
Died, and despairs; no son to come
Matters, no future heir, to a father
Forced to live through such misery. The place
Where his son once dwelled, before death compelled him
To journey away, is a windy wasteland,
Empty, cheerless; the childless father
Shudders, seeing it. So riders and ridden
Sleep in the ground; pleasure is gone,
The harp is silent, and hope is forgotten."

Anonymous

A WOMAN'S MESSAGE *(c.1000)*

MODERN ENGLISH VERSION BY BURTON RAFFEL

This song of journeys into sorrow
Is mine. I sing it. I alone
Can ravel out its misery, full-grown
When I was, and never worse than now.
The darkness of exile droops on my life.
His going began it, the tossing waves
Taking my lord. I was left in the dawn

Friendless where affection had been. I travelled
Seeking the sun of protection and safety,
Accepting the exile as payment for hope.
　　But the man's family was weaving plans
In the dark, intending to drive us apart
With a wedge the width of the world, condemning
Our love to a living death. I wept.
My new lord commanded me into a convent
Of wooden nuns, in a land where I knew
No lovers, no friends. So sadness was framed,
For I'd matched myself with a fitting man,
Born to misfortune, blessed with sorrow,
His mind close to me, mulling on murder.
How gaily, how often, we'd fashioned oaths
Defying everything but death to endanger
Our love; now only the words are left
And our friendship's a fable that time has forgotten
And never tells. For my well-belovèd
I've been forced to suffer, far and near.
　　I was ordered to live in a nun's-nest of leaves
In an earthen cavern under an oak.
I writhe with longing in this ancient hole;
The valleys seem leaden, the hills reared aloft,
And the bitter towns all bramble patches
Of empty pleasure. The memory of parting
Rips at my heart. My friends are out there,
Savouring their lives, secure in their beds,
While at dawn alone, I crawl miserably down
Under the oak growing out of my cave.
There I must squat the summer-long day,
There I can water the earth with weeping
For exile and sorrow, for sadness that can never
Find rest from grief nor from the famished
Desires that leap at unquenchable life.
　　May that man be always bent with misery,
With calloused thoughts; may he have to cling
To laughter and smiles when sorrow is clamouring
Wild for his blood; let him win his pleasures
Unfriended, alone; force him out
Into distant lands—as my lover dwells
In the shade of rocks the storm has frosted,
My downhearted lover in desolate hall
Lapped by floods. Christ, how he suffers,
Unable to smother swelling memories
Of a better place. There are few things more bitter
Than awaiting a love who is lost to hope.

[5]

William Langland (c.1332–c.1400)

From PIERS THE PLOUGHMAN

MODERN ENGLISH VERSION BY SELDEN RODMAN

Prologue

In a summer season, when soft was the sun
I dressed as a shepherd, all shaggy in bag-cloth:
The kind of a hermit who takes to the road
To see the world, wandering, in all its wonders,
Or pick up, in passing, the latest reports.
But on a May morning, in Malvern Hills,
From weariness of walking I fell asleep
And a strange thing happened, magical almost;
For weary of wandering, as I lay down
Under a broad bank by a burn's side,
I saw all the world's wealth and all of its woe,
The truth and the treachery, the treason smiling,
All in my sleeping, as I shall now tell you.
  Eastward I saw there, high in the sunlight
A tower on a hillside, constructed most cunningly,
And under it a cañon with a dungeon in it
Pitted and dark, and between these a plain:
A fair field of folk, going about their business,
Some rich and some poor, some ploughing, some sowing
With no time for pleasure, producing in their sweat
Enough for the squanderers, wasting as they wandered,
With those overdressed in the latest fashions.
Yet others seemed honest: their prayers and their penance,
Their working till sundown, were all for the Lord;
In hope to have bliss in the life after death,
Each of these kept to his task, as the anchorite
Keeps to his cell or the hermit his hovel,
With no anxiety to see or be seen
Or pleasure the body in lickerish living.

And some chose trade—the easy way out
For those with their eyes on earthly rewards.
And some made merry, as minstrels will,
And were well paid for it (guiltless, I guess)
Whereas others, children of Judas, made jokes
And told dirty stories, or posed as half-wits,
Clever enough to make an honest living
If they had to; their weakness I'll not weigh, but quote
St. Paul's 'The foul-mouthed are Lucifer's lackeys.'
  There I saw tramps, and beggars too, taking
Whatever their back-packs and bellies would hold,
Harranguing for hand-outs, hassling in ale-houses,
Ribald, besotted, and bedded down
Wherever Sleep happened (or Sloth) to seduce them.
  Pilgrims and palmers saw I at shrines
Or strung out from Rome to St. James Compostella,
Telling tall-tales enough to last a lifetime;
Hermits with hooked staves on their way by hundreds
To Walsingham, with their wenches in tow;
And aping them, even to their clerical habits,
Lubbers linked only by their hatred of work.
  There I saw Friars, of all four Orders,
Preaching for practical reasons, interpreting
The Scriptures as they chose, covering cunningly
With the colors of their capes their similarities;
For with Charity now so debased in the service
Of the lords, strange things are happening here,
And unless Holy Church shall chop down her betrayers
The world by their mounting mischief's undone.
  There preached a pardoner, pretending priesthood,
Who brought forth a bull with a bishop's seals,
Swearing that he would absolve them all
From falseness to fastings and broken promises.
The ignorant loved him. The laymen believed,
Kneeling before him, bussing his bulls,
He banged them with his brevet. He blurred their eyes,
Raking in their rings with his 'papal' parchment.
  So you give your gold pieces to gorge these gluttons?
You grant it to rascals, running after lechery?
Were the bishop devout and listening with both ears
His seal would not be serving to deceive the people,
Yet it's not by his leave that this rogue preaches
But the parish priest's, in the pardoner's pocket,
So that between them they divide the loot
Of the poor, who otherwise might be poor no longer.
  Parsons and parish priests complain to their bishops

[7]

That their parish has been poor since pestilence time,
Asking for time off, to loiter in London
And sing there for simony, for silver is sweet.
  Hangers-on by hundreds in silks stand swaying,
Sergeants-at-arms, lawyers babbling at bars,
Pleading their cases for fat fees, not for love
Of the Lord; you could easier measure the mist
At Malvern than get an opinion for free.
  Bishops I saw, and Doctors of Divinity
Taking mere clerkships to please the King;
Deacons and Archdeacons, preachers to the people,
Feeders of the hungry, now leaping to London
To serve the King's bench, not the courts of the countryside,
Barons, burgesses, bondsmen of thorps,
All I saw sleeping, as you shall hear shortly.
Bakers and brewers, butchers and such,
Weavers of woolen and weavers of linen,
Tailors and tanners, tillers of the earth,
Ditchers and delvers, alike in ill-doing;
Singers of low songs like 'Save you, Dame Emma,'
Cooks with their boys crying 'Hot pies, hot!
Fat pigs and geese for sale! Come and get it!'
Taverners trilling their wines of Moselle,
Gascoyne or Rochelle, or Rhenish for roasts.
  All this I saw sleeping—and seven times more.

From Passus 12: *The Poet, Rebuked, Responds*

"I am Imagination," he said, "I am never idle
Though I hold to myself, both in sickness and health
Following you faithfully, five years and forty,
Reminding you to remember your end,
The years that have vanished, the years still before you ...
Yet, for all this, you still play around
(Instead of reading your Psalter, instead of
Kneeling to those who nourish you) with your poems.
Are there not books enough already? Treatises,
Handbooks on how to be good, be better, be best?
And preachers to prove it? And friars praying in pairs?"
  Abashed though I was, I defended myself. "Did not Cato,"
I said, "though a man of learning, write poetry
To please his son—as I do? Did he not say
'Pleasures mix well with pains'? Did not even the saints
Indulge themselves sometimes to test out their truths?
Nevertheless, should someone truly illuminate
What *are* 'Do-well,' 'Do-better,' and 'Do-best'

Then I would give up this scribbling, cherish the Church,
Tell my beads all day long, and curl in my bed-roll . . .
   But meanwhile I shall praise Learning . . . For not by the
      shepherds
Only, but by the poets, was the angel seen!—
Bidding them take to Bethlehem the exultant tidings
Of the Lord's birth. Awake as they were to that glory,
While the rich lay in their beds and snored,
They sang their 'Glory-to-God-in-the-highest's,' their eyes
Dazzled by God's beautitude, while over the rim
Of the East came Men of Learning with their gifts for Him."

Anonymous

From SIR GAWAIN AND THE GREEN KNIGHT

MODERN ENGLISH VERSION BY BURTON RAFFEL

Gawain and the Temptress

   . . . She peered through the curtain, and courteous
Gawain gave her a warm welcome,
And she gave him back as good as she got,
Sat softly at his side, laughed lightly
And said, with a cheerful glance: "Ah sir,
Can you really be Gawain? Your soul reaches
Up for Goodness and Holiness, nothing
Else. Polite manners escape you;
Taught the truth you carefully forget it.
Yesterday I gave you instruction in the greatest
Of love's lessons, and today it's gone."
"What lesson?" he asked. "Tell me again:
Whatever I've lost the fault must be mine."
"And yet," said that lovely, "what I taught you was kissing:
Whenever a lady's looks ask it,
Claim it. That is courtesy, knight."
"Oh no," said that soldier, "you're wrong, my dear,
I cannot dare what I might be denied:

How wrong I would be to ask an unwanted
Kiss." "By our Lord," said that lord's wife,
"You're far too strong to accept a 'no'—
If anyone were boorish enough to deny you."
"You're right," Gawain exclaimed. "Except that
Force and threats are indecent, with friends,
And unwilling gifts are given in vain.
My lips are yours, to kiss on command,
Lady, as long as you like, or as short:
                    Just tell me."
            She bent to his face
            And kissed him well,
            Then they argued sadness and grace,
            Love's heavens and hells.

"Tell me, knight," said that noble lady,
"Without being angry, just why so young
And bold, so vigorous a man, so knightly,
So courteous—and your name is known far
And wide, and a knight's good name rests
Most on his loyalty to love, his learning
In its weaponry (and stories of love's true warriors
Are title and text inscribed in their love-deeds,
Risking their lives for a belovèd, enduring
In that great name great grief and pain,
Finally finding revenge and destroying
Sorrow, earning happiness in their true love's
Arms)—just why so young and handsome
A knight, so famous in your time, could find me
Sitting at your bedside, not once but twice,
And never reveal that your head could hold
A single word of love, not one?
A knight so ready with gracious vows
Should eagerly open his treasures to an innocent
Girl, teach her some signs of true love's
Skill. Hah! Is your heart unlettered
Despite your fame? Do I seem too stupid?
                    For shame!
            I've come alone, tame
            For the study of love's high game:
            Come, while we're still alone,
            Teach me till my husband comes home."

"Christ reward you!" said Gawain. "I can't
Tell you, lady, how delighted I am
That one so noble and knowing as you

Would come here, would care to sport with so humble
A knight, would grant me a single long glance.
But for to try to tell you true love's
Rules, repeat romances to you,
Knowing that you know everything I could say
And more, are wiser in love than a hundred
Like me could be if I lived to a hundred,
This would make me a hundredfold fool!
As best I can, I want to obey you;
This is my duty, now and forever,
To serve you, lady, so help me God!"
And so she tested him, pushed and probed,
Trying to tempt him, pretending love,
And Gawain so gracefully evasive that he seemed
Always polite, and nothing happened
                                    But happiness.
            They laughed and fenced,
            And at the end,
            Offering a courtly kiss,
            Off she went.

Geoffrey Chaucer (c.1340–1400)

From TROILUS AND CRESEYDE

MODERN ENGLISH VERSION BY BURTON RAFFEL AND
SELDEN RODMAN

Conclusion

Go, little book, go, my little tragedy
There where God, before your maker dies,
May send him, there to write some comedy!
But never, little book, never envy
Authors, bow to all great poetry,
Kissing the steps where Lucan walked, and where
Vergil walked too, and Statius, Ovid, Homer.

And since our English talks in many tongues,
Spoken and written, everywhere different, I pray

[11]

To God that no one, unknowing, scans you wrong,
Reads you aloud in some outlandish way—
But lettered, or read, or sung, it makes no difference,
So long as your sense is clear, oh God I beseech!
—And now, back to my story; I'd started this speech:

Troilus' anger, my story began to tell,
Cost the Greeks more than they had bargained for.
His quick hands sent thousands rolling to hell.
No one could match him, no one on the Trojan side
But Hector, while Hector could breathe and use his eyes.
But oh, he hung, all hangs, on God's sweet will
Whom fierce Achilles caught up with to kill.

And Troilus, after this fierce, this bitter death,
Ascended, a joyful spirit, a passing breath
Of light, high to the eighth and final sphere,
And earth, and water, and air, and fire stayed here;
And there he saw, and stared, and went on staring
At the erratic stars, and with his ears
Listened to the music of the heavenly spheres.

And then he turned, eager, anxious to watch
This tiny bit of ground, this earth, all washed
And held by the sea, and learn'd, at once, how botched
And miserable a world we hold, how couched
In heaven, he'd changed vanity for bliss, the best,
Most perfect bliss; and finally he sought
The field where his body lay, and stared, and thought.

And then he laughed and laughed, seeing the tears
Shed for his death, and the men who mourned his going;
And all we do for blind desire, or fear,
Or hate, or earthly love, is all unknown
In heaven, and heaven is all our hearts need know.
And off he went, to cut my story short,
To live where Mercury sets his house and court.

And that was the end of Troilus, who lived for love!
And that was the end of all his mighty virtue!
And that was the end of royalty, flown above!
And that was the end of desire, the end of worth, too!
And that was the end of earthly fickleness! And how
Troilus met Creseyde, how they loved, you've read
In this book, and how Troilus passed this life, now dead.

From THE CANTERBURY TALES

MODERN ENGLISH VERSION BY NEVILL COGHILL

Persons of the Prologue

There was a *Knight*, a most distinguished man,
Who from the day on which he first began
To ride abroad had followed chivalry ...
  He had his son with him, a fine young *Squire*,
A lover and cadet, a lad of fire
With locks as curly as if they had been pressed.
He was some twenty years of age, I guessed.
In stature he was of a moderate length,
With wonderful agility and strength.
He'd seen some service with the cavalry
In Flanders and Artois and Picardy
And had done valiantly in little space
Of time, in hope to win his lady's grace.
He was embroidered like a meadow bright
And full of freshest flowers, red and white.
Singing he was, or fluting all the day;
He was as fresh as is the month of May.
Short was his gown, the sleeves were long and wide;
He knew the way to sit a horse and ride.
He could make songs and poems and recite,
Knew how to joust and dance, to draw and write.
He loved so hotly that till dawn grew pale
He slept as little as a nightingale.
Courteous he was, lowly and serviceable,
And carved to serve his father at the table ...
  There also was a *Nun*, a Prioress,
Her way of smiling very simple and coy.
Her greatest oath was only 'By St Loy!'
And she was known as Madam Eglantyne.
And well she sang a service, with a fine
Intoning through her nose, as was most seemly,
And she spoke daintily in French, extremely,
After the school of Stratford-atte-Bowe;
French in the Paris style she did not know.
At meat her manners were well taught withal;
No morsel from her lips did she let fall,
Nor dipped her fingers in the sauce too deep;

But she would carry a morsel up and keep
The smallest drop from falling on her breast.
For courtliness she had a special zest,
And she would wipe her upper lip so clean
That not a trace of grease was to be seen
Upon the cup when she had drunk; to eat,
She reached a hand sedately for the meat.
She certainly was very entertaining,
Pleasant and friendly in her ways, and straining
To counterfeit a courtly kind of grace,
A stately bearing fitting to her place,
And to seem dignified in all her dealings.
As for her sympathies and tender feelings,
She was so charitably solicitous
She used to weep if she but saw a mouse
Caught in a trap, if it were dead or bleeding.
And she had little dogs she would be feeding
With roasted flesh, or milk, or fine white bread.
And bitterly she wept if one were dead
Or someone took a stick and made it smart;
She was all sentiment and tender heart.
Her veil was gathered in a seemly way,
Her nose was elegant, her eyes glass-grey;
Her mouth was very small, but soft and red,
Her forehead, certainly, was fair of spread,
Almost a span across the brows, I own;
She was indeed by no means undergrown.
Her cloak, I noticed, had a graceful charm.
She wore a coral trinket on her arm,
A set of beads, the gaudies tricked in green,
Whence hung a golden brooch of brightest sheen
On which there first was graven a crowned A,
And lower, *Amor vincit omnia* . . .

There was a *Friar*, a wanton one and merry,
A Limiter, a very festive fellow.
In all Four Orders there was none so mellow
So glib with gallant phrase and well-turned speech.
He'd fixed up many a marriage, giving each
Of his young women what he could afford her.
He was a noble pillar to his Order.
High beloved and intimate was he
With County folk within his boundary,
And city dames of honour and possessions;
For he was qualified to hear confessions,
Or so he said, with more than priestly scope
He had a special licence from the Pope.

Sweetly he heard his penitents at shrift
With pleasant absolution, for a gift.
He was an easy man in penance-giving
Where he could hope to make a decent living;
It's a sure sign whenever gifts are given
To a poor Order that a man's well shriven,
And should he give enough he knew in verity
The penitent repented in sincerity.
For many a fellow is so hard of heart
He cannot weep, for all his inward smart.
Therefore instead of weeping and of prayer
One should give silver for a poor Friar's care.
He kept his tippet stuffed with pins for curls,
And pocket-knives to give to pretty girls.
And certainly his voice was gay and sturdy,
For he sang well and played the hurdy-gurdy.
At sing-songs he was champion of the hour.
His neck was whiter than a lily-flower
But strong enough to butt a bruiser down.
He knew the taverns well in every town
And every innkeeper and barmaid too
Better than lepers, beggars and that crew,
For in so eminent a man as he
It was not fitting with the dignity
Of his position, dealing with the scum
Of wretched lepers; nothing good can come
Of dealings with the slum-and-gutter dwellers,
But only with the rich and victual-sellers.
But anywhere a profit might accrue
Courteous he was and lowly of service too.
Natural gifts like his were hard to match.
He was the finest beggar of his batch,
And, for his begging-district, payed a rent;
His brethren did no poaching where he went.
For though a widow mightn't have a shoe,
So pleasant was his holy how-d'ye-do
He got his farthing from her just the same
Before he left, and so his income came
To more than he laid out. And how he romped,
Just like a puppy! He was ever prompt
To arbitrate disputes on settling days
(For a small fee) in many helpful ways,
Not then appearing as your cloistered scholar
With threadbare habit hardly worth a dollar,
But much more like a Doctor or a Pope.
Of double-worsted was the semi-cope

Upon his shoulders, and the swelling fold
About him, like a bell about its mould
When it is casting, rounded out his dress.
He lisped a little out of wantonness
To make his English sweet upon his tongue.
When he had played his harp, or having sung,
His eyes would twinkle in his head as bright
As any star upon a frosty night . . .

There was a *Skipper* hailing from far west;
He came from Dartmouth, so I understood.
He rode a farmer's horse as best he could,
In a woolen gown that reached his knee.
A dagger on a lanyard falling free
Hung from his neck under his arm and down.
The summer heat had tanned his colour brown,
And certainly he was an excellent fellow.
Many a draught of vintage, red and yellow,
He'd drawn at Bordeaux, while the trader snored.
The nicer rules of conscience he ignored.
If, when he fought, the enemy vessel sank,
He sent his prisoners home: they walked the plank.
As for his skill in reckoning his tides,
Currents and many another risk besides,
Moons, harbours, pilots, he had such dispatch
That none from Hull to Carthage was his match.
Hardy he was, prudent in undertaking;
His beard in many a tempest had its shaking,
And he knew all the havens as they were
From Gottland to the Cape of Finisterre . . .

A *Doctor* too emerged as we proceeded;
No one alive could talk as well as he did
On points of medicine and of surgery,
For, being grounded in astronomy,
He watched his patient's favorable star
And, by his Natural Magic, knew what are
The lucky hours and planetary degrees
For making charms and magic effigies.
The cause of every malady you'd got
He knew, and whether dry, cold, moist or hot;
He knew their seat, their humour and condition.
He was a perfect practising physician.
These causes being known for what they were
He gave the man his medicine then and there.
All his apothecaries in a tribe
Were ready with the drugs he would prescribe
And each made money from the other's guile;

[16]

They had been friendly for a goodish while.
He was well-versed in Aesculapius too
And what Hippocrates and Rufus knew
And Dioscorides, now dead and gone,
Galen and Rhazes, Hali, Serapion,
Averroes, Avicenna, Constantine,
Scotch Bernard, John of Gaddesden, Gilbertine.
In his own diet he observed some measure;
There were not superfluities for pleasure,
Only digestives, nutritives and such.
He did not read the Bible very much.
In blood-red garments, slashed with bluish-grey
And lined with taffeta, he rode his way;
Yet he was rather close as to expenses
And kept the gold he won in pestilences.
Gold stimulates the heart, or so we're told.
He therefore had a special love of gold . . .

The *Miller* was a chap of sixteen stone,
A great stout fellow big in brawn and bone.
He did well out of them, for he could go
And win the ram at any wrestling show.
Broad, knotty, and short-shouldered, he would boast
He could have any door off hinge and post
Or take a run and break it with his head.
His beard, like any sow or fox, was red
And broad as well, as though it were a spade;
And at its very tip his nose displayed
A wart on which there stood a tuft of hair
Red as the bristles in an old sow's ear.
His nostrils were as black as they were wide.
He had a sword and buckler at his side.
His mighty mouth was like a furnace door.
A wrangler and buffoon, he had a store
Of tavern stories, filthy in the main.
He was a master-hand at stealing grain.
He felt it with his thumb and thus he knew
Its quality and took three times his due—
A thumb of gold, by God, to gauge an oat!
He wore a hood of blue and a white coat.
He liked to play his bagpipes up and down
And that was how he brought us out of town . . .

There was a *Summoner* with us in the place
Who had a fire-red cherubinnish face,
For he had carbuncles. His eyes were narrow.
He was as hot and lecherous as a sparrow.

Black, scabby brows he had, and a thin beard.
Children were afraid when he appeared ...
  He and a gentle *Pardoner* rode together
A bird from Charing Cross of the same feather,
Just back from visiting the Court of Rome.
He loudly sang *'Come hither, love, come home!'*
The Summoner sang deep seconds to this song,
No trumpet ever sounded half so strong.
This Pardoner had hair as yellow as wax,
Hanging down smoothly like a hank of flax.
In driblets fell his locks behind his head
Down to his shoulders which they overspread;
Thinly they fell, like rat-tails, one by one.
He wore no hood upon his head, for fun;
The hood inside his wallet had been stowed,
He aimed at riding in the latest mode;
But for a little cap his head was bare
And he had bulging eye-balls, like a hare.
He'd sewed a holy relic on his cap;
His wallet lay before him on his lap,
Brimful of pardons come from Rome all hot.
He had the same small voice a goat has got.
His chin no beard had harboured, nor would harbour,
Smoother than chin was ever left by barber.
I judge he was a gelding, or a mare.
As to his trade, from Berwick down to Ware
There was no Pardoner of equal grace,
For in his trunk he had a pillow-case
Which he asserted was Our Lady's veil.
He said he had a gobbet of the sail
Saint Peter had the time when he made bold
To walk the waves—till Jesus Christ took hold.
He had a cross of metal set with stones
And in a glass, a rubble of pigs' bones.
And with these relics, any time he found
Some poor up-country parson to astound,
On one short day, in money down, he drew
More than the parson in a month or two,
And by his flatteries and prevarication
Made monkeys of the priest and congregation.
But still to do him justice first and last
In church he was a noble ecclesiast.
How well he read a lesson or told a story!
But best of all he sang an Offertory,
For well he knew that when that song was sung
He'd have to preach and tune his honey-tongue

And (well he could) win silver from the crowd.
That's why he sang so merrily and loud.

From *The Knight's Tale*

In the third hour after Palamon
Had sought out Venus for his orison,
Up rose the sun, and up rose Emily
And hastened to Diana's sanctuary,
Taking such maidens as she might require
And they were ready furnished with the fire,
The incense and the vestments and a throng
Of other necessaries that belong
To sacrifices, horns of brimming mead,
As was the custom, all that they could need.
The Temple smoked and the adornments there
Glittered in beauty. Emily the fair
Joyfully washed her body in a well,
But how she did her rite I dare not tell
Save in a general way, though I for one
Think that to hear the detail would be fun.
If one means well why bother to feel queasy?
It's good for people to be free and easy.
Her shining hair untressed upon her cloak
They combed, and set a crown of cerrial oak
Green on her golden head with fitting grace.
Two fires she kindled in the proper place
And did her rites, as he will find who looks
In Statius' *Book of Thebes* and other books,
And when the fires were kindled she drew near
With piteous heart, and prayed as you shall hear:
   'O Goddess Chaste of all the woodlands green,
That seest earth and heaven and sea, O Queen
Of Pluto's kingdom, dark and deep below,
Goddess of virgins that from long ago
Hast known my heart, and knowest my desire,
As I may shun the vengeance of thine ire
Such as upon Actaeon once was spent,
Thou knowest well, O chaste omnipotent,
That I would be a virgin all my life
And would be neither mistress, no, nor wife,
I am, thou knowest, of thy company,
A huntress, still in my virginity,
And only ask to walk the woodlands wild,
And not to be a wife or go with child,
Nor would I know the company of man.

O help me, Goddess, for none other can,
By the three Forms that ever dwell in thee,
And as for Palamon who longs for me
And for Arcita's passion, I implore
This favour of thy grace and nothing more;
Set them in amity and let them be
At peace, and turn their hearts away from me.
Let all their violent loves and hot desires,
Their ceaseless torments and consuming fires,
Be quenched, or turned towards another face.
Yet if thou wilt not do me so much grace,
Or if my destiny ordains it so
That one shall have me whether I will or no,
Then send me him that shall desire me most . . .'

From *The Wife of Bath's Prologue*

'If there were no authority on earth
Except experience; mine, for what it's worth,
And that's enough for me, all goes to show
That marriage is a misery and woe;
For let me say, if I may make so bold,
My lords, since when I was but twelve years old,
Thanks be to God Eternal evermore,
Five husbands have I had at the church door;
Yet, it's a fact that I have had so many,
All worthy in their way, as good as any.
   'Someone said recently for my persuasion
That as Christ only went on one occasion
To grace a wedding—in Cana of Galilee—
He taught me by example there to see
That it is wrong to marry more than once.
Consider, too, how sharply, for the nonce,
He spoke, rebuking the Samaritan
Beside the well, Christ Jesus, God and man.
"Thou has had five men husband unto thee
And he that even now thou hast," said He,
"Is not thy husband." Such the words that fell;
But what He meant thereby I cannot tell.
Why was her fifth—explain it if you can—
No lawful spouse to the Samaritan?
How many might have had her then to wife?
I've never heard an answer all my life
To give the number final definition.
People may guess or frame a supposition,
But I can say for certain, it's no lie,

God bade us all to wax and multiply.
That kindly text I well can understand.
Is not my husband under God's command
To leave his father and mother and take me?
No word of what the number was to be,
Then why not marry two or even eight?
And why speak evil of the married state?
    'Take wise King Solomon of long ago;
We hear he had a thousand wives or so.
And would to God it were allowed to me
To be refreshed, aye, half as much as he!
He must have had a gift of God for wives,
No one to match him in a world of lives!
This noble king, one may as well admit,
On the first night threw many a merry fit
With each of them, he was so much alive.
Blessed be God that I have wedded five!
Welcome the sixth, whenever he appears.
I can't keep continent for years and years.
No sooner than one husband's dead and gone
Some other christian man shall take me on,
For then, so says the Apostle, I am free
To wed, o'God's name, where it pleases me.
Wedding's no sin, so far as I can learn.
Better it is to marry than to burn . . .
    'Tell me to what conclusion or in aid
Of what were generative organs made?
And for what profit were those creatures wrought?
Trust me, they cannot have been made for naught.
Gloze as you will and plead the explanation
That they were only made for the purgation
Of urine, little things of no avail
Except to know a female from a male,
And nothing else. Did somebody say no?
Experience knows well it isn't so.
The learned may rebuke me, or be loath
To think it so, but they were made for both,
That is to say both use and pleasure in
Engendering, except in case of sin.
Why else the proverb written down and set
In books: "A man must yield his wife her debt"?
What means of paying her can he invent
Unless he use his silly instrument?
It follows they were fashioned at creation
Both to purge urine and for procreation . . .
In wifehood I shall use my instrument

[21]

As freely as my Maker me it sent.
If I turn difficult, God give me sorrow!
Whenever he likes to come and pay his debt,
I won't prevent him! I'll have a husband yet
Who shall be both my debtor and my slave
And bear his tribulation to the grave
Upon his flesh, as long as I'm his wife.
For mine shall be the power all his life
Over his proper body, and not he
Thus the Apostle Paul has told it me,
And bade our husbands they should love us well;
There's a command on which I like to dwell . . .

'When my fourth husband lay upon his bier
I wept all day and looked as drear as drear,
As widows must, for it is quite in place,
And with a handkerchief I hid my face.
Now that I felt provided with a mate
I wept but little, I need hardly state.

'To church they bore my husband on the morrow
With all the neighbours round him venting sorrow,
And one of them of course was handsome Johnny.
So help me God, I thought he looked so bonny
Behind the coffin! Heavens, what a pair
Of legs he had! Such feet, so clean and fair!
I gave my whole heart up, for him to hold.
He was, I think, some twenty winters old,
And I was forty then, to tell the truth.
But still, I always had a coltish tooth.
Yes, I'm gap-toothed; it suits me well I feel,
It is the print of Venus and her seal.
So help me God I was a lusty one,
Fair, young and well-to-do, and full of fun!
And truly, as my husbands said to me
I had the finest *quoniam* that might be.
For Venus sent me feeling from the stars
And my heart's boldness came to me from Mars.
Venus gave me desire and lecherousness
And Mars my hardihood, or so I guess,
Born under Taurus and with Mars therein.
Alas, alas, that ever love was sin!
I ever followed natural inclination
Under the power of my constellation
And was unable to deny, in truth,
My chamber of Venus to a likely youth.
The mark of Mars is still upon my face
And also in another privy place.

For as I may be served by God above,
I never used discretion when in love
But ever followed on my appetite,
Whether the lad was short, long, black or white.

William Dunbar (1460?–1520?)

OF THE CHANGES OF LIFE

MODERN ENGLISH VERSION BY ANDREW GLAZE

I seek about this world unstable
to find one faithful moral fable,
but I can not for all my wit
so true one maxim find of it
but say, it is deceivable.

For yesterday I did declare
how that the season soft and fair
came in as fresh as peacock feather.
This day it stings me like an adder.
Things conclude me *au contraire*.

Yesterday fair upsprang the flowers,
this day they are all slain with shears;
and fowls in forests that sang clear
now wake up with a dreary cheer.
Full cold are both their beds and bowers.

Next after summer, winter lean,
next after comfort, care keen;
next to dark midnight, mirthful morrow;
next after joy cometh sorrow.
So is this world, and ever has been.

LAMENT FOR THE POETS

MODERN ENGLISH VERSION BY ANDREW GLAZE AND
SELDEN RODMAN

I that in health was, and gladness,
am troubled now with a great sickness
and feebled with infirmity.
Timor mortis conturbat me.

And pleasures here are all vain glory,
this false world is but transitory,
the flesh is feeble, the Fiend wily.
Timor mortis conturbat me.

The state of man does change and vary,
now sound, now sick, now blithe, now sorry,
now dancing merry, now ceasing to be.
Timor mortis conturbat me.

No state on earth stands as certain;
As with the wind waveth the curtain,
waveth this world, and its vanity.
Timor mortis conturbat me.

On to the dead go all Estates,
Princes, Prelates, Potentates,
rich and poor of every degree.
Timor mortis conturbat me.

He taketh the knight up from the field,
enamored under helm and shield,
victor though he at each melée.
Timor mortis conturbat me.

That alien merciless dynast
takes, even at the mother's breast,
the suckling babe, all innocent he.
Timor mortis conturbat me.

He takes the champion in the fight,
the captain armoured on his height,

the lady bowered in all her beauty.
Timor mortis conturbat me.

Clever magicians, cosmic quacks,
logicians, holy doctors, hacks,
give up—no matter how they try.
Timor mortis conturbat me.

Those who make the big decisions,
leeches, surgeons, all physicians,
themselves from death they cannot free.
Timor mortis conturbat me.

I see the poet, like the knave
playing his pageant, go to the grave:
Death spares him not for his degree.
Timor mortis conturbat me.

Did Death not pitilessly devour
the noble Chaucer, the lesser Gower,
not to mention the Monk of Berry?
Timor mortis conturbat me.

The good Sir Hugh of Eglinton
and also Heryot and also Wyntoun
he has removed from this country.
Timor mortis conturbat me.

That scorpion foul has cut the neck
of Master John Clerk and James Affleck
from ballad-making and tragedy.
Timor mortis conturbat me.

Holland and Barber he did bereave,
alack! and did not with us leave
Sir Mungo Lockhart of the Lee.
Timor mortis conturbat me.

Clerk of Tranent he has slain
that made 'The Adventures of Sir Gawain';
and Sir Gilbert Hay concluded has he.
Timor mortis conturbat me.

He has Blind Harry and Sandy Traill
slain with his shower of mortal hail,

while Patrick Johnston might not flee.
Timor mortis conturbat me.

Mercer he plunged into the night
that did of love so blithely write:
such short, such quick high thoughts had he:
Timor mortis conturbat me.

He has taken Reuel of Aberdeen,
and gentle Reuel of Corstophine:
two better fellows did no man see.
Timor mortis conturbat me.

In Dumfermline his talk is done
with Master Robert Henryson;
Sir John the Ross embrac'd has he.
Timor mortis conturbat me.

And he has now taken, last of all,
Gentle Stobo and Quentin Schall,
for whom all men of strength have pity.
Timor mortis conturbat me.

Good Master Walter Kennedy
at the point of death lies presently:
Great sorrow that it should have to be.
Timor mortis conturbat me.

Since he hath with my brethren flown
he will not let me live alone.
Perforce I must his next prey be.
Timor mortis conturbat me.

And since for death there is no cure,
best is that we for death prepare,
that after death we may still be.
Timor mortis conturbat me.

John Skelton (c.1460–1529)

GUP, SCOT

Gup, Scot,
Ye blot;
Laudate
Caudate,
Set in better
Thy pentameter.
This Dundas,
This Scottishe asse,
He rymes and railes
That Englishmen have tailes.

. . . . . .

Skelton laureat
After this rate
Defendeth with his pen
All English men
Agayn Dundas,
That Scottishe asse.
Shake thy tale, Scot, lyke a cur,
For thou beggest at every mannes dur:
Tut, Scot, I sey,
Go shake thy dog, hey!

. . . . . .

Dundas, dronken and drowsy,
Skabed, scurvy, and lowsy,
Of unhappy generacion
And most ungracious nation.
Dundas,
That dronke asse,
That ratis and rankis,
That prates and prankes
On Huntley bankes,

Take this our thankes;
Dunde, Dunbar,
Walke, Scot,
Walke, sot,
Rayle not so far.

Sir Thomas Wyatt (1503–1542)

VIXI PUELLIS NUPER IDONEUS . . .

They flee from me that sometime did me seek,
　With naked foot stalking within my chamber:
Once have I seen them gentle, tame, and meek,
　That now are wild, and do not once remember
　That sometime they have put themselves in danger
To take bread at my hand; and now they range,
Busily seeking in continual change.

Thankèd be fortune, it hath been otherwise
　Twenty times better; but once especial—
In thin array: after a pleasant guise,
　When her loose gown did from her shoulders fall,
　And she me caught in her arms long and small,
And therewithal so sweetly did me kiss,
And softly said, *'Dear heart, how like you this?'*

It was no dream; for I lay broad awaking:
　But all is turn'd now, through my gentleness,
Into a bitter fashion of forsaking;
　And I have leave to go of her goodnèss;
　And she also to use new-fangleness.
But since that I unkindly so am servèd,
'How like you this?'—what hath she now deservèd?

[28]

Sir Philip Sidney (1554–1586)

From ASTROPHEL AND STELLA

1

Loving in truth, and fain in verse my love to show,
That she, dear she, might take some pleasure of my
    pain:
Pleasure might cause her read, reading might make her
    know,
Knowledge might pity win, and pity grace obtain,
    I sought fit words to paint the blackest face of woe,
Studying inventions fine, her wits to entertain:
Oft turning others' leaves, to see if thence would flow
Some fresh and fruitful showers upon my sun-burn'd
    brain.
    But words came halting forth, wanting Invention's
    stay,
Invention Nature's child, fled step-dame Study's blows,
And others' feet still seem'd but strangers in my way.
Thus great with child to speak, and helpless in my
    throes,
    Biting my truant pen, beating myself for spite,
    Fool, said my Muse to me, look in thy heart and
    write.

31

With how sad steps, O moon, thou climb'st the skies,
    How silently, and with how wan a face,
    What may it be, that even in heav'nly place
That busy archer his sharp arrows tries?
Sure if that long-with-love-acquainted eyes
    Can judge of love, thou feel'st a lover's case;

I read it in thy looks, thy languisht grace
To me that feel the like, thy state descries.
    Then ev'n of fellowship, O moon, tell me
Is constant love deem'd there but want of wit?
Are beauties there as proud as here they be?
Do they above love to be lov'd, and yet
    Those lovers scorn whom that love doth possess?
    Do they call Virtue there ungratefulness?

107

Stella since thou so right a princess art
    Of all the powers which life bestows on me,
    That ere by them ought undertaken be,
They first resort unto that sovereign part;
Sweet, for a while give respite to my heart,
    Which pants as though it still should leap to thee:
    And on my thoughts give the lieftenancy
To this great cause, which needs both use and art.
    And as a queen, who from her presence sends
Whom she employs, dismiss from thee my wit,
Till it have wrought what thy own will attends.
On servant's shame oft master's blame doth sit;
    O let not fools in me thy works reprove,
    And scorning say, 'See what it is to love.'

Sir Walter Ralegh (1552?–1618)

THE PASSIONATE MANS PILGRIMAGE

Supposed to Be Written by One at the Point of Death

Give me my Scallop shell of quiet,
My staffe of Faith to walke upon,
My Scrip of Joy, Immortall diet,
My bottle of salvation:

My Gowne of Glory, hopes true gage,
And thus Ile take my pilgrimage.

Blood must be my bodies balmer,
No other balme will there be given
Whilst my soule like a white Palmer
Travels to the land of heaven,
Over the silver mountaines,
Where spring the Nectar fountaines:
And there Ile kisse
The Bowle of blisse,
And drinke my eternall fill
On every milken hill.
My soule will be a drie before,
But after it, will nere thirst more.

And by the happie blisfull way
More peacefull Pilgrims I shall see,
That have shooke off their gownes of clay,
And goe appareld fresh like mee.
Ile bring them first
To slake their thirst,
And then to taste those Nectar suckets
At the cleare wells
Where sweetnes dwells,
Drawne up by Saints in Christall buckets.

And when our bottle and all we
Are fild with immortalitie:
Then the holy paths weele travell
Strewde with Rubies thick as gravell,
Seelings of Diamonds, Saphire floores,
High walles of Corall and Pearl Bowres.

From thence to heavens Bribeles hall
Where no corrupted voyces brall,
No Conscience molten into gold,
Nor forg'd accusers bought and sold,
No cause deferd, nor vaine spent Jorney,
For there Christ is the Kings Atturney:
Who pleades for all without degrees,
And he hath Angells, but no fees.

When the grand twelve million Jury,
Of our sinnes with sinful fury,
Gainst our soules blacke verdicts give,

Christ pleades his death, and then we live,
Be thou my speaker taintles pleader,
Unblotted Lawyer, true proceeder,
Thou movest salvation even for almes:
Not with a bribèd Lawyers palmes.

And this is my eternall plea
To him that made Heaven, Earth and Sea,
Seeing my flesh must die so soone,
And want a head to dine next noone,
Just at the stroke when my vaines start and spred
Set my soul an everlasting head.
Then am I readie like a palmer fit,
To tread those blest paths which before I writ.

Edmund Spenser (1552?–1599)

From THE FAERIE QUEENE

Guyon's Temptation

There the most daintie Paradise on ground
   It selfe doth offer to his sober eye,
   In which all pleasures plenteously abound,
   And none does others happinesse envye:
   The painted flowres, the trees upshooting hye,
   The dales for shade, the hilles for breathing space,
   The trembling groves, the Christall running by;
   And that which all faire workes doth most aggrace,
The art, which all that wrought, appearèd in no place.

One would have thought, (so cunningly, the rude
   And scornèd parts were mingled with the fine,)
   That nature had for wantonnesse ensude
   Art, and that Art at nature did repine;
   So striving each th'other to undermine,
   Each did the others worke more beautifie;

So diff'ring both in willes, agreed in fine:
So all agreed through sweete diversitie,
This Gardin to adorne with all varietie.

And in the midst of all a fountaine stood,
Of richest substaunce that on earth might bee,
So pure and shiny that the silver flood
Through every channell running one might see;
Most goodly it with curious imageree
Was over-wrought, and shapes of naked boyes,
Of which some seemed with lively jollitee
To fly about playing their wanton toyes,
Whilst others did them selves embay in liquid joyes.

And over all, of purest gold was spred,
A trayle of yvie in his native hew;
For the rich metall was so colourèd,
That wight, who did not well avis'd it view,
Would surely deeme it to bee yvie trew;
Low his lascivious armes adown did creepe,
That themselves dipping in the silver dew,
Their fleecy flowres they tenderly did steepe,
Which drops of Christall seemed for wantonès to weepe.

Infinit streames continually did well
Out of this fountaine, sweet and faire to see,
The which into an ample laver fell,
And shortly grew to great a quantitie,
That like a litle lake it seemed to bee;
Whose depth exceeded not three cubits hight,
That through the waves one might the bottom see,
All pav'd beneath with Jaspar shining bright,
That seemd the fountaine in that sea did sayle upright.

And all the margent round about was set
With shady laurell trees, thence to defend
The sunny beames, which on the billowes bet,
And those which therein bathèd mote offend.
As *Guyon* hapned by the same to wend,
Two naked damzelles he therein espyde,
Which, therein bathing, seemèd to contend,
And wrestle wantonly, ne car'd to hyde
Their dainty partes from view of any which them eyed.

Sometimes the one would lift the other quight
Above the waters, and then down againe

Her plong, as over maisterèd by might,
Where both awhile would coverèd remaine,
And each the other from to rise restraine;
The whiles their snowy limbes, as through a vele,
So through the christall waves appearèd plaine;
Then suddeinly both would themselves unhele,
And th'amarous sweet spoiles to greedy eyes revele.

As that faire starre, the messenger of morne,
His deawy face out of the sea doth reare,
Or as the *Cyprian* goddesse, newly borne
Of th'oceans fruitfull froth, did first appeare,
Such seemèd they, and so their yellow heare
Christalline humour droppèd downe apace.
Whom such when *Guyon* saw, he drew him neare,
And somewhat gan relent his earnest pace;
His subborne brest gan secret pleasaunce to embrace.

The wanton maidens, him espying, stood
Gazing a while at his unwonted guise;
Then th'one her selfe low ducked in the flood,
Abasht, that her a straunger did avise;
But th'other rather higher did arise,
And her two lilly paps aloft displayd,
And all, that might his melting hart entyse
To her delights, she unto him bewrayd:
The rest hidd underneath, him more desirous made.

With that the other likewise up arose,
And her faire lockes, which formerly were bownd
Up in one knott, she low adowne did lose;
Which, flowing long and thick, her cloth'd arownd,
And th'yvorie in golden mantle gownd:
So that faire spectacle from him was reft,
Yet that which reft it no lesse faire was fownd:
So hidd in lockes and waves from lookers theft,
Nought but her lovely face she for his looking left.

Withall she laughèd, and she blusht withall,
That blushing to her laughter gave more grace,
And laughter to her blushing, as did fall.
Now when they spyde the knight to slacke his pace,
Them to behold, and in his sparkling face
The secret signes of kindled lust appeare,

Their wanton meriments they did encreace,
And to him beckned, to approch more neare,
And shewd him many sights, that corage cold could reare.

John Lyly (c.1554–1606)

From ALEXANDER AND CAMPASPE

Trico's Song

What bird so sings, yet so does wail?
O! 'tis the ravished nightingale.
"Jug, Jug, Jug, Jug, Tereu," she cries,
And still her woes at midnight rise.
Brave prick-song! Who is't now we hear?
None but the lark so shrill and clear;
Now at heaven's gate she claps her wings,
The morn not waking till she sings.
Hark, hark, with what a pretty throat
Poor robin redbreast tunes his note;
Hark how the jolly cuckoos sing
"Cuckoo," to welcome in the spring,
"Cuckoo," to welcome in the spring.

Fulke Greville, Lord Brooke (1554–1628)

"MERLIN, THEY SAY . . ."

Merlin, they say, an English Prophet borne,
When he was young and govern'd by his Mother,

Took great delight to laugh such fooles to scorne
As thought, by Nature we might know a Brother.

His Mother chid him oft, till on a day,
They stood, and saw a Coarse to buriall carried,
The Father teares his beard, doth weepe and pray;
The Mother was the woman he had married.

Merlin laughs out aloud in stead of crying;
His Mother chides him for that childish fashion;
Sayes, Men must mourne the dead, themselves are
 dying,
Good manners doth make answer unto passion.

The Child (for children see what should be hidden)
Replies unto his Mother by and by,
'Mother, if you did know, and were forbidden,
'Yet you would laugh as heartily, as I.'

Chidiock Tichborne (1558?–1586)

ON THE EVE OF HIS EXECUTION

My prime of youth is but a frost of cares,
 My feast of joy is but a dish of pain,
My crop of corn is but a field of tares,
 And all my good is but vain hope of gain;
  The day is past, and yet I saw no sun,
  And now I live, and now my life is done.

My tale was heard and yet it was not told,
 My fruit is fallen, yet my leaves are green,
My youth is spent and yet I am not old,
 I saw the world and yet I was not seen;
  My thread is cut and yet it is not spun,
  And now I live, and now my life is done.

I sought my death and found it in my womb,
I looked for life and saw it was a shade,
I trod the earth and knew it was my tomb,
And now I die, and now I was but made;
    My glass is full, and now my glass is run,
    And now I live, and now my life is done.

Robert Greene (1558?–1592)

From MENAPHON

Sephestia's Song to Her Childe

Weepe not my wanton! smile upon my knee!
When thou art olde, ther's grief inough for thee!
    Mothers wagge, pretie boy.
    Fathers sorrow, fathers joy.
    When thy father first did see
    Such a boy by him and mee,
    He was glad, I was woe,
    Fortune changde made him so,
    When he left his pretie boy,
    Last his sorowe, first his joy.

Weepe not my wanton! smile upon my knee!
When thou art olde, ther's grief inough for thee!
    Streaming teares that never stint,
    Like pearle drops from a flint,
    Fell by course from his eyes,
    That one anothers place supplies:
    Thus he grievd in everie part,
    Teares of bloud fell from his hart,
    When he left his pretie boy,
    Fathers sorrow, fathers joy.

Weep not my wanton! smile upon my knee!
When thou art olde, ther's grief inough for thee!
    The wanton smilde, father wept;

Mother cride, babie lept:
More he crowde, more we cride;
Nature could not sorrow hide.
He must goe, he must kisse
Childe and mother, babie blisse:
For he left his pretie boy,
Fathers sorowe, fathers joy.

Weepe not my wanton! smile upon my knee!
When thou art olde, ther's grief inough for thee!

Robert Southwell (1561–1595)

THE BURNING BABE

As I in hoary winter's night
   Stood shivering in the snow,
Surprised I was with sudden heat
   Which made my heart to glow;
And lifting up a fearful eye
   To view what fire was near,
A pretty babe all burning bright
   Did in the air appear;
Who scorchèd with excessive heat,
   Such floods of tears did shed,
As though His floods should quench His flames,
   Which with His tears were bred:
'Alas!' quoth He, 'but newly born
   In fiery heats I fry,
Yet none approach to warm their hearts
   Or feel my fire but I!

'My faultless breast the furnace is;
   The fuel, wounding thorns;
Love is the fire, and sighs the smoke;
   The ashes, shames and scorns;
The fuel Justice layeth on,

And Mercy blows the coals,
The metal in this furnace wrought
    Are men's defilèd souls:
For which, as now on fire I am
    To work them to their good,
So will I melt into a bath,
    To wash them in my blood.'
With this He vanish'd out of sight
    And swiftly shrunk away,
And straight I callèd unto mind
    That it was Christmas Day.

Mark Alexander Boyd (1563–1601)

SONET

Fra bank to bank, fra wood to wood I rin,
    Ourhailit with my feeble fantasie;
Like til a leaf that fallis from a tree,
    Or til a reed ourblowin with the win.

Twa gods guides me: the ane of tham is blin,
    Yea and a bairn brocht up in vanitie;
    The next a wife ingenrit of the sea,
And lichter nor a dauphin with her fin.

Unhappy is the man for evermair
    That tills the sand and sawis in the air;

    But twice unhappier is he, I lairn,
That feidis in his hairt a mad desire,
And follows on a woman throw the fire,
    Led by a blind and teachit by a bairn.

Christopher Marlowe (1564–1593)

OVID'S FIFTH ELEGY

In summers heate and mid-time of the day
To rest my limbes upon a bed I lay,
One window shut, the other open stood,
Which gives such light as twincles in a wood,
Like twilight glimps at setting of the Sunne
Or night being past, and yet not day begunne.
Such light to shamefast maidens must be shone,
Where they may sport, and seeme to be unknowne.
Then came *Corinna* in a long loose gowne,
Her white neck hid with tresses hanging downe:
Resembling fayre *Semiramis* going to bed
Or *Layis* of a thousand wooers sped.
I snacht her gowne, being thin, the harm was small.
Yet striv'd she to be covered there withall.
And striving thus as one that would be cast,
Betray'd herselfe, and yelded at the last.
Starke naked as she stood before mine eye,
Not one wen in her body could I spie.
What armes and shoulders did I touch and see,
How apt her breasts were to be prest by me?
How smooth a belly under her waist saw I?
How large a legge, and what a lustie thigh?
To leave the rest, al lik'd me passing well,
I cling'd her naked body, downe she fell,
Judge you the rest: being tirde she bad me kisse,
Jove send me more such after-noones as this.

From THE TRAGICALL HISTORIE OF DOCTOR FAUSTUS

Conclusion

The clocke strikes eleven.
FAUSTUS. Ah Faustus,
Now hast thou but one bare hower to live,
And then thou must be damnd perpetually:
Stand still you ever mooving spheres of heaven,
That time may cease, and midnight never come:
Faire Natures eie, rise, rise againe, and make
Perpetuall day, or let this houre be but
A yeere, a moneth, a weeke, a naturall day,
That Faustus may repent, and save his soule,
O lente, lente curite noctis equi:
The starres moove stil, time runs, the clock wil strike,
The divel wil come, and Faustus must be damnd.
O Ile leape up to my God: who pulles me downe?
See where Christs blood streames in the firmament.
One drop would have my soule, halfe a drop, ah my Christ.
Ah rend not my heart for naming of my Christ,
Yet wil I call on him: oh spare me *Lucifer*!
Where is it now? tis gone: And see where God
Stretcheth out his arme, and bends his irefull browes:
Mountaines and hilles, come, come, and fall on me,
And hide me from the heavy wrath of God.
No, no.
Then wil I headlong runne into the earth:
Earth gape. O no, it will not harbour me:
You starres that raignd at my nativitie,
Whose influence hath alotted death and hel,
Now draw up Faustus like a foggy mist,
Into the intrailes of yon labring cloude,
That when you vomite foorth into the ayre,
My limbes may issue from your smoaky mouthes,
So that my soule may but ascend to heaven:
Ah, halfe the houre is past: *The watch strikes*
Twil all be past anone:
O God,
If thou wilt not have mercy on my soule,
Yet for Christs sake, whose bloud hath ransomd me,
Impose some end to my incessant paine.

[41]

Let Faustus live in hel a thousand yeeres,
A hundred thousand, and at last be sav'd.
O no end is limited to damnèd soules,
Why wert thou not a creature wanting soule?
Or, why is this immortall that thou hast?
Ah *Pythagoras metemsucosis*, were that true,
This soule should flie from me, and I be changde
Unto some brutish beast: al beasts are happy,
For when they die,
Their soules are soone dissolved in elements,
But mine must still live to be plagde in hel:
Curst be the parents that engenderd me:
No, Faustus, curse thy selfe, curse *Lucifer*,
That hath deprivde thee of the joyes of heaven:
The clocke striketh twelve.
O it strikes, it strikes: now body turne to ayre,
Or *Lucifer* will beare thee quicke to hel:
Thunder and lightning.
O soule, be changde into little water drops,
And fall into the *Ocean*, nere be found:
My God, my God, looke not so fierce on me:
Enter divels.
Adders, and Serpents, let me breathe a while:
Ugly hell gape not, come not *Lucifer*,
Ile burne my bookes, ah *Mephastophilis*.
                                        Exeunt with him.

Enter Chorus.
CHORUS. Cut is the branch that might have growne full
        straight,
And burnèd is *Apolloes* Laurel bough,
That sometime grew within this learned man:
Faustus is gone, regard his hellish fall,
Whose fiendful fortune may exhort the wise,
Onely to wonder at unlawful things,
Whose deepnesse doth intise such forward wits,
To practise more than heavenly power permits.

Terminat hora diem, Terminat Author opus.

William Shakespeare (1564–1616)

SONNETS

138

When my love swears that she is made of truth,
I do believe her, though I know she lies,
That she might think me some untutor'd youth,
Unlearnèd in the world's false subtleties.
Thus vainly thinking that she thinks me young,
Although she knows my days are past the best,
Simply I credit her false-speaking tongue:
On both sides thus is simple truth supprest.
But wherefore says she not she is unjust?
And wherefore say not I that I am old?
O love's best habit is in seeming trust,
And age in love loves not to have years told:
　　Therefore I lie with her, and she with me,
　　And in our faults by lies we flatter'd be.

116

Let me not to the marriage of true minds
Admit impediments. Love is not love
Which alters when it alteration finds,
Or bends with the remover to remove:
O no! it is an ever-fixèd mark,
That looks on tempests and is never shaken;
It is the star to every wandering bark,
Whose worth's unknown, although his height be taken.
Love's not Time's fool, though rosy lips and cheeks
Within his bending sickle's compass come;
Love alters not with his brief hours and weeks,
But bears it out even to the edge of doom.
　　If this be error, and upon me prov'd,
　　I never writ, nor no man ever lov'd.

As an unperfect actor on the stage,
Who with his fear is put beside his part,
Or some fierce thing replete with too much rage,
Whose strength's abundance weakens his own heart;
So I, for fear of trust, forget to say
The perfect ceremony of love's rite,
And in mine own love's strength seem to decay,
O'ercharg'd with burden of mine own love's night.
O let my books be then the eloquence
And dumb presagers of my speaking breast,
Who plead for love and look for recompense,
More than that tongue that more hath more express'd.
   O learn to read what silent love hath writ:
   To hear with eyes belongs to love's fine wit.

When, in disgrace with fortune and men's eyes,
I all alone beweep my outcast state,
And trouble deaf heaven with my bootless cries,
And look upon myself, and curse my fate,
Wishing me like to one more rich in hope,
Featur'd like him, like him with friends possess'd,
Desiring this man's art, and that man's scope,
With what I most enjoy contented least;
Yet in these thoughts myself almost despising,
Haply I think on thee,—and then my state,
Like to the lark at break of day arising
From sullen earth, sings hymns at heaven's gate;
   For thy sweet love remember'd such wealth brings
   That then I scorn to change my state with kings.

That time of year thou mayst in me behold
When yellow leaves, or none, or few, do hang
Upon those boughs which shake against the cold,
Bare ruin'd choirs, where late the sweet birds sang.
In me thou see'st the twilight of such day
As after sunset fadeth in the west;
Which by and by black night doth take away,
Death's second self, that seals up all in rest.

In me thou see'st the glowing of such fire,
That on the ashes of his youth doth lie,
As the death-bed on which it must expire,
Consum'd with that which it was nourish'd by.
   This thou perceiv'st, which makes thy love more strong,
   To love that well which thou must leave ere long.

129

The expense of spirit in a waste of shame
Is lust in action; and till action, lust
Is perjur'd, murderous, bloody, full of blame,
Savage, extreme, rude, cruel, not to trust;
Enjoy'd no sooner but despisèd straight;
Past reason hunted, and no sooner had
Past reason hated, as a swallow'd bait
On purpose laid to make the taker mad;
Mad in pursuit, and in possession so;
Had, having, and in quest to have, extreme;
A bliss in proof, and prov'd, a very woe;
Before, a joy propos'd; behind, a dream.
   All this the world well knows; yet none knows well
   To shun the heaven that leads men to this hell.

146

Poor soul, the centre of my sinful earth,
Fool'd by these rebel powers that thee array,
Why dost thou pine within and suffer dearth,
Painting thy outward walls so costly gay?
Why so large cost, having so short a lease,
Dost thou upon thy fading mansion spend?
Shall worms, inheritors of this excess,
Eat up thy charge? Is this thy body's end?
Then, soul, live thou upon thy servant's loss,
And let that pine to aggravate thy store;
Buy terms divine in selling hours of dross;
Within be fed, without be rich no more:
   So shalt thou feed on Death that feeds on men,
   And Death once dead, there's no more dying then.

SONGS FROM THE PLAYS

From *Cymbeline*

Hark! hark! the lark at heaven's gate sings,
  And Phoebus 'gins arise
His steeds to water at those springs
  On chaliced flowers that lies;
And winking Mary-buds begin
  To ope their golden eyes
With every thing that pretty is,
  My lady sweet, arise;
    Arise, arise!

From *Love's Labour's Lost*

When daisies pied and violets blue
  And lady-smocks all silver-white
And cuckoo-buds of yellow hue
  Do paint the meadows with delight,
The cuckoo then on every tree,
Mocks married men, for thus sings he:
"Cuckoo! cuckoo!" O word of fear,
Unpleasing to a married ear!

When shepherds pipe on oaten straws
  And merry larks are ploughmen's clocks,
When turtles tread, and rooks, and daws,
  And maidens bleach their summer smocks,
The cuckoo then on every tree
Mocks married men, for thus sings he:
"Cuckoo! cuckoo!" O word of fear,
Unpleasing to a married ear.

From *Twelfth Night*

When that I was and a little tiny boy,
  With hey, ho, the wind and the rain,
A foolish thing was but a toy,
  For the rain it raineth every day.

But when I came to man's estate,
  With hey, ho, the wind and the rain,

'Gainst knaves and thieves men shut their gate,
    For the rain it raineth every day.

But when I came, alas, to wive,
    With hey, ho, the wind and the rain,
By swaggering could I never thrive,
    For the rain it raineth every day.

But when I came unto my beds,
    With hey, ho, the wind and the rain,
With tosspots still had drunken heads,
    For the rain it raineth every day.

A great while ago the world begun,
    With hey, ho, the wind and the rain,
But that's all one, our play is done,
    And we'll strive to please you every day.

From *A Midsummer Night's Dream*

Now the hungry lion roars,
    And the wolf behowls the moon;
Whilst the heavy ploughman snores,
    All the weary task foredone.
Now the wasted brands do glow,
    Whilst the screech-owl, screeching loud,
Puts the wretch that lies in woe
    In remembrance of a shroud.
Now it is the time of night
    That the graves, all gaping wide,
Every one lets forth his sprite,
    In the churchway paths to glide.
And we fairies, that do run
    By the triple Hecate's team
From the presence of the sun,
    Following darkness like a dream,
Now are frolic; not a mouse
Shall disturb this hallow'd house.
I am sent with broom before,
To sweep the dust behind the door.

From *The Winter's Tale*

When daffodils begin to peer,
With heigh! the Doxy over the dale,

Why then comes in the sweet o' the year;
For the red blood reigns in the winter's pale.

The white sheet bleaching on the hedge,
With heigh! the sweet birds, O how they sing!
Doth set my pugging tooth on edge;
For a quart of ale is a dish for a king.

The lark, that tirra-lyra chants,
With heigh, with heigh the thrush and the jay,
Are summer songs for me and my aunts,
While we lie tumbling in the hay.

From *Love's Labour's Lost*

When icicles hang by the wall,
  And Dick the shepherd blows his nail,
And Tom bears logs into the hall,
  And milk comes frozen home in pail;
When blood is nipp'd and ways be foul,
  Then nightly sings the staring owl
"To-whit! Tu-whoo!" A merry note,
While greasy Joan doth keel the pot.

When all around the wind doth blow,
  And coughing drowns the parson's saw,
And birds sit brooding in the snow,
  And Marian's nose looks red and raw;
When roasted crabs hiss in the bowl—
  Then nightly sings the staring owl
"To whit! Tu-whoo!" A merry note,
While greasy Joan doth keel the pot.

From *The Tempest*

Full fathom five thy father lies;
  Of his bones are coral made;
Those are pearls that were his eyes;
  Nothing of him that doth fade
But doth suffer a sea-change
Into something rich and strange.
Sea-nymphs hourly ring his knell.

Burthen: 'Ding-dong!'
"Hark! now I hear them,—Ding-dong, bell."

From *The Tempest*

The master, the swabber, the boatswain and I,
   The gunner and his mate,
Lov'd Mall, Meg, and Marian and Margery,
    But none of us car'd for Kate;
    For she had a tongue with a tang,
    Would cry to a sailor, "Go hang!"
She lov'd not the savour of tar nor of pitch,
Yet a tailor might scratch her where-e'er she did itch:
    Then to sea, boys, and let her go hang!

From *Cymbeline*

Fear no more the heat of the sun,
   Nor the furious winter's rages;
Thou thy worldly task hast done,
   Home art gone and ta'en thy wages.
Golden lads and girls all must,
As chimney-sweepers come to dust.

Fear no more the frown o' the great,
   Thou art past the tyrant's stroke;
Care no more to clothe and eat;
   To thee the reed is as the oak.
The sceptre, learning, physic, must
All follow this, and come to dust.

Fear no more the lightning-flash,
   Nor the all-dreaded thunder-stone;
Fear not slander, censure rash;
   Thou hast finished joy and moan.
All lovers young, all lovers must
Consign to thee, and come to dust.

No exorciser harm thee!
Nor no witchcraft charm thee!
Ghost unlaid forebear thee!
Nothing ill come near thee!
Quiet consummation have,
And renownèd be thy grave!

SPEECHES FROM A PLAY

King Lear: The Cycle of His Madness

LEAR *(to Cordelia, I, 1).* Let it be so; thy truth then be thy
    dower:
For, by the sacred radiance of the sun,
The mysteries of Hecate and the night,
By all the operation of the orbs
From whom we do exist and cease to be,
Here I disclaim all my paternal care,
Propinquity and property of blood,
And as a stranger to my heart and me
Hold thee from this for ever. The barbarous Scythian,
Or he that makes his generation messes
To gorge his appetite, shall to my bosom
Be as well neighbour'd, piti'd, and reliev'd,
As thou my sometime daughter.

LEAR *(to Albany, Goneril, I, iv).* It may be so, my lord.
Hear, Nature, hear! dear goddess, hear!
Suspend thy purpose, if thou didst intend
To make this creature fruitful!
Into her womb convey sterility!
Dry up in her the organs of increase,
And from her derogate body never spring
A babe to honour her! If she must teem,
Create her child of spleen, that it may live
And be a thwart disnatur'd torment to her!
Let it stamp wrinkles in her brow of youth,
With cadent tears fret channels in her cheeks,
Turn all her mother's pains and benefits
To laughter and contempt, that she may feel
How sharper than a serpent's tooth it is
To have a thankless child! ...

                                      I am asham'd
That thou hast power to shake my manhood thus;
That these hot tears, which break from me perforce,
Should make thee worth them. Blasts and fogs upon thee!
Th'untented woundings of a father's curse
Pierce every sense about thee! Old fond eyes,
Beweep this cause again, I'll pluck ye out,

And cast you, with the waters that you loose,
To temper clay. Ha! is it come to this?
Let it be so: I have another daughter,
Who, I am sure, is kind and comfortable:
When she shall hear this of thee, with her nails
She'll flay thy wolvish visage.

LEAR (*to Regan, II, iv*). Thou art a lady;
If only to go warm were gorgeous,
Why, nature needs not what thou gorgeous wear'st,
Which scarcely keeps thee warm. But, for true need,—
You heavens, give me that patience, patience I need!
You see me here, you gods, a poor old man,
As full of grief as age; wretched in both!
If it be you that stir these daughters' hearts
Against their father, fool me not so much
To bear it tamely; touch me with noble anger,
And let not women's weapons, water-drops,
Stain my man's cheeks! No, you unnatural hags,
I will have such revenges on you both
That all the world shall—I will do such things,—
What they are yet I know not,—but they shall be
The terrors of the earth. You think I'll weep;
No, I'll not weep:
I have full cause of weeping, but this heart

(*Storm and Tempest*)

Shall break into a hundred thousand flaws
Or ere I'll weep. O fool! I shall go mad.

LEAR (*and Fool, III, ii*). Blow, winds, and crack your cheeks!
    rage! blow!
You cataracts and hurricanoes, spout
Till you have drench'd our steeples, drown'd the cocks!
You sulpherous and thought-executing fires,
Vaunt-couriers of oak-cleaving thunderbolts,
Singe my white head! And thou, all-shaking thunder,
Strike flat the thick rotundity o' the world!
Crack nature's moulds, all germens spill at once
That make ungrateful man! . . .

Rumble thy bellyful! Spit fire! spout rain!
Nor rain, wind, thunder, fire, are my daughters:
I tax not you, you elements, with unkindness;
I never gave you kingdom, call'd you children;
You owe me no subscription. Then, let fall
Your horrible pleasure; here I stand, your slave,

A poor, infirm, weak, and despis'd old man.
But yet I call you servile ministers
That will with two pernicious daughters join
Your high-engender'd battles 'gainst a head
So old and white as this. O! O! 'tis foul.

LEAR (*to Kent, III, iv*). Thou thinkst 'tis much that this con-
    tentious storm
Invades us to the skin: so 'tis to thee;
But where the greater malady is fix't
The lesser is scarce felt. Thou'dst shun a bear;
But if thy flight lay toward the roaring sea,
Thou'dst meet the bear i' the mouth. When the mind's free
The body's delicate; the tempest in my mind
Doth from my senses take all feeling else
Save what beats there. Filial ingratitude!
Is it not as this mouth should tear this hand
For lifting food to 't? But I will punish home:
No, I will weep no more. In such a night
To shut me out! Pour on; I will endure
In such a night as this! O Regan, Goneril!
Your old kind father, whose frank heart gave all,—
O! that way madness lies; let me shun that;
No more of that.

LEAR (*to Gloucester, IV, vi*). Ay, every inch a king:
When I do stare, see how the subject quakes.
I pardon that man's life. What was thy cause?
Adultery?
Thou shalt not die; die for adultery! No:
The wren goes to 't, and the small gilded fly
Does lecher in my sight.
Let copulation thrive; for Gloucester's bastard son
Was kinder to his father than my daughters
Got 'tween the lawful sheets.
To 't luxury, pell-mell! for I lack soldiers.
Behold yond simpering dame
Whose face between her forks presageth snow;
That minces virtue, and does shake the head
To hear of pleasure's name;
The fitchew nor the soilèd horse goes to 't
With a more riotous appetite.
Down from the waist they are Centaurs,
Though women all above:
But to the girdle do the gods inherit,
Beneath is all the fiends':

There's hell, there's darkness, there is the sulphurous pit
Burning, scalding, stench, consumption; fie, fie, fie!
pah! pah! Give me an ounce of civet, good apothecary, to
sweeten my imagination: there's money for thee.

LEAR (*to Cordelia, V, iii*). No, no, no, no! Come, let's away
    to prison;
We two alone will sing like birds i' the cage:
When thou dost ask me blessing, I'll kneel down
And ask of thee forgiveness: so we'll live,
And pray, and sing, and tell old tales, and laugh
At gilded butterflies, and hear poor rogues
Talk of court news; and we'll talk with them too,
Who loses and who wins; who's in, who's out;
And take upon 's the mystery of things,
As if we were God's spies: and we'll wear out,
In a wall'd prison, packs and sets of great ones
That ebb and flow by the moon.

Thomas Nashe (1567–1601)

From SUMMER'S LAST WILL AND TESTAMENT

Song

Adieu, farewell earths blisse,
This world uncertaine is,
Fond are lifes lustfull joyes,
Death proves them all but toyes,
None from his darts can flye;
I am sick, I must dye:
    Lord, have mercy on us.

Rich men, trust not in wealth,
God cannot buy you health;
Phisick himselfe must fade.

[53]

All things to end are made,
The plague full swift goes bye;
I am sick, I must dye:
   Lord have mercy on us.

Beauty is but a flowre,
Which wrinckles will devoure,
Brightnesse falls from the ayre,
Queens have died yong and faire,
Dust hath closde *Helens* eye.
I am sick, I must dye:
   Lord, have mercy on us.

Strength stoopes unto the grave,
Wormes feed on *Hector* brave,
Swords may not fight with fate,
Earth still holds ope her gate.
Come, come, the bells do crye.
I am sick, I must dye:
   Lord, have mercy on us.

Haste therefore eche degree,
To welcome destiny:
Heaven is our heritage,
Earth but a players stage,
Mount wee unto the sky.
I am sick, I must dye:
   Lord, have mercy on us.

Sir John Davies (1569–1626)

From ORCHESTRA, or A POEME OF DAUNCING

Stanzas 34-37

Behold the *Worlde*, how it is *whirlèd round*,
And for it is so whirl'd, is namèd so;

In whose large volume many rules are found
Of this new Art, which it doth fairly show;
For your quick eyes in wandring too and fro
    From East to West, on no one thing can glaunce
    But if you marke it well, it seemes to daunce.

First you see fixt in this huge mirrour blew
Of trembling lights, a number numberlesse:
Fixt they are nam'd, but with a name untrue,
For they all moove and in a Daunce expresse
That *great long yeare,* that doth containe no lesse
    Then threescore hundreds of those yeares in all,
    Which the sunne makes with his course naturall.

What if to you these sparks disordered seeme
As if by chaunce they had been scattered there?
The gods a solemne measure doe it deeme,
And see a just proportion every where,
And know the points whence first their movings were;
    To which first points when all returne againe,
    The axel-tree of Heav'n shall breake in twaine.

Under that spanggled skye, five wandring flames
Besides the King of Day, and Queene of Night,
Are wheel'd around, all in their sundry frames,
And all in sundry measures doe delight,
Yet altogether keepe no measure right;
    For by it selfe each doth it selfe advance,
    And by it selfe each doth a galliard daunce . . .

Stanzas 57-60

Harke how the birds doe sing, and marke then how
Jumpe with the modulation of their layes,
They lightly leape, and skip from bow to bow:
Yet doe the cranes deserve a greater praise
Which keepe such measure in their ayrie wayes,
    As when they all in order rankèd are,
    They make a perfect forme triangular.

In the chief angle flyes the watchfull guide,
And all the followers their heads doe lay
On their foregoers backs, on eyther side;
But for the captaine hath no rest to stay,
His head forewearied with the windy way,
    He back retires, and then the next behind,

As his lieutenaunt leads them through the wind.

But why relate I every singular?
Since all the World's great fortunes and affaires
Forward and backward rapt and whirlèd are
According to the musicke of the spheares:
And Chaunge herselfe her nimble feete upbeares
    On a round slippery wheele that rowleth ay,
    And turnes all States with her impervous sway.

Learne then to daunce, you that are Princes borne,
And lawfull lords of earthly creatures all;
Imitate them, and thereof take no scorne,
For this new art to them is naturall—
And imitate the stars coelestiall:
    For when pale Death your vital twist shall sever,
    Your better parts must daunce with them for ever.

Ben Jonson (1572–1637)

TO THE MEMORY OF MY BELOVED, THE AUTHOR MR. WILLIAM SHAKESPEARE: AND WHAT HE HATH LEFT US

To draw no envy (*Shakespeare*) on thy name,
    Am I thus ample to thy Booke, and Fame:
While I confesse thy writings to be such,
    As neither *Man*, nor *Muse*, can praise too much.
'Tis true, and all mens suffrage. But these wayes
    Were not the paths I meant unto thy praise:
For seeliest Ignorance on these may light,
    Which, when it sounds at best, but eccho's right;
Or blinde Affection, which doth ne're advance
    The truth, but gropes, and urgeth all by chance;
Or crafty Malice, might pretend this praise,
    And thinke to ruine, where it seem'd to raise.
These are, as some infamous Baud, or Whore,

Should praise a Matron. What could hurt her
    more?
But thou art proofe against them, and indeed
    Above th'll fortune of them, or the need.
I, therefore will begin. Soule of the Age!
    The applause! delight! the wonder of our Stage!
My Shakespeare, rise; I will not lodge thee by
    Chaucer, or *Spenser*, or bid *Beaumont* lye
A little further, to make thee a roome:
    Thou art a Moniment, without a tombe,
And art alive still, while thy Booke doth live,
    And we have wits to read, and praise to give.
That I not mixe thee so, my braine excuses;
    I meane with great, but disproportion'd *Muses*:
For, if I thought my judgement were of yeeres,
    I should commit thee surely with thy peeres,
And tell, how farre thou dist our *Lily* out-shine,
    Or sporting *Kid*, or *Marlowes* mighty line.
And though thou hadst small *Latine*, and lesse *Greeke*,
    From thence to honour thee, I would not seeke
For names; but call forth thund'ring *Aeschilus*,
    Euripides, and *Sophocles* to us,
Paccuvius, *Accius*, him of Cordova dead
    To life againe, to heare thy Buskin tread,
And shake a Stage: Or, when thy Sockes were on,
    Leave thee alone, for the comparison
Of all, that insolent *Greece*, or haughtie *Rome*
    Sent forth, or since did from their ashes come.
Triúmph, my *Britaine*, thou hast one to showe,
    To whom all Scenes of *Europe* homage owe.
He was not of an age, but for all time!
    And all the *Muses* still were in their prime,
When like *Apollo* he came forth to warme
    Our eares, or like a *Mercury* to charme!
Nature her selfe was proud of his designes,
    And joy'd to weare the dressing of his lines!
Which were so richly spun, and woven so fit,
    As, since, she will vouchsafe no other Wit.
The merry *Greeke*, tart *Aristophanes*,
    Neat *Terence*, witty *Plautus*, now not please;
But antiquated, and deserted lye
    As they were not of Natures family.
Yet must I not give Nature all: Thy Art,
    My gentle *Shakespeare*, must enjoy a part.
For though the Poets matter, Nature be,
    His Art doth give the fashion. And, that he,

[57]

Who casts to write a living line, must sweat,
  (Such as thine are) and strike the second heat
Upon the *Muses* anvile: turne the same,
  (And himselfe with it) that he thinkes to frame;
Or for the lawrell, he may gaine a scorne,
  For a good *Poet's* made, as well as borne.
And such wert thou. Looke how the fathers face
  Lives in his issue, even so, the race
Of *Shakespeares* minde, and manners brightly shines
  In his well torned, and true-filed lines:
In each of which, he seemes to shake a Lance,
  As brandish't at the eyes of Ignorance.
Sweet Swan of *Avon!* what a sight it were
  To see thee in our waters yet appeare,
And make those flights upon the bankes of *Thames,*
  That so did take *Eliza,* and our *James!*
But stay, I see thee in the *Hemisphere*
  Advanc'd, and make a Constellation there!
Shine forth, thou Starre of *Poets,* and with rage,
  Or influence, chide, or cheere the drooping Stage;
Which, since thy flight from hence, hath mourn'd like
    night,
  And despaires day, but for thy Volumes light.

ON MY FIRST SONNE

Farewell, thou child of my right hand, and joy;
  My sinne was too much hope of thee, lov'd boy,
Seven yeeres tho'wert lent to me, and I thee pay,
  Exacted by thy fate, on the just day.
O, could I loose all father, now. For why
  Will man lament the state he should envie?
To have so soone scap'd worlds, and fleshes rage,
  And, if no other miserie, yet age?
Rest in soft peace, and, ask'd, say here doth lye
  BEN. JONSON his best piece of *poetrie,*
For whose sake, hence-forth, all his vowes be such,
  As what he loves may never like too much.

From EPICENE; OR, THE SILENT WOMAN

Simplex Munditiis

Still to be neat, still to be drest,
As you were going to a feast;
Still to be powder'd, still perfumed:
Lady, it is to be presumed,
Though art's hid causes are not found,
All is not sweet, all is not sound.

Give me a look, give me a face
That makes simplicity a grace;
Robes loosely flowing, hair as free:
Such sweet neglect more taketh me
Than all th'adulteries of art;
They strike mine eyes, but not my heart.

John Donne (1572–1631)

ELEGIE 19: TO HIS MISTRIS GOING TO BED

Come, Madam, come, all rest my powers defie,
Until I labour, I in labour lie.
The foe oft-times having the foe in sight,
Is tir'd with standing though he never fight.
Off with that girdle, like heaven's Zone glistering,
But a far fairer world incompassing.
Unpin that spangled breastplate which you wear,
That th' eyes of busy fools may be stopt there.
Unlace yourself, for that harmonious chyme,
Tells me from you that now it is bed time.
Off with that happy busk, which I envie,
That still can be, and still can stand so high.
Your gown going off, such beautious state reveals,

As when from flowry meads th'hills shadow steales.
Off with that wyerie Coronet and shew
The haiery Diademe which on you doth grow:
Now off with those shooes, and then safely tread
In this loves hallow'd temple, this soft bed.
In such white robes, heaven's Angels us'd to be
Receavd by men; Thou Angel bringst with thee
A heaven like Mahomets paradice; and though
Ill spirits walk in white, we easly know,
By this these Angels from an evil sprite,
Those set our hairs, but these our flesh upright.
     Licence my roaving hands, and let them go,
Before, behind, between, above, below.
O my America! my new-found-land,
My kingdome, safeliest when with one man man'd,
My Myne of precious stones, My Emperie,
How blest am I in this discovering thee!
To enter in these bonds, is to be free;
Then where my hand is set, my seal shall be.
     Full nakedness! All joyes are due to thee,
As souls unbodied, bodies uncloth'd must be,
To taste whole joyes. Gems which you women use
Are like Atlanta's balls, cast in mens views,
That when a fools eye lighteth on a Gem,
His earthly soul may covet theirs, not them.
Like pictures, or like books' gay coverings made
For lay-men, are all women thus array'd;
Themselves are mystick books, which only wee
(Whom their imputed grace will dignifie)
Must see reveal'd. Then since that I may know;
As liberally, as to a Midwife, shew
Thy self: cast all, yea, this white lynnen hence,
There is no pennance due to innocence.
     To teach thee, I am naked first; why then
What needst thou have more covering than a man.

SONG

Goe, and catche a falling starre,
     Get with child a mandrake root,
Tell me, where all past yeares are,
     Or who cleft the Divels foot,
Teach me to heare Mermaides singing,

Or to keep off envies stinging,
          And finde
          What winde
Serves to advance an honest mind.

If thou beest borne to strange sights,
    Things invisible to see,
Ride ten thousand daies and nights,
    Till age snow white haires on thee,
Thou, when thou retorn'st, wilt tell mee
All strange wonders that befell thee,
          And sweare
          No where
Lives a woman true, and faire.

If thou findst one, let mee know,
    Such a Pilgrimage were sweet;
Yet doe not, I would not goe,
    Though at next doore wee might meet,
Though shee were true, when you met her,
And last, till you write your letter,
          Yet shee
          Will bee
False, ere I come, to two, or three.

A NOCTURNALL UPON S. LUCIES DAY,
BEING THE SHORTEST DAY

Tis the yeares midnight, and it is the dayes,
Lucies, who scarce seaven houres herself unmaskes,
    The Sunne is spent, and now his flasks
    Send forth light squibs, no constant rayes;
    The worlds whole sap is sunke:
The generall balme th'hydroptique earth hath drunk,
Wither, as to the beds-feet, life is shrunke,
Dead and enterr'd; yet all these seeme to laugh,
Compar'd with mee, who am their Epitaph.

Study mee then, you who shall lovers bee
At the next world, that is, at the next Spring:
    For I am every dead thing,
    In whom love wrought new Alchimie.
    For his art did expresse

A quintessence even from nothingnesse,
From dull privations, and leane emptinesse:
He ruin'd mee, and I am re-begot
Of absence, darknesse, death; things which are not.

All others, from all things, draw all that's good,
Life, soule, forme, spirit, whence they beeing have;
   I, by love's limbecke, am the grave
  Of all, that's nothing. Oft a flood
    Have wee too wept, and so
Drownd the whole world, us two; oft did we grow
To be two Chaosses, when we did show
Care to ought else; and often absences
Withdrew our soules, and made us carcasses.

But I am by her death, (which word wrongs her)
Of the first nothing, the Elixir grown;
   Were I a man, that I were one,
  I needst must know; I should preferre,
    If I were any beast,
Some ends, some means; Yea plants, yea stones detest,
And love; All, all some properties invest;
If I an ordinary nothing were,
As shadow, a light, and body must be here.

But I am None; nor will my Sunne renew.
You lovers, for whose sake, the lesser Sunne
   At this time to the Goat is runne
  To fetch new lust, and give it you,
    Enjoy your summer all;
Since shee enjoyes her long nights festivall,
Let me prepare towards her, and let mee call
This houre her Vigill, and her Eve, since this
Both the yeares, and the dayes deep midnight is.

ELEGIE 16: ON HIS MISTRIS

By our first strange and fatall interview,
By all desires which thereof did ensue,
By our long starving hopes, by that remorse
Which my words masculine perswasive force
Begot in thee, and by the memory
Of hurts, which spies and rivals threatened me,
I calmly beg: But by thy fathers wrath,

By all paines, which want and divorcement hath,
I conjure thee, and all the oathes which I
And thou have sworne to seale joynt constancy,
Here I unsweare, and overswear them thus,
Thou shalt not love by wayes so dangerous.
Temper, ô faire Love, loves impetuous rage,
Be my true Mistris still, not my faign'd page;
I'll goe, and, by thy kinde leave, leave behinde
Thee, onely worthy to nurse in my minde,
Thirst to come backe; ô if thou die before,
My soule from other lands to thee shall soare.
Thy (else Almighty) beautie cannot move
Rage from the Seas, nor thy love teach them love,
Nor tame wilde Boreas harshnesse; Thou hast reade
How roughly hee in peeces shiverèd
Faire Orithea, whom he swore he lov'd.
Fall ill or good, 'tis madnesse to have prov'd
Dangers unurg'd; Feed on this flattery,
That absent Lovers one in th'other be.
Dissemble nothing, not a boy, nor change
Thy bodies habite, nor mindes; bee not strange
To thy selfe onely; All will spie in thy face
A blushing womanly discovering grace;
Richly cloath'd Apes, are call'd Apes, and as soone
Ecclips'd as bright we call the Moone the Moone.
Men of France, changeable Camelions,
Spittles of diseases, shops of fashions,
Loves fuellers, and the rightest company
Of Players, which upon the worlds stage be,
Will quickly know thee, and no lesse, alas!
Th'indifferent Italian, as we passe
His warme land, well content to thinke thee page,
Will hunt thee with such lust, and hideous rage,
As *Lots* faire guests were vext. But none of these
Nor spungy hydroptique Dutch shall thee displease,
If thou stay here. O stay here, for, for thee
England is onely a worthy Gallerie,
To walke in expectation, till from thence
Our greatest King call thee to his presence.
When I am gone, dreame me some happinesse,
Nor let thy lookes our long hid love confesse,
Nor praise, nor dispraise me, nor blesse nor curse
Openly loves force, nor in bed fright thy Nurse
With midnight startings, crying out, oh, oh
Nurse, ô my love is slaine, I saw him goe
O'r the white Alpes alone; I saw him I,

Assail'd, fight, taken, stabb'd, bleed, fall, and die.
Augure me better chance, except dread *Jove*
Thinke it enough for me to'have had thy love.

From THE PROGRESSE OF THE SOULE

The Whale

At every stroake his brazen finnes do take
More circles in the broken sea they make
Than cannons' voices, when the aire they teare:
His ribs are pillars, and his high arch'd roofe
Of barke that blunts best steele, is thunder-proofe:
Swimme in him swallow'd Dolphins, without feare,
And feele no sides, as if his vast wombe were
Some inland sea, and ever as he went
Hee spouted rivers up, as if he meant
　　To joyne our seas, with seas above the firmament.

He hunts not fish but as an officer,
Stayes in his court, at his own net, and there
All suitors of all sorts themselves enthrall;
So on his backe lies this whale wantoning,
And in his gulfe-like throat, sucks every thing
That passeth neare. Fish chaseth fish, and all,
Flyer and follower, in this whirlpool fall . . .

The Elephant

Nature's great masterpiece, an elephant
(The only harmless great thing), the giant
Of beasts, who thought none had to make him wise,
But to be just and thankful, loth to offend
(Yet nature hath given him no knees to bend)
Himself he up-props, on himself relies,
And, foe to none, suspects no enemies,
Still sleeping stood; vex'd not his fantasy
Black dreams; like an unbent bow carelessly
His sinewy proboscis did remissly lie.

THE EXTASIE

Where, like a pillow on a bed,
   A Pregnant banke swel'd up, to rest
The violets reclining head,
   Sat we two, one anothers best.
Our hands were firmly cìmented
   With a fast blame, which thence did spring,
Our eye-beames twisted, and did thread
   Our eyes, upon one double string;
So to'entergraft our hands, as yet
   Was all the meanes to make us one,
And pictures in our eyes to get
   Was all our propagation.
As 'twixt two equall Armies, Fate
   Suspends uncertaine victorie,
Our soules, (which to advance their state,
   Were gone out,) hung 'twixt her, and mee.
And whilst our soules negotiate there,
   Wee like sepulchrall statues lay;
All day, the same our postures were,
   And wee said nothing, all the day.
If any, so by love refin'd,
   That he soules language understood,
And by good love were growen all minde,
   Within convenient distance stood,
He (though he knew not which soul spake,
   Because both meant, both spake the same)
Might thence a new concoction take,
   And part farre purer than he came.
This Extasie doth unperplex
   (We said) and tell us what we love,
Wee see by this, it was not sexe,
   Wee see, we saw not what did move:
But as all severall soules containe
   Mixture of things, they know not what,
Love, these mixt soules, doth mixe againe,
   And makes both one, each this and that.
A single violet transplant,
   The strength, the colour, and the size,
(All which before was poore, and scant,)
   Redoubles still, and multiplies.
When love, with one another so

Interinanimates two soules,
That abler soule, which thence doth flow,
  Defects of lonelinesse controules,
Wee then, who are this new soule, know
  Of what we are compos'd, and made,
For, th'Atomies of which we grow,
  Are soules, whom no change can invade.
But O alas, so long, so farre
  Our bodies why do wee forbeare?
They are ours, though they are not wee, Wee are
  The intelligences, they the spheares.
We owe them thankes, because they thus,
  Did us, to us, at first convay,
Yeelded their forces, sense, to us,
  Nor are drosse to us, but allay.
On man heavens influence workes not so,
  But that it first imprints the ayre,
Soe soule into the soule may flow,
  Though it to body first repaire.
As our blood labours to beget
  Spirits, as like soules as it can,
Because such fingers need to knit
  That subtile knot, which makes us man:
So must pure lovers soules descend
  T'affections, and to faculties,
Which sense may reach and apprehend,
  Else a great Prince in prison lies.
To'our bodies turne wee then, that so
  Weake men on love reveal'd may looke;
Loves mysteries in soules doe grow,
  But yet the bodie is his booke.
And if some lover, such as wee,
  Have heard this dialogue of one,
Let him still marke us, he shall see
  Small change, when we'are to bodies gone.

HOLY SONNETS

7

At the round earths imagin'd corners, blow
Your trumpets, Angells, and arise, arise
From death, you numberlesse infinities
Of soules, and to your scattred bodies goe,

All whom the flood did, and fire shall o'erthrow,
All whom warre, dearth, age, agues, tyrannies,
Despaire, law, chance, hath slaine, and you whose eyes,
Shall behold God, and never taste deaths woe.
But let them sleepe, Lord, and mee mourne a space,
For, if above all these, my sinnes abound,
'Tis late to aske abundance of thy grace,
When wee are there; here on this lowly ground,
Teach mee how to repent; for that's as good
As if thou'hadst seal'd my pardon, with thy blood.

10

Death be not proud, though some have callèd thee
Mighty and dreadful, for, thou art not soe,
For, those, whom thou think'st, thou dost overthrow,
Die not, poore death, nor yet canst thou kill mee.
From rest and sleepe, which but thy pictures bee,
Much pleasure, then from thee, much more must flow,
And sonnest our best men with thee doe goe,
Rest of their bones, and soules deliverie.
Thou art slave to Fate, Chance, kings, and desperate men,
And dost with poyson, warre, and sicknesse dwell,
And poppie, or charmes can make us sleepe as well,
And better than thy stroake; why swell'st thou then?
One short sleepe past, wee wake eternally,
And death shall be no more; death, thou shalt die.

14

Batter my heart, three-person'd God; for, you
As yet but knocke, breathe, shine, and seeke to mend;
That I may rise, and stand, o'erthrow mee,'and bend
Your force, to breake, blowe, burn and make me new.
I, like an usurpt towne, to'another due,
Labour to'admit you, but Oh, to no end,
Reason your viceroy in mee, mee should defend,
But is captiv'd, and proves weake or untrue.
Yet dearely'I love you,'and would be loved faine,
But am betroth'd unto your enemie:
Divorce mee,'untie, or breake that knot againe,
Take me to you, imprison mee, for I
Except you'enthrall mee, never shall be free,
Nor ever chaste, except you ravish mee.

Cyril Tourneur (1575?–1626)

From THE REVENGER'S TRAGEDY

*Vendice, with the skull of his Betrothed, to his brother,
Hippolito*

... age and bare bone

Are e'er allied in action. Here's an eye,
Able to tempt a great man—to serve God:
A pretty hanging lip, that has forgot now to dissemble.
Methinks this mouth should make a swearer tremble;
A drunkard clasp his teeth, and not undo 'em.
To suffer wet damnation to run through 'em.
Here's a cheek keeps her colour, let the wind go whistle:
Spout, rain, we fear thee not: be hot or cold,
All's one with us; and is not he absurd,
Whose fortunes are upon their faces set,
That fear no other god but wind and wet?
  HIPPOLITO Brother, you've spoke that right:
Is this the form that, living, shone so bright?
  VENDICE The very same.
And now methinks I could e'en chide myself
For doating on her beauty, though her death
Shall be revenged after no common action.
Does the silkworm expend her yellow labours
For thee? For thee does she undoe herself?
Are lordships sold to maintain ladyships,
For the poor benefit of a bewildering minute?
Why does yon fellow falsify highways,
And put his life between the judge's lips,
To refine such a thing—keeps horse and men
To beat their valours for her?
Surely we are mad people, and they
Whom we think are, are not: we mistake those;

[68]

'Tis we are mad in sense, they but in clothes.
HIPPOLITO Faith, and in clothes too we, give us our due.
VENDICE Does every proud and self-affecting dame
Camphire her face for this, and grieve her Maker
In sinful baths of milk, when many an infant starves
For her superfluous outside—all for this?
Who now bids twenty pounds a night? prepares
Music, perfumes, and sweetmeats? All are hushed.
Thou may'st lie chaste now! It was fine, methinks,
To have thee seen at revels, forgetful feasts,
And unclean brothels! sure, 'twould fright the sinner,
And make him a good coward: put a reveller
Out of his antic amble,
And cloy an epicure with empty dishes.
Here might a scornful and ambitious woman
Look through and through herself. See, ladies with false
    forms
You deceive men, but cannot deceive worms. . . .

John Webster (c.1580–1638?)

From THE WHITE DEVIL

A Dirge

Call for the robin-redbreast and the wren,
Since o'er shady groves they hover,
And with leaves and flowers do cover
The friendless bodies of unburied men.
Call unto his funeral dole
The ant, the field-mouse, and the mole,
To rear him hillocks that shall keep him warm,
And (when gay tombs are robb'd) sustain no harm;
But keep the wolf far thence, that's foe to men,
For with his nails he'll dig them up again.

From THE DEVIL'S LAW-CASE

Vanitas Vanitatum

All the flowers of the spring
Meet to perfume our burying;
These have but their growing prime,
And man does flourish but his time:
Survey our progress from our birth—
We are set, we grow, we turn to earth.
Courts adieu, and all delights,
All bewitching appetites!
Sweetest breath and clearest eye
Like perfumes go out and die;
And consequently this is done
As shadows wait upon the sun.
Vain the ambition of kings
Who seek by trophies and dead things
To leave a living name behind,
And weave but nets to catch the wind.

From THE DUCHESS OF MALFI

From *Act IV, Scene 2*

[*Scene: A Room in the Duchess of Malfi's Lodging.*
Characters: The Duchess of Malfi; Daniel de Bosola (one of
her household); and Cariola (her woman).]

BOSOLA. I am come to make thy tomb.
DUCHESS. Ha! My tomb!
 Thou speak'st as if I lay upon my deathbed,
 Gasping for breath: dost thou perceive me sick?
BOSOLA. Yes, and the more dangerously, since thy sickness is
 insensible.
DUCHESS. Thou art mad, sure: dost know me?
BOSOLA. Yes.
DUCHESS. Who am I?
BOSOLA. Thou art a box of worm-seed, at best but a salvatory
 of green mummy. What's this flesh? a little crudded
 milk, fantastical puff-paste. Our bodies are weaker than
 those paper-prisons boys use to keep flies in; more con-

temptible, since ours is to preserve earth-wormes. Didst ever see a lark in a cage? Such is the soul in the body: this world is like her little turf of grass, and the Heaven o'er our heads, like her looking-glass, only gives us a miserable knowledge of the small compass of our prison.

DUCHESS. Am I not thy duchess?

BOSOLA. Thou art some great woman, sure, for riot begins to sit on thy forehead (clad in grey hairs) twenty years sooner than on a merry milkmaid's. Thou sleepest worse than if a mouse should be forced to take up her lodging in a cat's ear: a little infant that breeds its teeth, should it lie with thee, would cry out, as if thou wert the more unquiet bedfellow.

DUCHESS. I am Duchess of Malfi still.

BOSOLA. That makes thy sleep so broken:
Glories, like glow-worms, afar off shine bright,
But looked too near have neither heat nor light.

DUCHESS. Thou art very plain.

BOSOLA. My trade is to flatter the dead, not the living; I am a tomb maker.

DUCHESS. And thou comest to make my tomb?

BOSOLA. Yes.

DUCHESS. Let me be a little merry:—of what stuff wilt thou make it?

BOSOLA. Nay, resolve me first, of what fashion?

DUCHESS. Why do we grow fantastical in our death-bed?
Do we affect fashion in the grave?

BOSOLA. Most ambitiously. Princes images on their tombs do not lie, as they were wont, seeming to pray up to Heaven; but with their hands under their cheeks, as if they died of the toothache: they are not carved with their eyes fixed upon the stars; but as their minds were wholly bent upon the world, the self-same way they seem to turn their faces.

DUCHESS. Let me know fully therefore the effect
Of this thy dismal preparation,
This talk fit for a charnel.

BOSOLA. Now I shall:—

Enter executioners, with a coffin, cords, and a bell.

Here is a present from your princely brothers;
And may it arrive welcome, for it brings
Last benefit, last sorrow.

[71]

DUCHESS. Let me see it:
    I have so much obedience in my blood,
    I wish it in their veins to do them good.
BOSOLA. This is your last presence-chamber.
CARIOLA. O my sweet lady!
DUCHESS. Peace; it afrights not me.
BOSOLA. I am the common bellman,
    That usually is sent to condemned persons
    The night before they suffer.
DUCHESS. Even now thou said'st
    Thou wast a tomb-maker.
BOSOLA. 'Twas to bring you
    By degrees to mortification. Listen.
    Hark, now every thing is still
    The screech-owl and the whistler shrill
    Call upon our dame aloud,
    And bid her quickly don her shroud!
    Much you had of land and rent;
    Your length in clay's now competent:
    A long war disturbed your mind;
    Here your perfect peace is signed.
    Of what is't fools make such vain keeping?
    Sin their conception, their birth weeping,
    Their life a general mist of error,
    Their death a hideous storm of terror.
    Strew your hair with powders sweet,
    Don clean linen, bathe your feet,
    And (the foul fiend more to check)
    A crucifix let bless your neck:
    'Tis now full tide 'tween night and day;
    End your groan, and come away.
CARIOLA. Hence, villains, tyrants, murderers! alas!
    What will you with my lady?—Call for help!
DUCHESS. To whom? to our next neighbours? They are mad-
    folk.
BOSOLA. Remove that noise.
DUCHESS. Farewell, Cariola.
    In my last will I have not much to give:
    A many hungry guests have fed upon me;
    Thine will be a poor reversion.
CARIOLA. I will die with her.
DUCHESS. I pray thee, look thou giv'st my little boy
    Some syrup for his cold, and let the girl
    Say her prayers ere she sleep.

    [*Cariola is forced out by the executioners.*]

Now what you please:
What death?
BOSOLA. Strangling; here are your executioners.
DUCHESS. I forgive them:
The apoplexy, catarrh, or cough o' the lungs,
Would do as much as they do.
BOSOLA. Doth not death fright you?
DUCHESS. Who would be afraid on't,
Knowing to meet such excellent company
In the other world?
BOSOLA. Yet, methinks,
The manner of your death should much afflict you:
This cord should terrify you.
DUCHESS. Not a whit:
What would it pleasure me to have my throat cut
With diamonds? or to be smotherèd
With cassia? or to be shot to death with pearls?
I know death hath ten thousand several doors
For men to take their exits; and 'tis found
They go on such strange geometrical hinges
You may open them both ways; any way, for Heaven's
sake,
So I were out of your whisperings. Tell my brothers
That I perceive death, now I am well awake,
Best gift they can give or I can take.
I would fain put off my last woman's fault,
I'd not be tedious to you.
1ST EXECUTIONER. We are ready.
DUCHESS. Dispose my breath how please you; but my body
Bestow upon my women, will you?
1ST EXECUTIONER. Yes.
DUCHESS. Pull, and pull strongly, for your able strength
Must pull down Heaven upon me:—
Yet stay; Heaven-gates are not so highly arched
As princes' palaces; they that enter there
Must go upon their knees [*kneels*].—Come, violent
death,
Serve for mandragora to make me sleep!
Go tell my brothers, when I am laid out,
They then may feed in quiet.

[*The executioners strangle the duchess.*]

Francis Beaumont (1584?–1616)

ON THE TOMBS IN WESTMINSTER ABBEY

Mortality, behold and fear!
What a change of flesh is here!
Think how many royal bones
Sleep within this heap of stones:
Here they lie had realms and lands,
Who now want strength to stir their hands:
Where from their pulpits seal'd with dust
They preach, 'In greatness is no trust.'
Here's an acre sewn indeed
With the richest, royall'st seed
That the earth did e'er suck in
Since the first man died for sin:
Here the bones of birth have cried—
'Though gods they were, as men they died.'
Here are sands, ignoble things,
Dropt from the ruin'd sides of kings;
Here's a world of pomp and state
Buried in dust, once dead by fate.

William Drummond, of Hawthornden (1585–1649)

SAINT JOHN BAPTIST

The last and greatest Herald of Heaven's King,
Girt with rough skins, hies to the deserts wild,
Among that savage brood the woods forth bring,
Which he than man more harmless found and mild.
His food was locusts, and what young doth spring
With honey that from virgin hives distill'd;
Parch'd body, hollow eyes, some uncouth thing
Made him appear, long since from earth exiled.
There burst he forth: 'All ye whose hopes rely
On God, with me amidst these deserts mourn;
Repent, repent, and from old errors turn!'
—Who listen'd to his voice, obey'd his cry?
  Only the echoes, which he made relent,
  Rung from their marble caves 'Repent! Repent!'

Robert Herrick (1591–1674)

THE ARGUMENT OF HIS BOOK

I sing of Brooks, of Blossoms, Birds, and Bowers:
Of April, May, of June, and July-Flowers.
I sing of May-poles, Hock-carts, Wassails, Wakes,

Of Bride-grooms, Brides, and of their Bridal-cakes.
I write of Youth, of Love, and have access
By these, to sing of cleanly-wantonness.
I sing of Dews, of Rains, and piece by piece
Of Balm, of Oil, of Spice, of Amber-Greece.
I sing of Time's transhifting; and I write
How Roses first came red, and Lilies white.
I write of Groves, of Twilights, and I sing
The Court of Mab, and of the Fairie-King.
I write of Hell. I sing (and ever shall)
Of Heaven, and hope to have it after all.

From A NUPTIALL SONG, OR EPITHALAMIE, ON SIR CLIPSEBY CREW AND HIS LADY

8

To bed, to bed, kind Turtles, now, and write
This the short'st day, and this the longest night;
But yet too short for you: 'tis we
Who count this night as long as three,
Lying alone,
Telling the Clock strike Ten, Eleven, Twelve, One.
Quickly, quickly then prepare;
And let the Young-men and the Bride-maids share
Your Garters; and their joynts
Encircle with the Bride-grooms Points.

9

By the Brides eyes, and by the teeming life
Of her green hopes, we charge ye, that no strife
(Farther then Gentlenes tends) gets place
Among ye, striving for her lace:
O doe not fall
Foule in these noble pastimes, lest ye call
Discord in, and so divide
The youthfull Bride-groom, and the fragrant Bride:
Which Love fore-fend; but spoken,
Be't to your praise, no peace was broken.

Strip her of Spring-time, tender-whimpring-maids,
Now *Autumne's* come, when all those flowrie aids
    Of her Delayes must end; Dispose
      That *Lady-smock,* that *Pansie,* and that *Rose*
        Neatly apart;
But for *Prick-madam,* and for *Gentle-heart*;
      And soft-*Maidens-blush,* the Bride
Makes holy these, all others lay aside:
      Then strip her, or unto her
        Let him come, who dares undo her.

11

And to enchant ye more, see every where
About the Roofe a *Syren* in a Sphere;
    (As we think) singing to the dinne
      Of many a warbling *Cherubim*:
        O marke yee how
The soule of Nature melts in numbers: now
      See, a thousand *Cupids* flye
To light their Tapers at the Brides bright eye.
        To Bed; or her they'l tire,
        Were she an Element of fire.

William Browne (c.1591–c.1643)

ON THE COUNTESS DOWAGER OF PEMBROKE

Underneath this sable Herse
Lies the subject of all Verse;
Sidney's sister, Pembroke's mother:
Death, ere thou hast slaine another,

Faire, and learn'd, and good as she,
Time shall throw a dart at thee.

Marble piles let no man raise
To her name, for after-dayes:
Some kind woman borne as she,
Reading this, (like Niobe)
Shall turne Marble, and become
Both her mourner and her tombe.

Henry King, Bishop of Chichester (1592–1669)

EXEQUY ON HIS WIFE

Accept thou Shrine of my dead Saint,
Instead of Dirges this complaint;
And for sweet flowres to crown thy hearse,
Receive a strew of weeping verse
From thy griev'd friend, whom thou might'st see
Quite melted into tears for thee.

Dear loss! since thy untimely fate
My task hath been to meditate
On thee, on thee: thou art the book,
The library whereon I look
Though almost blind. For thee (lov'd clay)
I languish out not live the day,
Using no other exercise
But what I practise with mine eyes:
By which wet glasses I find out
How lazily time creeps about
To one that mourns: this, onely this
My exercise and bus'ness is:
So I compute the weary houres
With sighs dissolvèd into showres.

Nor wonder if my time go thus

Backward and most preposterous;
Thou hast benighted me, thy set
This Eve of blackness did beget,
Who was't my day, (though overcast
Before thou hads't thy Noon-tide past)
And I remember must in tears,
Thou scarce hads't seen so many years
As Day tells houres. By thy cleer Sun
My love and fortune first did run;
But thou wilt never more appear
Folded within my Hemisphear,
Since both thy light and motiòn
Like a fled Star is fall'n and gone,
And twixt me and my soules dear wish
The earth now interposèd is,
With such a strange eclipse doth make
As ne'er was read in Almanake.

I could follow thee for a time
To darken me and my sad Clime,
Were it a month, a year, or ten,
I would thy exile live till then;
And all that space my mirth adjourn,
So thou wouldst promise to return;
And putting off thy ashy shrowd
At length disperse this sorrows cloud.

But woe is me! The longest date
Too narrow is to calculate
These empty hopes: never shall I
Be so much blest as to descry
A glimpse of thee, till that day come
Which shall the earth to cinders doom,
And a fierce Feaver must calcine
The body of this world like thine,
(My Little World!) that fit of fire
Once off, our bodies shall aspire
To our soules bliss: then we shall rise
And view ourselves with cleerer eyes
In that calm Region, where no night
Can hide us from each others sight.

Mean time, thou hast her earth: much good
May my harm do thee. Since it stood
With Heavens will I might not call
Her longer mine, I give thee all

My short-liv'd right and interest
In her, whom living I lov'd best:
With a most free and bounteous grief,
I give thee what I could not keep.
Be kind to her, and prethee look
Thou write into thy Dooms-day book
Each parcell of this Rarity
Which in thy Casket shrin'd doth ly:
See that thou make thy reck'ning streight,
And yield her back again by weight;
For thou must audit on thy trust
Each graine and atome of this dust,
As thou wilt answer *Him* that lent,
Not gave thee my dear Monument.

So close the ground, and 'bout her shade
Black curtains draw, my *Bride* is laid.

Sleep on my *Love* in thy cold bed
Never to be disquieted!
My last good night! Thou wilt not wake
Till I thy fate shall overtake:
Till age, or grief, or sickness must
Marry my body to that dust
It so much loves; and fill the room
My heart keeps empty in thy Tomb.
Stay for me there; I will not faile
To meet thee in that hollow Vale.
And think not much of my delay;
I am already on the way,
And follow thee with all the speed
Desire can make, or sorrows breed.
Each minute is a short degree,
And ev'ry houre a steep towards thee.
At night when I betake to rest,
Next morn I rise neerer my West
Of life, almost by eight houres saile,
Then when sleep breath'd his drowsie gale.

Thus from the Sun my Bottom stears,
And my dayes Compass downward bears:
Nor labour I to stem the tide
Through which to *Thee* I swiftly glide.

'Tis true, with shame and grief I yield,
Thou like the *Vann* first took'st the field,

And gotten hast the victory
In thus adventuring to die
Before me, whose more years might crave
A just precedence in the grave.
But heark! My pulse like a soft Drum
Beats my approach, tells *Thee* I come;
And slow howere my marches be,
I shall at last sit down by *Thee*.

The thought of this bids me go on,
And wait my dissolution
With hope and comfort. *Dear* (forgive
The crime) I am content to live
Divided, with but half a heart,
Till we shall meet and never part.

George Herbert (1593–1633)

JORDAN

Who sayes that fictions onely and false hair
Become a verse? Is there in truth no beautie?
Is all good structure in a winding stair?
May no lines passe, except they do their dutie
    Not to a true, but painted chair?

Is it no verse, except enchanted groves
And sudden arbours shadow course-spunne lines?
Must purling streams refresh a lovers loves?
Must all be vail'd, while he that reads divines,
    Catching the sense at two removes?

Shepherds are honest people; let them sing:
Riddle who list for me, and pull for Prime:
I envie no man's nightingale or spring;

Nor let them punish me with loss of rime
  Who plainly say, *My God, My King.*

THE COLLAR

I struck the board, and cry'd, No more.
          I will abroad.
    What? shall I ever sigh and pine?
My lines and life are free; free as the rode,
    Loose as the winde, as large as store.
          Shall I be still in suit?
Have I no harvest but a thorn
To let me bloud, and not restore
What I have lost with cordiall fruit?
          Sure there was wine
Before my sighs did drie it: there was corn
          Before my tears did drown it.
    Is the yeare onely lost to me?
          Have I no bayes to crown it?
No flowers, no garlands gay? all blasted?
          All wasted?
    Not so, my heart: but there is fruit,
          And thou hast hands.
    Recover all thy sigh-blown age
On double pleasures: leave thy cold dispute
Of what is fit, and not. Forsake thy cage,
          Thy rope of sands,
Which pettie thoughts have made, and made to thee
    Good cable, to enforce and draw,
          And be thy law,
    While thou didst wink and wouldst not see.
          Away; take heed:
          I will abroad.
Call in thy deaths head there: tie up thy fears.
          He that forbears
    To suit and serve his need,
          Deserves his load.
But as I rav'd and grew more fierce and wilde
          At every word,
    Me thought I heard one calling, *Child!*
          And I reply'd *My Lord.*

Thomas Carew (1595?–1639?)

THE SPRING

Now that the winter's gone, the earth hath lost
Her snow-white robes; and now no more the frost
Candies the grasse, or casts an ycie creame
Upon the silver lake or chrystall streame:
But the warme sunne thawes the benummèd earth,
And makes it tender; gives a second birth
To the dead swallow; wakes in hollow tree
The drowsie cuckow and the humble-bee.
Now doe a quire of chirping minstrels sing
In triumph to the world, the youthfull Spring:
The vallies, hills, and woods in rich araye
Welcome the comming of the long'd-for May.
Now all things smile; onely my Love doth lowre;
Nor hath the scalding noon-day sunne the power
To melt that marble yce, which still doth hold
Her heart congeal'd, and makes her pittie cold.
The oxe, which lately did for shelter flie
Into the stall, doth now securely lie
In open field; and love no more is made
By the fire-side, but in the cooler shade.
Amyntas now doth by his Cloris sleepe
Under a sycamoure, and all things keepe
Time with the season: only she doth carry
June in her eyes, in her heart January.

A SONG

Aske me no more where Jove bestowes,
When June is past, the fading rose;

For in your beautie's orient deepe
These flowers, as in their causes, sleepe.

Aske me no more whither doth stray
The golden atoms of the day;
For, in pure love, heaven did prepare
Those powders to inrich your haire.

Aske me no more whither doth hast
The nightingale when May is past;
For in your sweet dividing throat
She winters and keepes warm her note.

Aske me no more where those starres light,
That downewards fall in dead of night;
For in your eyes they sit, and there
Fixèd become as in their sphere.

Aske me no more if east or west
The Phoenix builds her spicy nest;
For unto you at last shee flies,
And in your fragrant bosome dies.

James Shirley (1596–1666)

From THE CONTENTION OF AJAX AND ULYSSES

Dirge

The glories of our blood and state,
　Are shadows, not substantial things,
There is no armour against fate,
　Death lays his icy hand on Kings,
　　Scepter and crown,
　　Must tumble down,
And in the dust be equal made,

With the poor crooked sithe and spade.

Some men with swords may reap the field,
   And plant fresh laurels where they kill,
But their strong nerves at last must yield,
   They tame but one another still;
      Early or late,
      They stoop to fate,
And must give up their murmuring breath,
When they pale Captives creep to death.

The Garlands wither on your brow,
   Then boast no more your mighty deeds,
Upon Deaths purple Altar now,
   See where the Victor-victim bleeds,
      Your heads must come
      To the cool Tomb,
Onely the actions of the just
Smell sweet, and blossom in their dust.

Anonymous

TOM O' BEDLAM'S SONG

From the hag and hungry goblin
   That into rags would rend ye,
And the spirit that stands by the naked man
   In the book of moons, defend ye,
That of your five sound senses
   You never be forsaken,
Now wander from yourselves with Tom,
   Abroad to beg your bacon.
      While I do sing: Any food,
      Any feeding, drink, or clothing?
    Come, dame or maid, be not afraid,
      Poor Tom will injure nothing.

Of thirty bare years have I
  Twice twenty been enragèd,
And of forty been three times fifteen
  In durance soundly cagèd
On the lordly lofts of Bedlam,
  With stubble soft and dainty,
Brave bracelets strong, sweet whips, ding-dong,
  With wholesome hunger plenty.
    And now I sing: Any food, etc.

With a thought I took for Maudlin,
  And a cruse of cockle pottage,
With a thing thus tall, sky bless you all,
  I befell into this dotage.
I slept not since the Conquest,
  Till then I never wakèd,
Till the roguish boy of love where I lay
  Me found and stripped me naked.
    And now I sing: Any food, etc.

When I short have shorn my sour-face,
  And swigged my horny barrel,
In an oaken inn I poured my skin,
  As a suit of gilt apparel.
The moon's my constant mistress,
  And the lowly owl my morrow;
The flaming drake and the night-crow make
  Me music to my sorrow.
    While I do sing: Any food, etc.

The palsy plagues my pulses,
  When I prig your pigs or pullen,
Your culvers take, or matchless make
  Your chanticleer or sullen.
When I want provant, with Humphry
  I sup, and when benighted,
I repose in Powles with waking souls,
  Yet never am affrighted.
    But I do sing: Any food, etc.

I know more than Apollo,
  For oft when he lies sleeping,
I see the stars at bloody wars
  In the wounded welkin weeping,
The moon embrace her shepherd,
  And the queen of love her warrior,

While the first doth horn the star of morn,
  And the next the heavenly Farrier.
    While I do sing: Any food, etc.

The gipsy Snap and Pedro
  Are none of Tom's comradoes,
The punk I scorn, and the cutpurse sworn,
  And the roaring boys' bravadoes.
The meek, the white, the gentle,
  Me handle, touch, and spare not;
But those that cross Tom Rhinoceros
  Do what the panther dare not.
    Although I sing: Any food, etc.

With an host of furious fancies
  Whereof I am commander,
With a burning spear and a horse of air
  To the wilderness I wander.
By a knight of ghosts and shadows
  I summoned am to tourney
Ten leagues beyond the wide world's end,
  Methinks it is no journey.
    Yet will I sing: Any food, etc.

Edmund Waller (1606–1687)

SONG

  Go lovely Rose,
Tell her that wastes her time and me,
  That now she knows
When I resemble her to thee,
  How sweet and fair she seems to be.

  Tell her that's young,
And shuns to have her Graces spy'd,

That hadst thou sprung
In Desarts, where no men abide,
  Thou must have uncommended dy'd.

  Small is the worth
Of Beauty from the light retir'd;
  Bid her come forth,
Suffer herself to be desir'd,
  And not blush so to be admir'd.

  Then die, that she,
The common fate of all things rare,
  May read in thee
How small a part of time they share,
  That are so wondrous sweet and fair.

OF ENGLISH VERSE

Poets may boast, as safely vain,
Their words shall with the world remain;
Both, bound together, live or die,
The verses and the prophecy.

But who can hope his lines should long
Last in a daily changing tongue?
While they are new, envy prevails;
And as that dies, our language fails.

When architects have done their part,
The matter may betray their art;
Time, if we use ill-chosen stone,
Soon brings a well-built palace down.

Poets that lasting marble seek
Must carve in Latin or in Greek;
We write in sand, our language grows,
And, like the tide, our work o'erflows.

Chaucer his sense can only boast,
The glory of his numbers lost!
Years have defaced his matchless strain,
And yet he did not sing in vain.

The beauties which adorned that age,
The shining subjects of his rage,
Hoping they should immortal prove,
Rewarded with success his love.

This was the generous poet's scope,
And all an English pen can hope,
To make the fair approve his flame,
That can so far extend their fame.

Verse, thus designed, has no ill fate
If it arrive but at the date
Of fading beauty; if it prove
But as long-lived as present love.

William Davenant (1606–1668)

WAKE ALL THE DEAD

Wake all the dead! what ho! what ho!
   How soundly they sleep whose pillows lie low?
They mind not poor lovers who walk above
On the decks of the world in storms of love.
   No whisper now nor glance shall pass
   Through thickets or through panes of glass;
For our windows and doors are shut and barred.
Lie close in the church, and in the churchyard.
   In every grave, make room, make room!
   The world's at an end, and we come, we come.

John Milton (1608-1674)

LYCIDAS

In this Monody the Author bewails a learned Friend, unfortunately drown'd in his passage from Chester on the Irish Seas, 1637. And by occasion foretells the ruine of our corrupted Clergie then in their height.

Yet once more, O ye Laurels, and once more
Ye Myrtles brown, with Ivy never-sear,
I com to pluck your Berries harsh and crude,
And with forc'd fingers rude,
Shatter your leaves before the mellowing year.
Bitter constraint, and sad occasion dear,
Compells me to disturb your season due:
For *Lycidas* is dead, dead ere his prime,
Young *Lycidas*, and hath not left his peer:
Who would not sing for *Lycidas*? he knew
Himself to sing, and build the lofty rhyme.
He must not flote upon his watry bear
Unwept, and welter to the parching wind,
Without the meed of som melodious tear.
  Begin then, Sisters of the sacred well,
That from beneath the seat of *Jove* doth spring,
Begin, and somewhat loudly sweep the string.
Hence with denial vain, and coy excuse,
So may some gentle Muse
With lucky words favour my destin'd Urn,
And as he passes turn,
And bid fair peace be to my sable shrowd.
For we were nurst upon the self-same hill,
Fed the same flock; by fountain, shade, and rill.
  Together both, ere the high Lawns appear'd
Under the opening eye-lids of the morn,

We drove a field, and both together heard
What time the Gray-fly winds her sultry horn,
Batt'ning our flocks with the fresh dews of night,
Oft till the Star that rose, at Ev'ning bright,
Toward Heav'ns descent had slop'd his westering wheel.
Mean while the Rural ditties were not mute,
Temper'd to th'oaten Flute,
Rough *Satyrs* danc'd, and *Fauns* with clov'n heel,
From the glad sound would not be absent long,
And old *Damœtas* lov'd to hear our song.
 But O the heavy change, now thou art gon,
Now thou art gon, and never must return!
Thee Shepherd, thee the Woods, and desert Caves,
With wilde Thyme and the gadding Vine o'regrown,
And all their echoes mourn.
The Willows, and the Hazle Copses green,
Shall now no more be seen,
Fanning their joyous Leaves to thy soft layes.
As killing as the Canker to the Rose,
Or Taint-worm to the weanling Herds that graz,
Or Frost to Flowers, that their gay wardrop wear,
When first the White Thorn blows;
Such, *Lycidas*, thy loss to Shepherds ear.
 Where were ye Nymphs when the remorseless deep
Clos'd o're the head of your lov'd *Lycidas*?
For neither were ye playing on the steep,
Where your old *Bards*, the famous *Druids*, ly,
Nor on the shaggy top of *Mona* high,
Nor yet where *Deva* spreads her wisard stream:
Ay me, I fondly dream!
Had ye been there—for what could that have don?
What could the Muse her self that *Orpheus* bore,
The Muse her self for her inchanting son
Whom Universal nature did lament,
When by the rout that made the hideous roar,
His goary visage down the stream was sent,
Down the swift *Hebrus* to the *Lesbian* shore.
 Alas! What boots it with uncessant care
To tend the homely slighted Shepherds trade,
And strictly meditate the thankles Muse,
Were it not better don as others use,
To sport with *Amaryllis* in the shade,
Or with the tangles of *Neæra's* hair?
Fame is the spur that the clear spirit doth raise
(That last infirmity of Noble mind)
To scorn delights, and live laborious dayes;

But the fair Guerdon when we hope to find,
And think to burst out into sudden blaze,
Comes the blind *Fury* with th'abhorred shears,
And slits the thin-spun life. But not the praise,
Phœbus repli'd, and touch'd my trembling ears;
Fame is no plant that grows on mortal soil,
Nor in the glistering foil
Set off to th'world, nor in broad rumour lies,
But lives and spreads aloft by those pure eyes,
And perfet witnes of all-judging *Jove*;
As he pronounces lastly on each deed,
Of so much fame in Heav'n expect thy meed.

   O Fountain *Arethuse*, and thou honour'd floud,
Smooth-sliding *Mincius*, crown'd with vocal reeds,
That strain I heard was of a higher mood:
But now my Oat proceeds,
And listens to the Herald of the Sea
That came in *Neptune's* plea,
He ask'd the Waves, and ask'd the Fellon winds,
What hard mishap hath doom'd this gentle swain?
And question'd every gust of rugged wings
That blows from off each beakèd Promontory;
They knew not of his story.
And sage *Hippotades* their answer brings,
That not a blast was from his dungeon stray'd,
The Ayr was calm, and on the level brine,
Sleek *Panope* with all her sisters play'd.
It was that fatall and perfidious Bark
Built in th'eclipse, and rigg'd with curses dark,
That sunk so low that sacred head of thine.

   Next *Camus,* reverend Sire, went footing slow,
His Mantle hairy, and his Bonnet sedge,
Inwrought with figures dim, and on the edge
Like to that sanguine flower inscrib'd with woe.
Ah; Who hath reft (quoth he) my dearest pledge?
Last come, and last did go,
The Pilot of the *Galilean* lake,
Two massy Keyes he bore of metals twain,
(The Golden opes, the Iron shuts amain)
He shook his Miter'd locks, and stern bespake,
How well could I have spar'd for thee young swain,
Anow of such as for their bellies sake,
Creep and intrude, and climb into the fold?
Of other care they little reck'ning make,
Then how to scramble at the shearers feast,
And shove away the worthy bidden guest.

Blind mouthes! that scarce themselves know how to hold
A Sheep-hook, or have learn'd ought els the least
That to the faithfull Herdmans art belongs!
What recks it them? What need they? They are sped;
And when they list, their lean and flashy songs
Grate on their scrannel Pipes of wretched straw,
The hungry Sheep look up, and are not fed,
But swoln with wind, and the rank mist they draw,
Rot inwardly, and foul contagion spread;
Besides what the grim Woolf with privy paw
Daily devours apace, and nothing sed,
But that two-handed engine at the door,
Stands ready to smite once, and smite no more.
    Return *Alphaeus*, the dread voice is past,
That shrunk thy streams; return *Sicilian* Muse,
And call the Vales, and bid them hither cast
Their Bels, and Flourets of a thousand hues.
Ye valleys low where the milde whispers use,
Of shades and wanton winds, and gushing brooks,
On whose fresh lap the swart Star sparely looks,
Throw hither all your quaint enameld eyes,
That on the green terf suck the honied showres,
And purple all the ground with vernal flowres.
Bring the rathe Primrose that forsaken dies.
The tufted Crow-toe, and pale Gessamine,
The white Pink, and the Pansie freakt with jet,
The glowing Violet.
The Musk-rose, and the well attir'd Woodbine,
With Cowslips wan that hang the pensive head,
And every flower that sad embroidery wears:
Big *Amaranthus* all his beauty shed,
And Daffadillies fill their cups with tears,
To strew the Lureat Herse where *Lycid* lies.
For so to interpose a little ease,
Let our frail thoughts dally with false surmise.
Ay me! Whilst thee the shores, and sounding Seas
Wash far away, where ere thy bones are hurl'd,
Whether beyond the stormy *Hebrides*
Where thou perhaps under the whelming tide
Visit'st the bottom of the monstrous world;
Or whether thou to our moist vows deny'd,
Sleep'st by the fable of *Bellerus* old,
Where the great vision of the guarded Mount
Looks toward *Namancos* and *Bayona's* hold;
Look homeward Angel now, and melt with ruth.
And, O ye *Dolphins*, waft the haples youth.

Weep no more, woful Shepherds weep no more,
For *Lycidas* your sorrow is not dead,
Sunk though he be beneath the watry floar,
So sinks the day-star in the Ocean bed,
And yet anon repairs his drooping head,
And tricks his beams, and with new spangled Ore,
Flames in the forehead of the morning sky:
So *Lycidas* sunk low, but mounted high,
Through the dear might of him that walk'd the waves
Where other groves, and other streams along,
With *Nectar* pure his oozy Lock's he laves,
And hears the unexpressive nuptial Song,
In the blest Kingdoms meek of joy and love.
There entertain him all the Saints above,
In solemn troops, and sweet Societies
That sing, and singing in their glory move,
And wipe the tears for ever from his eyes.
Now *Lycidas* the Shepherds weep no more;
Hence forth thou art the Genius of the shore,
In thy large recompense, and shalt be good
To all that wander in that perilous flood.

    Thus sang the uncouth Swain to th'Okes and rills,
While the still morn went out with Sandals gray,
He touch'd the tender stops of various Quills,
With eager thought warbling his *Dorick* lay:
And now the Sun had stretch'd out all the hills,
And now was dropt into the Western Bay;
At last he rose, and twitch'd, his Mantle blew:
To morrow to fresh Woods, and Pastures new.

SONNETS

To Oliver Cromwell

Cromwell our Chief of Men, that through a Cloud,
   Not of War only, but distractions rude;
    Guided by Faith, and Matchless Fortitude;
   To Peace and Truth, they Glorious way hast Plough'd,
And on the neck of crownèd Fortune proud
   Hast rear'd God's Trophies, and his Work pursu'd,
    While *Darwen* Stream with Blood of *Scots* imbru'd;
   And *Dunbarfield* resound thy Praises loud,
And *Worcester's* Laureat Wreath; yet much remains
   To Conquer still; Peace hath her Victories

No less than those of War; new Foes arise
Threat'ning to bind our Souls in secular Chains,
  Help us to save Free Conscience from the paw
  Of Hireling Wolves, whose Gospel is their Maw.

On the late Massacher in Piemont

Avenge O Lord thy slaughter'd Saints, whose bones
  Lie scatter'd on the Alpine mountains cold,
  Ev'n them who kept thy truth so pure of old
When all our Fathers worship'd Stocks and Stones,
Forget not: in thy book record their groanes
  Who were thy Sheep and in their antient Fold
  Slayn by the bloody *Piemontese* that roll'd
Mother with Infant down the Rocks. Their moans
The Vales redoubl'd to the Hills, and they
  To Heav'n. Their martyr'd blood and ashes sow
  O're all th'*Italian* fields where still doth sway
The triple Tyrant: that from these may grow
  A hunder'd-fold, who having learnt thy way
  Early may fly the *Babylonian* woe.

"Methought I saw my late espousèd Saint"

Methought I saw my late espousèd Saint
  Brought to me like *Alcestis* from the grave,
  Whom *Jove's* great Son to her glad Husband gave,
  Rescu'd from death by force though pale and faint.
Mine as whom washt from spot of child-bed taint
  Purification in the old Law did save,
  And such, as yet once more I trust to have
  Full sight of her in Heaven without restraint,
Came vested all in white, pure as her mind:
  Her face was veil'd, yet to my fancied sight,
  Love, sweetness, goodness, in her person shin'd
So clear, as in no face with more delight.
  But O as to embrace me she enclin'd
  I wak'd, she fled, and day brought back my night.

"When I consider how my light is spent"

When I consider how my light is spent,
  E're half my days, in this dark world and wide,
  And that one Talent which is death to hide,
  Lodg'd with me useless, though my Soul more bent

[95]

To serve therewith my Maker, and present
My true account, lest he returning chide,
Doth God exact day-labour, light deny'd,
I fondly ask; but Patience to prevent
That murmur, soon replies, God doth not need
Either man's work or his own gifts, who best
Bears his milde yoak, they serve him best, his State
Is Kingly. Thousands at his bidding speed
And post o're Land and Ocean without rest:
They also serve who only stand and waite.

From PARADISE LOST

Invocation

Of Mans First Disobedience, and the Fruit
Of that Forbidden Tree, whose mortal taste
Brought Death into the World, and all our woe,
With loss of *Eden*, till one greater Man
Restore us, and regain the blissful Seat,
Sing Heav'nly Muse, that on the secret top
Of *Oreb*, or of *Sinai*, didst inspire
That Shepherd, who first taught the chosen Seed,
In the Beginning how the Heav'ns and Earth
Rose out of *Chaos*: or if *Sion* Hill
Delight thee more, and *Siloa's* Brook that flow'd
Fast by the Oracle of God; I thence
Invoke thy aid to my adventrous Song,
That with no middle flight intends to soar
Above th'*Aonian* Mount, while it pursues
Things unattempted yet in Prose or Rhime.
And chiefly Thou O Spirit, that dost prefer
Before all Temples th'upright heart and pure,
Instruct me, for Thou know'st; Thou from the first
Wast present, and with mighty wings outspread
Dove-like satst brooding on the vast Abyss
And mad'st it pregnant: What in me is dark
Illumin, what is low raise and support;
That to the height of this great Argument
I may assert Eternal Providence,
And justifie the wayes of God to men.

Satan as Rebel-Liberator

Is this the Region, this the Soil, the Clime,
Said then the lost Arch-Angel, this the seat
That we must change for Heav'n, this mournful gloom
For that celestial light? Be it so, since he
Who now is Sovran can dispose and bid
What shall be right; fardest from him is best
Whom reason hath equalld, force hath made supream
Where Joy for ever dwells: Hail horrours, hail
Infernal world, and thou profoundest Hell
Receive thy new Possessor: One who brings
A mind not to be chang'd by Place or Time.
The mind is its own place, and in it self
Can make a Heav'n of Hell, a Hell of Heav'n.
What matter where, if I be still the same,
And what I should be, all but less than he
Whom Thunder hath made greater? Here at least
We shall be free; th'Almighty hath not built
Here for his envy, will not drive us hence:
Here we may reign secure, and in my choyce
To reign is worth ambition though in Hell:
Better to reign in Hell, than serve in Heav'n.

The Poet's Blindness

Hail, holy light, offspring of Heav'n first-born,
Or of th'Eternal Coeternal beam
May I express thee unblam'd? since God is light,
And never but in unapproachèd light
Dwelt from Eternitie, dwelt then in thee,
Bright effluence of bright essence increate.
Or hear'st thou rather pure Ethereal stream,
Whose Fountain who shall tell? before the Sun,
Before the heavens thou wert, and at the voice
Of God, as with a Mantle didst invest
The rising world of water dark and deep,
Won from the void and formless infinite.
Thee I re-visit now with bolder wing,
Escap't the *Stygian* Pool, though long detain'd
In that obscure sojourn, while in my flight
Through utter and through middle darkness borne
With other notes than to th'*Orphean* Lyre
I sung of *Chaos* and *Eternal Night*,
Taught by the heav'nly Muse to venture down
The dark descent, and up to reascend,

Though hard and rare: thee I revisit safe,
And feel thy sovran vital Lamp; but thou
Revisit'st not these eyes, that rowle in vain
To find thy piercing ray, and find no dawn;
So thick a drop serene hath quencht their Orbs,
Or dim suffusion veild. Yet not the more
Cease I to wander where the Muses haunt
Cleer Spring, or shadie Grove, or Sunnie Hill,
Smit with the love of sacred song; but chief
Thee *Sion* and the flowrie Brooks beneath
That wash thy hallowd feet, and warbling flow,
Nightly I visit: nor somtimes forget
Those other two equal'd with me in Fate,
So were I equal'd with them in renown,
Blind *Thamyris* and blind *Maeonides*,
And *Tiresias* and *Phineus* Prophets old.
Then feed on thoughts, that voluntarie move
Harmonious numbers; as the wakeful Bird
Sings darkling, and in shadiest Covert hid
Tunes her nocturnal Note. Thus with the Year
Seasons return, but not to me returns
Day, or the sweet approach of Ev'n or Morn,
Or sight of vernal bloom, or Summers Rose,
Or flocks, or herds, or human face divine;
But cloud instead, and ever-during dark
Surrounds me, from the chearful wayes of men
Cut off, and for the Book of knowledg fair
Presented with a Universal blanc
Of Natures works to mee expung'd and ras'd,
And wisdome at one entrance quite shut out.
So much the rather thou Celestial light
Shine inward, and the mind through all her powers
Irradiate, there plant eyes, all mist from thence
Purge and disperse, that I may see and tell
Of things invisible to mortal sight.

Evening in Eden

Now came still Evening on, and Twilight gray
Had in her sober Liverie all things clad;
Silence accompanied, for Beast and Bird,
They to their grassie Couch, these to thir Nests
Were slunk, all but the wakeful Nightingale;
She all night long her amorous descant sung;
Silence was pleas'd: Now glow'd the Firmament
With living Saphirs: *Hesperus* that led

The starrie Host, rode brightest, till the Moon
Rising in clouded Majestie, at length
Apparent Queen unvail'd her peerless light,
And o're the dark her Silver Mantle threw.

War in Heaven

Of Battel: whereat Michaël bid sound
Th'Arch-angel trumpet; through the vast of Heav'n
It sounded, and the faithful Armies rung
Hosanna to the Highest: nor stood at gaze
Th'adverse Legions, nor less hideous joyn'd
The horrid shock: now storming furie rose,
And clamour such as heard in Heav'n till now
Was never. Arms on Armour clashing bray'd
Horrible discord, and the madding Wheeles
Of brazen Chariots rag'd; dire was the noise
Of conflict; over head the dismal hiss
Of fiery Darts in flaming volies flew,
And flying vaulted either Host with fire;
So under fiery Cope together rush'd
Both Battels maine, with ruinous assault
And inextinguishable rage; all Heaven
Resounded, and had Earth been then, all Earth
Had to her Center shook.

Eve Contemplates Sharing Her Sin

"And I perhaps am secret; Heav'n is high,
High and remote to see from thence distinct
Each thing on Earth; and other care perhaps
May have diverted from continual watch
Our great Forbidder, safe with all his Spies
About him. But to *Adam* in what sort
Shall I appeer? shall I to him make known
As yet my change, and give him to partake
Full happiness with mee, or rather not,
But keep the odds of Knowledge in my power
Without Copartner? so to add what wants
In Female Sex, the more to draw his Love,
And render me more equal, and perhaps,
A thing not undesireable, sometime
Superior: for inferior who is free?
This may be well: but what if God have seen,
And Death ensue? then I shall be no more,
And *Adam* wedded to another *Eve*,

Shall live with her enjoying, I extinct;
A death to think. Confirm'd then I resolve,
Adam shall share with me in bliss or woe:
So dear I love him, that with him all deaths
I could endure, without him live no life."

Conclusion

                              High in Front advanc'd
The brandisht Sword of God before them blaz'd
Fierce as a Comet; which with torrid heat,
And vapour as the *Libyan* Air adust,
Began to parch that temperate Clime; whereat
In either hand the hastning Angel caught
Our lingring Parents, and to th'Eastern Gate
Led them direct, and down the Cliff as fast
To the subjected Plaine; then disappeer'd.
They looking back, all th'Eastern side beheld
Of Paradise, so late thir happie seat,
Wav'd over by that flaming Brand, the Gate
With dreadful Faces throng'd and fierie Armes:
Some natural tears they drop'd, but wip'd them soon;
The World was all above them, where to choose
Thir place of rest, and Providence thir guide:
They hand in hand with wandring steps and slow,
Through *Eden* took thir solitarie way.

Translators of the King James BIBLE (1606–1611)

From ISAIAH

Because the daughters of Zion are haughty,
And walk with stretched forth necks and wanton eyes,
Walking and mincing as they go,
And making a tinkling with their feet:
Therefore the Lord will smite with a scab

The crown of the head of the daughters of Zion,
And the Lord will discover their secret parts.
In that day the Lord will take away
The bravery of their tinkling ornaments about their feet,
And their cauls, and their round tires like the moon,
The chains, and the bracelets, and the mufflers,
The bonnets, and the ornaments of the legs,
And the headbands, and the tablets, and the earrings,
The rings, and nose jewels,
The changeable suits of apparel,
And the mantles, and the wimples, and the crisping pins,
The glasses, and the fine linen, and the hoods, and the veils.
And it shall come to pass,
That instead of sweet smell there shall be stink;
And instead of a girdle a rent;
And instead of well-set hair baldness;
And instead of a stomacher a girding of sackcloth;
And burning instead of beauty.
Thy men shall fall by the sword,
And thy mighty in the war.
And her gates shall lament and mourn;
And she being desolate shall sit upon the ground.

From PSALMS

The heavens declare the glory of God;
And the firmament showeth his handiwork.
Day unto day uttereth speech,
And night unto night showeth knowledge.
There is no speech nor language,
Where their voice is not heard.
Their line is gone out through all the earth,
And their words to the end of the world.
In them hath he set a tabernacle for the sun,
Which is as a bridegroom coming out of his chamber,
And rejoiceth as a strong man to run a race.
His going forth is from the end of the heaven,
And his circuit unto the ends of it:
And there is nothing hid from the heat thereof.
The law of the Lord is perfect, converting the soul:
The testimony of the Lord is sure, making wise the simple.
The statutes of the Lord are right, rejoicing the heart:
The commandment of the Lord is pure, enlightening the eyes.
The fear of the Lord is clean, enduring for ever:

The judgments of the Lord are true and righteous altogether.
More to be desired are they than gold, yea, than much fine
 gold:
Sweeter also than honey and the honeycomb.
Moreover by them is thy servant warned:
In keeping of them there is great reward.
Who can understand his errors?
Cleanse thou me from secret faults.
Keep back thy servant also from presumptuous sins;
Let them not have dominion over me: then shall I be up-
 right,
And I shall be innocent from the great transgression.
Let the words of my mouth, and the meditation of my heart,
 be acceptable in thy sight,
O Lord, my strength, and my redeemer.

From JOB

Canst thou bind the cluster of the Pleiades,
Or loose the bands of Orion?
Canst thou lead forth the Mazzaroth in their season?
Or canst thou guide the Bear with her train?
Knowest thou the ordinances of the heavens?
Canst thou establish the dominion thereof in the earth?
Canst thou lift up thy voice to the clouds,
That abundance of waters may cover thee? . . .
Hast thou given the horse his might?
Has thou clothed his neck with the quivering mane?
Has thou made him to leap as a locust?
The glory of his snorting is terrible.
He paweth in the valley, and rejoiceth in his strength:
He goeth out to meet the armed men.
He mocketh at fear, and is not dismayed;
Neither turneth he back from the sword.
The quiver rattleth against him,
The flashing spear and the javelin.
He swalloweth the ground with fierceness and rage;
Neither believeth he that it is the voice of the trumpet.
As oft as the trumpet soundeth he saith, "Aha!"
And he smelleth the battle afar off,
The thunder of the captains, and the shouting.

From THE SONG OF SONGS

How beautiful are thy feet in sandals, O prince's daughter!
The joints of thy thighs are like jewels,
The work of the hands of a cunning workman.
Thy navel is like a round goblet,
Wherein no mingled wine is wanting;
Thy belly is like a heap of wheat
Set about with lilies.

Thy two breasts are like two fawns
That are twins of a roe.
Thy neck is like the tower of ivory;
Thine eyes as the pools in Heshbon, by the gate of Bath-rab-
    bim;
Thy nose is like the tower of Lebanon
Which looketh toward Damascus.

Thine head upon thee is like Carmel,
And the hair of thine head like purple;
The king is held captive in the tresses thereof.
How fair and how pleasant art thou,
O love, for delights!
This thy stature is like to a palm tree,
And thy breasts to clusters of grapes.

I said, "I will climb up into the palm tree,
I will take hold of the branches thereof";
Let thy breasts be as clusters of the vine,
And the smell of thy breath like apples;
And thy mouth like the best wine,
That goeth down smoothly for my beloved,
Gliding through the lips of those who are asleep.

From ECCLESIASTES

Remember also thy Creator in the days of thy youth,
Or ever the evil days come,
And the years draw nigh, when thou shalt say,
"I have no pleasure in them";
Or ever the sun, and the light,

And the moon, and the stars, be darkened,
And the clouds return after the rain;
In the days when the keepers of the house shall tremble,
And the strong men shall bow themselves,
And the grinders cease because they are few,
And those that look out of the windows be darkened,
And the doors shall be shut in the street;
When the sound of the grinding is low,
And one shall rise up at the voice of a bird,
And all the daughters of music shall be brought low;
Yea, they shall be afraid of that which is high,
And terrors shall be in the way;
And the almond tree shall blossom,
And the grasshopper shall be a burden,
And the caper-berry shall fail:
Because man goeth to his long home,
And the mourners go about the streets:
Or ever the silver cord be loosed,
Or the golden bowl be broken,
Or the pitcher be broken at the fountain,
Or the wheel broken at the cistern;
And the dust return to the earth as it was,
And the spirit return unto God who gave it.

Richard Crashaw (1613?–1649)

From THE FLAMING HEART

Upon the Book and Picture of the Seraphical Saint Teresa

Conclusion

O Heart! the equal poise of love's both parts,
Big alike with wound and darts,
Live in these conquering leaves; live all the same;
And walk through all tongues one triumphant flame.
Live here, great Heart, and love and die and kill,
And bleed and wound, and yield and conquer still,
Let this immortal life, where e'er it comes,
Walk in a crowd of loves and martyrdoms.

Let mystic deaths wait on't, and wise souls be
The love-slain witnesses of this life of thee.
O sweet incendiary! show here thy art
Upon this carcass of a hard cold heart!
Let all thy scattered shafts of light, that play
Among the leaves of thy large books of day,
Combined against this breast, at once break in
And take away from me my self and sin!
This gracious robbery shall thy bounty be,
And my best fortunes such fair spoils of me.

O thou undaunted daughter of desires,
By all thy dower of lights and fires,
By all the eagle in thee, all the dove,
By all thy lives and deaths of love,
By thy large draughts of intellectual day,
And by thy thirsts of love more large than they,
By all thy brim-filled bowls of fierce desire,
By thy last morning's draught of liquid fire;
By the full kingdom of that final kiss
That seized thy parting soul and sealed thee His,
By all the heaven thou hast in Him—
Fair sister of the Seraphim!—
By all of Him we have in thee,
Leave nothing of myself in me.
Let me so read thy life that I
Unto all life of mine may die.

From TO THE NOBLEST AND BEST OF LADIES, THE COUNTESS OF DENBIGH

Persuading her to resolution in religion, and to render herself without further delay into the communion of the Catholic Church

... The astonished nymphs their flood's strange fate deplore,
To see themselves their own severer shore.
Thou that alone canst thaw this cold,
And fetch the heart from its stronghold,
Almighty Love! end this long war,
And of a meteor make a star.
Oh, fix this fair indefinite,
And, 'mongst thy shafts of sovereign light

Choose out that sure decisive dart
Which has the key of this close heart,
Knows all the corners of't, and can control
The self-shut cabinet of an unsearched soul . . .
Disband dull fears, give faith the day;
To save your life, kill your delay.
It is Love's siege, and sure to be
Your triumph, through His victory.
'Tis cowardice that keeps this field,
And want of courage not to yield.
Yield then, O yield, that Love may win
The fort at last, and let life in;
Yield quickly, lest perhaps you prove
Death's prey, before the prize of Love.
This fort of your fair self, if't be not won,
He is repulsed indeed, but you're undone.

Abraham Cowley (1618–1667)

ANACREONTICS: DRINKING

The thirsty earth soaks up the rain,
And drinks and gapes for drink again;
The plants suck in the earth, and are
With constant drinking fresh and fair;
The sea itself (which one would think
Should have but little need of drink)
Drinks twice ten thousand rivers up,
So fill'd that they o'erflow the cup.
The busy Sun (and one would guess
By 's drunken fiery face no less)
Drinks up the Sea, and when he's done
The Moon and Stars drink up the Sun:
They drink and dance by their own light,
They drink and revel all the night:
Nothing in Nature's sober found,

But an eternal health goes round.
Fill up the bowl, then, fill it high,
Fill all the glasses there—for why
Should every creature drink but I?
Why, man of morals, tell me why?

Richard Lovelace (1618–1657)

LA BELLA BONA ROBA

I cannot tell who loves the Skeleton
Of a poor Marmoset, nought but boan, boan.
Give me a nakednesse with her cloath's on.

Such whose white-sattin upper coat of skin,
Cuts upon Velvet rich Incarnadin,
Ha's yet a Body (and of Flesh) within.

Sure it is meant good Husbandry in men,
Who do incorporate with Aëry leane,
T' repair their sides, and get their Ribb agen.

Hard hap unto that Huntsman that Decrees
Fat joys for all his swet, when as he sees,
After his 'Say, nought but his Keepers Fees.

Then Love I beg, when next thou tak'st thy Bow,
Thy angry shafts, and dost Heart-chasing go,
Passe *Rascall Deare*, strike me the largest Doe.

TO LUCASTA, GOING TO THE WARRES

Tell me not (Sweet) I am unkinde,
  That from the Nunnerie

Of thy chaste breast, and quiet minde,
    To Warre and Armes I flie.

True; a new Mistresse now I chase,
    The first Foe in the Field;
And with a stronger Faith imbrace
    A Sword, a Horse, a Shield.

Yet this Inconstancy is such,
    As you too shall adore;
I could not love thee (Deare) so much,
    Lov'd I not Honour more.

Andrew Marvell (1621–1678)

TO HIS COY MISTRESS

Had we but World enough, and Time,
This coyness Lady were no crime.
We would sit down, and think which way
To walk, and pass our long Love's Day.
Thou by the *Indian Ganges* side
Should'st Rubies find: I by the Tide
Of *Humber* would complain. I would
Love you ten years before the Flood:
And you should if you please refuse
Till the Conversion of the Jews.
My vegetable Love should grow
Vaster than Empires, and more slow.
An hundred years should go to praise
Thine Eyes, and on thy Forehead Gaze.
Two hundred to adore each Breast:
But thirty thousand to the rest.
An Age at least to every part,
And the last Age should show your Heart.
For Lady you deserve this State;

Nor would I love at slower rate.
    But at my back I always hear
Time's wingèd Charriot hurrying near:
And yonder all before us lye
Deserts of vast Eternity.
Thy Beauty shall no more be found;
Nor, in thy marble Vault, shall sound
My echoing Song: then Worms shall try
That long preserv'd Virginity:
And your quaint Honour turn to dust;
And into ashes all my Lust.
The Grave's a fine and private place,
But None I think do there embrace.
    Now therefore, while the youthful hew
Sits on thy skin like morning dew,
And while thy willing Soul transpires
At every pore with instant Fires,
Now let us sport us while we may;
And now, like am'rous birds of prey,
Rather at once our Time devour,
Than languish in his slow-chapt power.
Let us roll all our Strength, and all
Our sweetness, up into one Ball:
And tear our Pleasures with rough strife,
Thorough the Iron gates of Life.
Thus, though we cannot make our Sun
Stand still, yet we will make him run.

AN HORATION ODE UPON CROMWELL'S
RETURN FROM IRELAND

The forward youth that would appear,
Must now forsake his Muses dear,
        Nor in the shadows sing
        His numbers languishing:

'Tis time to leave the books in dust,
And oil the unusèd armour's rust;
        Removing from the wall
        The corselet of the hall.

So restless Cromwell could not cease
In the inglorious arts of peace,

But through adventurous war
Urgèd his active star;

And, like the three-forked lightning, first
Breaking the clouds where it was nursed,
Did thorough his own side
His fiery way divide:

(For 'tis all one to courage high,
The emulous, or enemy;
And with such, to enclose,
Is more than to oppose;)

Then burning through the air he went,
And palaces and temples rent;
And Caesar's head at last
Did through his laurels blast.

'Tis madness to resist or blame,
The face of the angry Heaven's flame;
And if we would speak true
Much to the man is due,

Who from his private gardens, where
He lived reservèd and austere,
(As if his highest plot
To plant the bergamot;)

Could by industrious valour climb
To ruin the great work of Time,
And cast the kingdoms old,
Into another mould;

Though Justice against Fate complain,
And plead the ancient rights in vain;
(But those do hold or break,
As men are strong or weak.)

Nature that hateth emptiness,
Allows of penetration less,
And therefore must make room
Where greater spirits come.

What field of all the civil wars,
Where his were not the deepest scars?

And Hampton shows what part
He had of wiser art;

Where, twining subtle fears with hope,
He wove a net of such a scope
    That Charles himself might chase
    To Caresbrooke's narrow case,

That thence the royal actor borne,
The tragic scaffold might adorn;
    While round the armèd bands
    Did clap their bloody hands.

He nothing common did, or mean,
Upon that memorable scene,
    But with his keener eye
    The axe's edge did try;

Nor called the gods with vulgar spite
To vindicate his helpless right;
    But bowed his comely head
    Down, as upon a bed.

This was that memorable hour
Which first assured the forcèd power;
    So, when they did design
    The capitol's first line,

A bleeding head, where they begun,
Did fright the architects to run;
    And yet in that happy state
    Foresaw its happy fate.

And now the Irish are ashamed
To see themselves in one year tamed;
    So much one man can do,
    That does both act and know.

They can affirm his praises best,
And have, though overcome, confessed
    How good he is, how just
    And fit for highest trust.

Nor yet grown stiffer with command,
But still in the republic's hand—

How fit he is to sway,
That can so well obey!

He to the Common's feet presents
A kingdom for his first year's rents;
    And, what he may, forbears
    His fame, to make it theirs;

And has his sword and spoils ungirt,
To lay them at the public's skirt:
    So when the falcon high
    Falls heavy from the sky,

She, having killed, no more doth search,
But on the next green bough to perch;
    Where, when he first does lure,
    The falconer has her sure.

What may not then our isle presume,
While victory his crest does plume?
    What may not others fear,
    If thus he crowns each year?

As Caesar, he, ere long, to Gaul,
To Italy an Hannibal,
    And to all states not free,
    Shall climactèric be.

The Pict no shelter now shall find
Within his parti-coloured mind,
    But, from this valour sad,
    Shrink underneath the plaid;

Happy, if in the tufted brake,
The English hunter him mistake,
    Nor lay his hounds in near
    The Caledonian deer.

But thou, the war's, and fortune's son,
March indefatigably on;
    And for the last effect,
    Still keep the sword erect;

Besides the force it has to fright
The spirits of the shady night,

The same arts that did gain
A power must it maintain.

Henry Vaughan (1622–1695)

THE RETREATE

Happy those early dayes! when I
Shin'd in my Angell-infancy.
Before I understood this place
Appointed for my second race,
Or taught my soul to fancy ought
But a white, Celestiall thought,
When yet I had not walkt above
A mile, or two, from my first love,
And looking back (at that short space,)
Could see a glimpse of his bright-face;
When on some *gilded Cloud*, or *flowre*
My gazing soul would dwell an houre,
And in those weaker glories spy
Some shadows of eternity;
Before I taught my tongue to wound
My Conscience with a sinful sound,
Or had the black art to dispence
A sev'rall sinne to ev'ry sence,
But felt through all this fleshly dresse
Bright *shootes* of everlastingnesse.
  O how I long to travell back
And tread again that ancient track!
That I might once more reach that plaine,
Where first I left my glorious traine,
From whence th'Inlightned spirit sees
That shady City of Palme trees;
But (ah!) my soul with too much stay
Is drunk, and staggers in the way.
Some men a forward motion love,

[113]

But I by backward steps would move,
And when this dust falls to the urn
In that state I came return.

THE WORLD

I saw Eternity the other night
Like a great *Ring* of pure and endless light,
    All calm, as it was bright,
And round beneath it, Time in hours, days, years
      Driv'n by the spheres
Like a vast shadow mov'd, In which the world
      And all her train were hurl'd;
The doting Lover in his quaintest strain
      Did there Complain,
Neer him, his Lute, his fancy, and his flights,
      With sour delights,
With gloves, and knots the silly snares of pleasure
      Yet his dear Treasure
All scatter'd lay, while he his eys did pour
      Upon a flowr.

The darksome States-man hung with weights and woe
Like a thick midnight-fog mov'd there so slow
      He did not stay, nor go;
Condemning thoughts (like sad Ecclipses) scowl
      Upon his soul,
And Clouds of crying witnesses without
      Pursued him with one shout.
Yet dig'd the Mole, and lest his ways be found
      Workt under ground,
Where he did Clutch his prey, but one did see
      That policie,
Churches and altars fed him, Perjuries
      Where gnats and flies,
It rain'd about him bloud and tears, but he
      Drank them as free.

The fearfull miser on a heap of rust
Sate pining all his life there, did scarce trust
      His own hands with the dust,
Yet would not place one peece above, but lives
      In feare of thieves.

Thousands there were as frantick as himself
    And hug'd each one his pelf,
The down-right Epicure plac'd heaven in sense
    And scornd pretence
While others slipt into a wide Excesse
    Said little lesse;
The weaker sort slight, triviall wares Inslave
    Who think them brave,
And poor, despisèd truth sate Counting by
    Their victory.

Yet some, who all this while did weep and sing,
And sing, and weep, soar'd up into the *Ring*.
    But most would use no wing.
O fools (said I,) thus to prefer dark night
    Before true light,
To live in grots, and caves, and hate the day
    Because it shows the way,
The way that from this dead and dark abode
    Leads up to God,
A way where you might tread the Sun, and be
    More bright than he.
But as I did their madness so discusse
    One whisper'd thus,
This Ring the Bride-groome did for none provide
    But for his bride.

John Dryden (1631–1700)

From MAC FLECKNOE

Shadwell Anatomized

All human things are subject to decay,
And when fate summons, monarchs must obey.
This Flecknoe found, who, like Augustus, young

Was call'd to empire, and had govern'd long;
In prose and verse was own'd, without dispute,
Thro' all the realms of *Nonsense*, absolute.

●

But let no alien Sedley interpose,
To lard with wit thy hungry *Epsom* prose.
And when false flowers of rhetoric thou wouldst cull,
Trust nature, do not labour to be dull.
But write thy best, and top; and in each line,
Sir Formal's oratory will be thine:
Sir Formal, tho' unsought, attends thy quill,
And does thy northern dedications fill.
Nor let false friends seduce thy mind to fame,
By arrogating Jonson's hostile name.
Let father Flecknoe fire thy mind with praise,
And Uncle Ogleby thy envy raise.
Thou art my blood, where Jonson has no part:
What share have we in nature or in art?
Where did his wit on learning fix a brand,
And rail at arts he did not understand?
Where made he love in Prince Nicander's vein,
Or swept the dust in *Psyche's* humble strain?
Where sold he bargain, 'whip-stitch, kiss my arse,'
Promis'd a play and dwindled to a farce? . . .

●

A tun of man in thy large bulk is writ,
Be sure thou'rt but a kilderkin of wit.
Like mine, thy gentle numbers feebly creep;
Thy tragic Muse gives smiles, thy comic sleep.
With whate'er gall thou sett'st thyself to write,
Thy inoffensive satires never bite.
In thy felonious heart tho' venom lies,
It does not touch thy Irish pen, and dies.
Thy genius calls thee not to purchase fame
In keen iambics, but mild anagram.
Leave writing plays, and choose for thy command
Some peaceful province in acrostic land . . .

From ABSALOM AND ACHITOPHEL, PART 2

Let him rail on, let his invective Muse
Have four and twenty letters to abuse,
Which if he jumbles to one line of sense,
Indict him of a capital offense.
In fireworks give him leave to vent his spite,
Those are the only serpents he can write;
The height of his ambition is, we know,
But to be master of a puppet show:
On that one stage his works may yet appear,
And a month's harvest keeps him all the year.
   Now stop your noses, readers, all and some,
For here's a tun of midnight work to come,
Og[1], from a treason-tavern rolling home.
Round as a globe, and liquor'd ev'ry chink,
Goodly and great he sails behind his link.
With all this bulk there's nothing lost in Og,
For every inch that is not fool is rogue:
A monstrous mass of foul corrupted matter,
As all the devils had spew'd to make the batter.
When wine has given him courage to blaspheme,
He curses God, but God before curs'd him;
And if man could have reason, none has more,
That made his paunch so rich, and him so poor.
With wealth he was not trusted, for Heav'n knew
What 'twas of old to pamper up a Jew;
To what would he on quail and pheasant swell,
That even on tripe and carrion could rebel?
But tho' Heav'n made him poor, (with rev'rence speaking,)
He never was a poet of God's making.
The midwife laid her hand on his thick skull
With this prophetic blessing: *Be thou dull;*
Drink, swear, and roar, forebear no lewd delight,
Fit for thy bulk, do anything but write:
Thou art of lasting make, like thoughtless men,
A strong nativity—but for the pen;
Eat opium, mingle arsenic in thy drink,
Still thou mayst live, avoiding pen and ink.
I see, I see, 'tis counsel given in vain,
For treason botch'd in rhyme will be thy bane;

---

[1] Shadwell.

Rhyme is the rock on which thou art to wreck,
'Tis fatal to thy fame and to thy neck. . . .

THE SECULAR MASQUE

Enter Janus.
JANUS. *Chronos, Chronos,* mend thy Pace,
An hundred times the rowling Sun
Around the Radiant Belt has run
In his revolving Race.
Behold, behold the Goal in sight,
Spread thy Fans, and wing thy flight.
Enter Chronos, with a Scythe in his hand, and a
great Globe on his Back, which he sets down at his entrance.
CHRONOS. Weary, weary of my weight,
Let me, let me drop my Freight,
    And leave the World behind.
I could not bear
Another Year
The Load of Human-kind.
Enter Momus Laughing.
MOMUS. Ha! ha! ha! Ha! ha! ha! well hast thou done,
    To lay down thy Pack,
    And lighten thy Back,
The World was a Fool, o'er since it begun,
And since neither *Janus,* nor *Chronos,* nor I.
    Can hinder the Crimes,
    Or mend the Bad Times,
'Tis better to Laugh than to Cry.
CHORUS OF ALL 3. *'Tis better to Laugh than to Cry.*
JANUS. Since *Momus* comes to laugh below,
    Old Time begin the Show,
That he may see, in every Scene,
What Changes in this Age have been.
CHRONOS. Then Goddess of the Silver Bow begin.
                    Horns, or Hunting-Musique within.

Enter Diana.
DIANA. With Horns and with Hounds I waken the Day,
And hye to my Woodland walks away;
I tuck up my Robe, and am buskin'd soon,
And tye to my Forehead a wexing Moon.
I course the fleet Stagg, unkennel the Fox,
And chase the wild Goats o'er summets of Rocks,

With shouting and hooting we pierce thro' the Sky;
And Eccho turns Hunter, and doubles the Cry.
CHORUS OF ALL. *With shouting and hooting, we pierce*
through the Skie,
And Eccho turns Hunter, and doubles the Cry.
JANUS. Then our Age was in it's Prime,
CHRONOS. Free from Rage.
DIANA. And free from Crime.
MOMUS. A very Merry, Dancing, Drinking,
Laughing, Quaffing, and unthinking Time.
CHORUS OF ALL. *Then our Age was in its Prime,*
Free from Rage and free from Crime,
A very Merry, Dancing, Drinking,
Laughing, Quaffing, and unthinking Time.

> *Dance of Diana's Attendants. Enter Mars.*

MARS. Inspire the Vocal Brass, Inspire;
The World is past its Infant Age:
   Arms and Honour,
   Arms and Honour,
Set the Martial Mind on Fire,
And kindle Manly Rage.
Mars has lookt the Sky to Red;
And Peace, the Lazy Good, is fled.
Plenty, Peace, and Pleasure fly;
   The Sprightly Green
In *Woodland-Walks*, no more is seen;
The Sprightly Green, has drunk the *Tyrian* Dye.
CHORUS OF ALL. *Plenty, Peace, etc.*
MARS. Sound the Trumpet, Beat the Drum,
Through all the World around;
Sound a Reveille, Sound, Sound,
   The Warrior God is come.
CHORUS OF ALL. *Sound the Trumpet, etc.*
MOMUS. Thy Sword within the Scabbard keep,
   And let Mankind agree;
Better the World were fast asleep,
   Than kept awake by Thee.
The Fools are only thinner,
   With all our Cost and Care;
But neither side a winner.
   For Things are as they were.
CHORUS OF ALL. *The Fools are only, etc.*
Enter Venus.
VENUS. Calms appear, when Storms are past;
Love will have his Hour at last:
Nature is my kindly Care;

Mars destroys, and I repair;
Take me, take me, while you may,
Venus comes not ev'ry Day.
CHORUS OF ALL. *Take her, take her, etc.*
CHRONOS. The World was then so light,
I scarcely felt the Weight;
Joy rul'd the Day, and Love the Night.
But since the Queen of Pleasure left the Ground,
 I faint, I lag,
 And feebly drag
The pond'rous Orb around.
MOMUS. All, all, of a piece throughout;
Pointing to Diana. Thy Chase had a Beast in View;
To Mars. Thy Wars brought nothing about;
To Venus. Thy Lovers were all untrue.
JANUS. 'Tis well an Old Age is out,
CHRONOS. And time to begin a New.
CHORUS OF ALL. *All, all, of a piece throughout;*
Thy Chase had a Beast in View;
Thy Wars brought nothing about;
Thy Lovers were all untrue.
'Tis well an Old Age is out,
And time to begin a New.

 Dance of Huntsmen, Nymphs, Warriours and Lovers.

John Wilmot, Earl of Rochester (1647–1680)

EPITAPH ON CHARLES II

 Here lies our Sovereign Lord, the King,
  Whose word no man relies on,
 Who never said a foolish thing,
  Nor ever did a wise one.

UPON LEAVING HIS MISTRESS

'Tis not that I am weary grown,
Of being yours, and yours alone;
But with what face can I incline
To damn you to be only mine—
You, whom some kinder power did fashion,
By merit, and by inclination,
The joy at least of a whole nation?

Let meaner spirits of your sex
With humble aims their thoughts perplex,
And boast if by their arts they can
Contrive to make one happy man;
While, moved by an impartial sense,
Favors, like Nature, you dispense
With universal influence.
See, the kind seed-receiving earth
To every grain affords a birth:
On her no showers unwelcome fall;
He willing womb retains them all.
And shall my Celia be confined?
No, live up to thy mighty mind,
And be the mistress of mankind!

George Berkeley, Bishop of Cloyne (1685–1753)

ON THE PROSPECT OF PLANTING ARTS
AND LEARNING IN AMERICA

The Muse, disgusted at an age and clime
    Barren of every glorious theme,
In distant lands now waits a better time,
    Producing subjects worthy fame:

In happy climes the seat of innocence,
    Where nature guides and virtue rules,
Where men shall not impose for truth and sense,
    The pedantry of courts and schools:

There shall be sung another golden age,
    The rise of empire and of arts,
The good and great inspiring epic rage,
    The wisest heads and noblest hearts.

Not such as Europe breeds in her decay;
    Such as she bred when fresh and young,
When heavenly flame did animate her clay,
    By future poets shall be sung.

Westward the course of empire takes its way;
    The four first acts already past,
A fifth shall close the drama with the day;
    Time's noblest offspring is the last.

Alexander Pope (1688–1744)

from EPISTLE TO DR. ARBUTHNOT

Curst be the Verse, how well so'er it flow,
That tends to make one worthy man my foe,
Give Virtue scandal, Innocence a fear,
Or from the soft-ey'd Virgin steal a tear!
But he who hurts a harmless neighbour's peace,
Insults fall'n worth, or Beauty in distress,
Who loves a Lye, lame slander helps about,
Who writes a Libel, or who copies out:
That Fop, whose pride affects a Patron's name,
Yet absent, wounds an Author's honest fame:
Who can your merit *selfishly* approve,
And show the *sense* of it without the *love*;

Who has the vanity to call you friend,
Yet wants the honour, injur'd, to defend;
Who tells whate'er you think, whate'er you say,
And if he lye not, must at least betray:
Who to the *Dean* and *silver bell* can swear,
And sees at *Cannons* what was never there;
Who reads, but with a lust to misapply,
Makes Satire a Lampoon, and fiction Lye.
A lash like mine no honest man shall dread,
But all such babbling blockheads in his stead.

    Let *Sporus* tremble—*A.* What? that thing of silk,
Sporus, that mere white curd of ass's milk?
Satire or sense, alas! can *Sporus* feel?
Who breaks a butterfly upon a wheel?
P. Yet let me flap this bug with gilded wings,
This painted child of Dirt, that stinks and stings;
Whose buzz the witty and the fair annoys,
Yet wit ne'er tastes, and beauty ne'er enjoys;
So well-bred spaniels civilly delight
In mumbling of the game they dare not bite.
Eternal smiles his emptiness betray,
As shallow streams run dimpling all the way.
Whether in florid impotence he speaks,
And as the prompter breathes, the puppet squeaks;
Or at the ear of *Eve*, familiar Toad,
Half froth, half venom, spits himself abroad,
In puns, or politics, or tales, or lies,
Or spite, or smut, or rhymes, or blasphemies.
His wit all see-saw, between *that* and *this*,
Now high, now low, now master up, now miss,
And he himself one vile Antithesis.
Amphibious thing! that acting either part,
The trifling head, or the corrupted heart,
Fop at the toilet, flatt'rer at the board,
Now trips a Lady, and now struts a Lord.
Eve's tempter thus the Rabbins have exprest,
A Cherub's face, a Reptile all the rest,
Beauty that shocks you, parts that none will trust,
Wit that can creep, and pride that licks the dust.

Thomas Gray (1716–1771)

ELEGY WRITTEN IN A COUNTRY CHURCH-YARD

The Curfew tolls the knell of parting day,
The lowing herd wind slowly o'er the lea,
The plowman homeward plods his weary way,
And leaves the world to darkness and to me.

Now fades the glimmering landscape on the sight,
And all the air a solemn stillness holds,
Save where the beetle wheels his droning flight,
And drowsy tinklings lull the distant folds;

Save that from yonder ivy-mantled tow'r
The mopeing owl does to the moon complain
Of such, as wand'ring near her secret bow'r,
Molest her ancient solitary reign.

Beneath those rugged elms, that yew-tree's shade,
Where heaves the turf in many a mould'ring heap,
Each in his narrow cell for ever laid,
The rude Forefathers of the hamlet sleep.

The breezy call of incense-breathing Morn,
The swallow twitt'ring from the straw-built shed,
The cock's shrill clarion, or the echoing horn,
No more shall rouse them from their lowly bed.

For them no more the blazing hearth shall burn,
Or busy housewife ply her evening care:
No children run to lisp their sire's return,
Or climb his knees the envied kiss to share.

Oft did the harvest to their sickle yield,
Their furrow oft the stubborn glebe has broke;

How jocund did they drive their team afield!
How bow'd the woods beneath their sturdy stroke!

Let not Ambition mock their useful toil,
Their homely joys, and destiny obscure;
Nor Grandeur hear with a disdainful smile,
The short and simple annals of the poor.

The boast of heraldry, the pomp of pow'r,
And all that beauty, all that wealth e'er gave,
Awaits alike th'inevitable hour.
The paths of glory lead but to the grave.

Nor you, ye Proud, impute to These the fault,
If Mem'ry o'er their Tomb, no Trophies raise,
Where thro' the long-drawn isle and fretted vault
The pealing anthem swells the note of praise.

Can storied urn or animated bust
Back to its mansion call the fleeting breath?
Can Honour's voice provoke the silent dust,
Or Flatt'ry soothe the dull cold ear of Death?

Perhaps in this neglected spot is laid
Some heart once pregnant with celestial fire;
Hands, that the rod of empire might have sway'd,
Or wak'd to extasy the living lyre.

But Knowledge to their eyes her ample page
Rich with the spoils of time did ne'er unroll;
Chill Penury repress'd their noble rage,
And froze the genial current of the soul.

Full many a gem of purest ray serene,
The dark unfathom'd caves of ocean bear:
Full many a flower is born to blush unseen,
And waste its sweetness on the desert air.

Some village-Hampden, that with dauntless breast
The little Tyrant of his fields withstood;
Some mute inglorious Milton here may rest,
Some Cromwell guiltless of his country's blood.

Th'applause of list'ning senates to command,
The threats of pain and ruin to despise,

To scatter plenty o'er a smiling land,
And read their hist'ry in a nation's eyes,

Their lot forbad: nor circumscrib'd alone
Their growing virtues, but their crimes confin'd;
Forbad to wade through slaughter to a throne,
And shut the gates of mercy on mankind,

The struggling pangs of conscious truth to hide,
To quench the blushes of ingenuous shame,
Or heap the shrine of Luxury and Pride
With incense kindled at the Muse's flame.

Far from the madding crowd's ignoble strife,
Their sober wishes never learn'd to stray;
Along the cool sequester'd vale of life
They kept the noiseless tenor of their way.

Yet ev'n these bones from insult to protect
Some frail memorial still erected nigh,
With uncouth rhimes and shapeless sculpture deck'd,
Implores the passing tribute of a sigh.

Their name, their years, spelt by th'unletter'd muse,
The place of fame and elegy supply:
And many a holy text around she strews,
That teach the rustic moralist to die.

For who to dumb Forgetfulness a prey,
This pleasing anxious being e'er resign'd,
Left the warm precincts of the chearful day,
Nor cast one longing ling'ring look behind?

On some fond breast the parting soul relies,
Some pious drops the closing eye requires;
Ev'n from the tomb the voice of Nature cries,
Ev'n in their Ashes live their wonted Fires.

For thee, who mindful of th'unhonour'd Dead
Dost in these lines their artless tale relate;
If chance, by lonely contemplation led,
Some kindred Spirit shall inquire thy fate,

Happly some hoary-headed Swain may say,
"Oft have we seen him at the peep of dawn
Brushing with hasty steps the dews away

To meet the sun upon the upland lawn.

"There at the foot of yonder nodding beech
That wreaths its old fantastic roots so high,
His listless length at noontide would he stretch,
And pore upon the brook that babbles by.

"Hard by yon wood, now smiling as in scorn,
Mutt'ring his wayward fancies he would rove,
Now drooping, woeful wan, like one forlorn,
Or craz'd with care, or cross'd in hopeless love.

"One morn I miss'd him on the custom'd hill,
Along the hill and near his fav'rite tree;
Another came; not yet beside the rill,
Nor up the lawn, nor at the wood was he;

"The next with dirges due in sad array
Slow through the church-way path we saw him born.
Approach and read (for thou can'st read) the lay,
Grav'd on the stone beneath yon agèd thorn."

THE EPITAPH

*Here rests his head upon the lap of Earth
A Youth to Fortune and to Fame unknown.
Fair Science frown'd not on his humble birth,
And Melancholy mark'd him for her own.*

*Large was his bounty, and his soul sincere,
Heav'n did a recompence as largely send:
He gave to Mis'ry all he had, a tear,
He gain'd from Heav'n ('twas all he wish'd) a friend.*

*No further seek his merits to disclose,
Or draw his frailties from their dread abode,
(There they alike in trembling hope repose,)
The bosom of his Father and his God.*

William Collins (1721–1759)

ODE TO EVENING

If aught of oaten stop, or pastoral song,
May hope, chaste Eve, to soothe thy modest ear,
   Like thy own solemn springs,
   Thy springs and dying gales;

O nymph reserved, while now the bright-haired sun
Sits in yon western tent, whose cloudy skirts,
   With brede etherreal wove,
   O'erhang his wavy bed:

Now air is hush'd, save where the weak-eyed bat
With short shrill shrieks flits by on leathern wing,
   Or where the beetle winds
   His small but sullen horn,

As oft he rises, midst the twilight path
Against the pilgrim borne in heedless hum:
   Now teach me, maid composed,
   To breathe some soften'd strain,

Whose numbers, stealing through thy darkening vale,
May not unseemly with its stillness suit,
   As, musing slow, I hail
   Thy genial loved return!

For when thy folding-star arising shows
His paly circlet, at his warning lamp
   The fragrant hours, and elves
   Who slept in buds the day,

And many a nymph who wreaths her brow with sedge,

And sheds the freshening dew, and, lovelier still,
  The pensive pleasures sweet,
    Prepare thy shadowy car:

Then lead, calm votaress, where some sheety lake
Cheers the lone heath, or sometime-hallowed pile,
  Or upland fallows grey
    Reflect its last cool gleam.

Or if chill blustering winds, or driving rain,
Prevent my willing feet, be mine the hut
  That from the mountain's side
    Views wilds and swelling floods,

And hamlets brown, and dim-discover'd spires,
And hears their simple bell, and marks o'er all
  Thy dewy fingers draw
    The gradual dusky veil.

While spring shall pour his show'rs, as oft he wont,
And bathe thy breathing tresses, meekest Eve!
  While Summer loves to sport
    Beneath thy lingering light;

While sallow Autumn fills thy lap with leaves,
Or Winter, yelling through the troublous air,
  Afrights thy shrinking train,
    And rudely rends thy robes:

So long, regardful of thy quiet rule,
Shall Fancy, Friendship, Science, rose-lipp'd Health,
  Thy gentlest influence own,
    And hymn thy favorite name!

Christopher Smart (1722–1771)

HYMN 32: THE NATIVITY OF OUR LORD AND SAVIOUR JESUS CHRIST

Where is this stupendous stranger,
  Swains of Solyma, advise,
Lead me to my Master's manger,
  Shew me where my Saviour lies?

O Most Mighty, O most holy!
  Far beyond the seraph's thought,
Art thou then so mean and lowly
  As unheeded prophets taught?

O the magnitude of meekness!
  Worth from worth immortal sprung;
O the strength of infant weakness,
  If eternal is so young!

If so young and thus eternal,
  Michael tune the shepherd's reed,
Where the scenes are ever vernal,
  And the loves be love indeed!

See the God blasphem'd and doubted
  In the schools of Greece and Rome;
See the pow'rs of darkness routed,
  Taken at their utmost gloom.

Nature's decorations glisten
  Far above their usual trim;
Birds on box and laurel listen
  As so near the cherubs hymn.

Boreas now no longer winters
  On the desolated coast;

Oaks no more are riv'n in splinters
  By the whirlwind and his host.

Spinks and ouzles sing sublimely,
  'We too have a Saviour born';
Whiter blossoms burst untimely
  On the blest Mosaic thorn.

God all-bounteous, all-creative,
  Whom no ills from good dissuade,
Is incarnate, and a native
  Of the very world he made.

From A SONG TO DAVID

Fruits of the Earth

... The world—the clust'ring spheres he made,
The glorious light, the soothing shade,
  Dale, champaign, grove, and hill;
The multitudinous abyss,
Where secrecy remains in bliss,
  And wisdom hides her skill.

Trees, plants, and flow'rs—of virtuous root;
Gem yielding blossom, yielding fruit,
  Choice gums and precious balm;
Bless ye the nosegay in the vale,
And with the sweetness of the gale
  Enrich the thankful psalm.

Of fowl—e'en ev'ry beak and wing
Which cheer the winter, hail the spring,
  That live in peace or prey;
They that make music, or that mock,
The quail, the brave domestic cock,
  The raven, swan, and jay.

Of fishes—ev'ry size and shape,
Which nature frames of light escape,
  Devouring man to shun:
The shells are in the wealthy deep,
The shoals upon the surface leap,
  And love the glancing sun.

Of beasts—the beaver plods his task;
While the sleek tigers roll and bask,
    Nor yet the shades arouse;
Her cave the mining coney scoops;
Where o'er the mead the mountain stoops,
    The kids exult and brouse.

Of gems—their virtue and their price,
Which hid in earth from man's device,
    Their darts of lustre sheathe;
The jasper of the master's stamp,
The topaz blazing like a lamp
    Among the mines beneath.

Blest was the tenderness he felt
When to his graceful harp he knelt,
    And did for audience call;
When Satan with his hand he quell'd,
And in serene suspence he held
    The frantic throes of Saul.

His furious foes no more malign'd
As he such melody divin'd,
    And sense and soul detain'd;
Now striking strong, now soothing soft,
He sent the godly sounds aloft,
    Or in delight refrain'd.

When up to heaven his thoughts he pil'd
From fervant lips fair Michael smil'd,
    As blush to blush she stood;
And chose herself the queen, and gave
Her utmost from her heart, 'so brave,
    And plays his hymns so good.'

The pillars of the Lord are seven,
Which stand from earth to topmost heav'n;
    His wisdom drew the plan;
His WORD accomplished the design,
From brightest gem to deepest mine,
    From CHRIST enthroned to man.

Alpha, the cause of causes, first
In station, fountain, whence the burst
    Of light, and blaze of day;

Whence bold attempt, and brave advance,
Have motion, life, and ordinance,
    And heaven itself its stay.

Gamma supports the glorious arch
On which angelic legions march,
    And is with sapphires pav'd;
Thence the fleet clouds are sent adrift,
And thence the painted folds, that lift
    The crimson veil, are wav'd.

Eta with living sculpture breathes,
With verdant carvings, flow'ry wreaths,
    Of never-wasting bloom;
In strong relief his goodly base
All instruments of labour grace,
    The trowel, spade, and loom.

Next Theta stands to the Supreme—
Who formed, in number, sign, and scheme,
    Th'illustrious lights that are;
And one address'd his saffron robe,
And one, clad in a silver globe,
    Held rule with ev'ry star.

Iota's tuned to choral hymns
Of those that fly, while he that swims
    In thankful safety lurks;
And foot, and chapitre, and niche,
The various histories enrich
    Of God's recorded works.

Sigma presents the social droves
With him that solitary roves,
    And man of all the chief;
Fair on whose face, and stately frame,
Did God impress his hallow'd name,
    For ocular belief.

OMEGA! GREATEST and the BEST,
Stands sacred to the day of rest,
    For gratitude and thought;
Which blest the world upon his pole,
And gave the universe his goal,
    And clos'd th' infernal draft. . . .

Praise above all—for praise prevails;
Heap up the measure, load the scales,
  And good to goodness add:
The generous soul her Saviour aids,
But peevish obloquy degrades;
  The Lord is great and glad.

For ADORATION all the ranks
Of angels yield eternal thanks,
  And DAVID in the midst;
With God's good poor, which, last and least
In man's esteem, thou to thy feast,
  O blessed bridegroom, bidst.

For ADORATION seasons change,
And order, truth, and beauty range,
  Adjust, attract, and fill:
The grass the polyanthus cheques;
And polish'd porphyry reflects,
  By the descending rill.

Rich almonds colour to the prime
For ADORATION; tendrils climb,
  And fruit-trees pledge their gems;
And Ivis, with her gorgeous vest,
Builds for her eggs her cunning nest,
  And bell-flow'rs bow their stems.

With vinous syrup cedars spout;
From rocks pure honey gushing out,
  For ADORATION springs:
All scenes of painting crowd the map
Of nature; to the mermaid's pap
  The scalèd infant clings.

The spotted ounce and playsome cubs
Run rustling 'mongst the flow'ring shrubs,
  And lizards feed the moss;
For ADORATION beasts embark,
While waves upholding halcyon's ark
  No longer roar and toss.

While Israel sits beneath his fig,

With coral root and amber sprig
    The wean'd adven'rer sports;
Where to the palm the jasmine cleaves,
For ADORATION 'mongst the leaves
    The gale his peace reports.

Increasing days their reign exalt,
Nor in the pink and mottled vault
    The opposing spirits tilt;
And, by the coasting reader spied,
The silverlings and crusions glide
    For ADORATION gilt.

For ADORATION rip'ning canes,
And cocoa's purest milk detains
    The western pilgrim's staff;
Where rain in clasping boughs inclos'd,
And vines with oranges dispos'd,
    Embow'r the social laugh.

Now labour his reward receives,
For ADORATION counts his sheaves,
    To peace, her bounteous prince;
The nectarine his strong tint imbibes,
And apples of ten thousand tribes,
    And quick peculiar quince.

The wealthy crops of whit'ning rice,
'Mongst thyine woods and groves of spice,
    For ADORATION grow;
And, marshall'd in the fencèd land,
The peaches and pomegranates stand,
    Where wild carnations blow.

The laurels with the winter strive;
The crocus burnishes alive
    Upon the snow-clad earth:
For ADORATION myrtles stay
To keep the garden from dismay,
    And bless the sight from dearth.

The pheasant shows his pompous neck;
And ermine jealous of a speck,
    With fear eludes offense:
The sable, with his glossy pride,

For ADORATION is descried,
  Where frosts the waves condense.

The cheerful holly, pensive yew,
And holy thorn, their trim renew;
  The squirrel hoards his nuts.
All creatures batten o'er their stores,
And careful nature all her doors
  For ADORATION shuts.

For ADORATION, David's Psalms
Lift up the heart to deeds of alms;
  And he who kneels and chants,
Prevails his passions to control,
Finds meat and med'cine to the soul,
  Which for translation pants.

For ADORATION, beyond match,
The scholar bullfinch aims to catch
  The soft flute's iv'ry touch;
And, careless on the hazel spray
The daring redbreast keeps at bay
  The damsel's greedy clutch.

For ADORATION, in the skies,
The Lord's philosopher espies
  The Dog, the Ram, the Rose;
The planet's ring, Orion's sword;
Nor is his greatness less ador'd
  In the vile worm that glows.

For ADORATION, on the strings,
The western breezes work their wings,
  The captive ear to soothe.—
Hark! 'tis a voice—how still, and small—
That makes the cataracts to fall,
  Or bids the sea be smooth!

For ADORATION, incense comes
From bezoar, and Arabian gums;
  And on the civet's furr.
But as for prayer, or e're it faints,
Far better is the breath of saints
  Than galbanum or myrrh.

For ADORATION from the down
Of dam'sins to th'anana's crown,
 God sends to tempt the taste;
And while the luscious zest invites,
The sense, that in the scene delights,
 Commands desire be chaste.

For ADORATION, all the paths
Of grace are open, all the baths
 Of purity refresh;
And all the rays of glory beam
To deck the man of God's esteem,
 Who triumphs o'er the flesh.

For ADORATION, in the dome
Of Christ, the sparrow's find an home;
 And on his olives perch:
The swallow also dwells with thee,
O man of God's humility,
 Within his Saviour CHURCH. ...

Gloria

Glorious the sun in mid career;
Glorious th' assembled fires appear;
 Glorious the comet's train:
Glorious the trumpet and alarm;
Glorious th' almighty stretch'd-out arm;
 Glorious th' enraptur'd main:

Glorious the northern lights a-stream;
Glorious the song, when God's the theme;
 Glorious the thunder's roar:
Glorious hosannah from the den;
Glorious the catholic amen;
 Glorious the martyr's gore:

Glorious—more glorious is the crown
Of Him that brought salvation down,
 By meekness, called thy Son:
Thou at stupendous truth believ'd,
And now the matchless deed's atchiev'd,
 DETERMINED, DARED, and DONE.

From JUBILATE AGNO

Section 7

For I am not without authority in my jeopardy, which I derive inevitably from the glory of the name of the Lord.

For I bless God whose name is Jealous—and there is a zeal to deliver us from everlasting burnings.

For my existimation is good even among the slanderers and my memory shall arise for a sweet savour unto the Lord.

For I bless the PRINCE OF PEACE and pray that all the guns may be nail'd up, save such are for the rejoicing days.

For I have abstained from the blood of the grape and that even at the Lord's table.

For I have glorified God in GREEK and LATIN, the consecrated languages spoken by the Lord on earth.

For I meditate the peace of Europe amongst family bickerings and domestic jars.

For the HOST is in the WEST—The Lord make us thankful unto salvation.

For I preach the very GOSPEL OF CHRIST without comment & with this weapon shall I slay envy.

For I bless God in the rising generation, which is on my side.

For I have translated in the charity, which makes things better & I shall be translated myself at the last.

For he that walked upon the sea hath prepared the floods with the Gospel of peace.

For the merciful man is merciful to his beast, and to the trees that give them shelter.

For he hath turned the shadow of death into the morning, the Lord is his name.

For I am come home again, but there is nobody to kill the calf or to pay the musick.

For the hour of my felicity, like the womb of Sarah, shall come at the latter end.

For I shall have avail'd myself of waggery, had not malice been multitudinous.

For there are still serpents that can speak—God bless my head, my heart & my heel.

For I bless God that I am of the same seed with Ehud, Mutius Scaevola, and Colonel Draper.

For the word of God is a sword on my side—no matter what other weapon a stick or a straw.

For I have adventured myself in the name of the Lord, and he hath mark'd me for his own.

For I bless God for the Postmaster general & all conveyancers of letters under his care especially Allen & Shelvock.

For my grounds in New Canaan shall infinitely compensate for the flats and maynes of Staindrop Moor.

For the praise of God can give to a mute fish the notes of a nightingale.

For I have seen the White Raven & Thomas Hall of Willingham & am myself a greater curiosity than both.

For I look up to heaven which is my prospect to escape envy by surmounting it.

For if Pharaoh had known Joseph, he would have blessed God & me for the illumination of the people.

For I pray God to bless improvements in gardening till London be a city of palm-trees.

For I pray to give his grace to the poor of England, that Charity be not offended & that benevolence may increase.

For in my nature I quested for beauty, but God, God hath sent me to sea for pearls.

For there is a blessing from the STONE OF JESUS which is founded upon hell to the precious jewell on the right hand of God.

For the nightly visitor is at the window of the impenitent, while I sing a psalm of my own composing.

For there is a note added to the scale, which the Lord hath made fuller, stronger & more glorious.

For I offer my goat as he browses the vine, bless the Lord from chambering & drunkeness.

For there is a traveling for the glory of God without going to Italy or France.

For I bless the children of Asher for the evil I did them & the good I might have received at their hands.

For I rejoice like a worm in the rain in him that cherishes and from him that tramples.

For I am ready for the trumpet & alarm to fight to die & to rise again.

For the banish'd of the Lord shall come about again, for so he hath prepared for them.

For sincerity is a jewel which is pure & transparent, eternal & inestimable.

[139]

For my hands and my feet are perfect as the sublimity of Naphthali and the felicity of Asher.

For the names and numbers of animals are as the names and numbers of the stars.

For I pray the Lord Jesus to translate my MAGNIFICAT into verse and represent it.

For I bless the Lord Jesus from the bottom of Royston Cave to the top of King's Chapel.

For I am a little fellow, which is entitled to the great mess by the benevolence of God my father.

For I this day made over my inheritance to my mother in consideration of her infirmities.

For I this day made over my inheritance to my mother in consideration of her age.

For I this day made over my inheritance to my mother in consideration of her poverty.

For I bless the thirteenth of August, in which I had the grace to obey the voice of Christ in my conscience.

For I bless the thirteenth of August, in which I was willing to run all hazards for the sake of the name of the Lord.

For I bless the thirteenth of August, in which I was willing to be called a fool for the sake of Christ.

For I lent my flocks and herds and my lands at once unto the Lord.

For nature is more various than observation tho' observors be innumerable.

For Agricola is Γεωργος.

For I pray God to bless Polly in the blessing of Naomi and asign her to the house of DAVID.

For I am in charity with the French who are my foes and Moabites because of the Moabitish woman.

For my Angel is always ready at a pinch to help me out and to keep me up.

For CHRISTOPHER must slay the Dragon with a PAEON's head.

For they have seperated me and my bosom, whereas the right comes by setting us together.

For Silly fellow! Silly Fellow! is against me and belongeth neither to me nor my family.

For he that scorneth the scorner hath condescended to my low estate.

For Abiah is the father of Joab and Joab of all Romans and English Men.

For they pass by me in their tour, and the good Samaritan is not yet come.

For I bless God in behalf of TRINITY COLLEGE in CAMBRIDGE & the society of PURPLES in LONDON.

For I have a nephew CHRISTOPHER to whom I implore the grace of God.

For I pray God bless the CAM—Mr. Higgs & Mr. & Mrs. Washbourne as the drops of the dew.

For I pray God bless the King of Sardinia and make him an instrument of his peace.

For I am possessed of a cat, surpassing in beauty, from whom I take occasion to bless Almighty God.

For I pray God for the professors of the University of Cambridge to attend & to amend.

For the Fatherless Children and widows are never deserted of the Lord.

Anonymous

FOLK POEMS AND NURSERY RHYMES

Westron Winde

Westron winde, when will thou blow,
The smalle raine downe can raine?
Crist, if my love wer in my armis,
And I in my bed againe.

I Saw a Peacock

I saw a peacock with a fiery tail
I saw a blazing comet drop down hail
I saw a cloud with ivy circled round
I saw a sturdy oak tree on the ground
I saw a pismire swallow up a whale
I saw a raging sea brim full of ale
I saw a Venice glass sixteen foot deep
I saw a well full of men's tears that weep
I saw their eyes all in a flame of fire
I saw a house as big as the moon and higher

I saw the sun even in the midst of night
I saw the man that saw this wondrous sight.

Brill

At Brill on the hill
The wind blows shrill,
The cook no meat can dress;
At Stowe-on-the-Wold
The wind blows cold,
I know no more than this.

If All the World Were Paper

If all the world were paper,
And all the sea were ink;
If all the trees were bread and cheese,
How should we do for drink.

If all the world were sand'o,
Oh then what should we lack'o;
If as they say there were no clay
How should we take Tobacco?

If all our vessels ran'a,
If none had but a crack'a;
If Spanish Apes eate all the Grapes,
How should we do for Sack'a.

If Fryers had no bald pates,
Nor Nuns had no dark Cloysters;
If all the Seas were Beanes and Pease,
How should we do for Oysters.

If there had been no projects,
Nor none that did great wrongs.
If Fiddlers shall turne Players all,
How should we doe for songs?

If all things were eternall,
And nothing there end bringing;
If this should be, then how should we
Here make an end of singing.

Cock Robin

Who killed Cock Robin?
I, said the Sparrow,
With my bow and arrow,
I killed Cock Robin.

Who saw him die?
I, said the Fly,
With my little eye,
I saw him die.

Who caught his blood?
I, said the Fish,
With my little dish
I caught his blood.

Who'll make the shroud?
I, said the Beetle,
With my thread and needle
I'll make the shroud.

Who'll dig his grave?
I, said the Owl,
With my pick and shovel,
I'll dig his grave.

Who'll be the parson?
I, said the Rook,
With my little book
I'll be the parson.

Who'll be the clerk?
I, said the Lark,
If it's not in the dark,
I'll be the clerk.

Who'll carry the link?
I, said the Linnet,
I'll fetch it in a minute,
I'll carry the link.

Who'll be chief mourner?
I, said the Dove,
I'll mourn for my love,
I'll be chief mourner.

Who'll carry the coffin?
I, said the Kite,
If it's not through the night,
I'll carry the coffin.

Who'll bear the pall?
We, said the Wren,
Both the cock and the hen,
We'll bear the pall.

Who'll sing a psalm?
I, said the Thrush,
As she sat on a bush,
I'll sing a psalm.

Who'll toll the bell?
I, said the Bull,
Because I can pull,
I'll toll the bell.

All the birds of the air
Fell a-sighing and a-sobbing,
When they heard the bell toll
For poor Cock Robin.

Johnny, I Hardly Knew Ye

While going the road to sweet Athy,
   Hurroo! Hurroo!
While going the road to sweet Athy,
   Hurroo! Hurroo!
While going the road to sweet Athy,
A stick in my hand and a drop in my eye,
A doleful damsel I heard cry:—
   'Och, Johnny, I hardly knew ye,
With drums and guns, and guns and drums
   The enemy nearly slew ye,
   My darling dear, you look so queer,
   Och, Johnny, I hardly knew ye!

'Where are your eyes that looked so mild?
   Hurroo! Hurroo!
Where are your eyes that looked so mild?
   Hurroo! Hurroo!
Where are your eyes that looked so mild?
When my poor heart you first beguiled?

Why did you run from me and the child?
　　Och, Johnny, I hardly knew ye!
With drums, &c.

'Where are the legs with which you run?
　　Hurroo! Hurroo!
Where are the legs with which you run?
　　Hurroo! Hurroo!
Where are the legs with which you run?
When you went to carry a gun?—
Indeed your dancing days are done!
　　Och, Johnny, I hardly knew ye!
With drums, &c.

'It grieved my heart to see you sail,
　　Hurroo! Hurroo!
It grieved my heart to see you sail,
　　Hurroo! Hurroo!
It grieved my heart to see you sail
Though from my heart you took leg bail,—
Like a cod you're doubled up head and tail.
　　Och, Johnny, I hardly knew ye!
With drums, &c.

'You haven't an arm and you haven't a leg,
　　Hurroo! Hurroo!
You haven't an arm and you haven't a leg,
　　Hurroo! Hurroo!
You haven't an arm and you haven't a leg,
You're an eyeless, noseless, chickenless egg;
You'll have to be put in a bowl to beg;
　　Och, Johnny, I hardly knew ye!
With drums, &c.

'I'm happy for to see you home,
　　Hurroo! Hurroo!
I'm happy for to see you home,
　　Hurroo! Hurroo!
I'm happy for to see you home,
All from the island of Sulloon,
So low in flesh, so high in bone,
　　Och, Johnny, I hardly knew ye!
With drums, &c.

'But sad as it is to see you so,
　　Hurroo! Hurroo!

But sad as it is to see you so,
  Hurroo! Hurroo!
But sad as it is to see you so,
And to think of you now as an object of woe,
Your Peggy'll still keep ye on as her beau;
  Och, Johnny, I hardly knew ye!
With drums and guns, and guns and drums
  The enemy nearly slew ye,
  My darling dear, you look so queer,
  Och, Johnny, I hardly knew ye!

Thomas Chatterton (1752–1770)

THE MINSTREL'S SONG

Oh! sing unto my roundelay;
  Oh! drop the briny tear with me;
Dance no more at holiday;
  Like a running river be.
    My love is dead,
    Gone to his death-bed,
    All under the willow-tree.

Black his hair as the winter night,
  White his skin as the summer snow,
Red his face as the morning light;
  Cold he lies in the grave below.
    My love is dead,
    Gone to his death-bed,
    All under the willow-tree.

Sweet his tongue as the throstle's note,
  Quick in dance as thought can be,
Deft his tabor, cudgel stout;
  Oh! he lies by the willow-tree.
    My love is dead,

Gone to his death-bed,
All under the willow-tree.

Hark! the raven flaps his wing,
  In the briarèd dell below;
Hark! the death-owl loud doth sing
  To the night-mares, as they go.
    My love is dead,
      Gone to his death-bed,
      All under the willow-tree.

See! the white moon shines on high,
  Whiter is my true love's shroud,
Whiter than the morning sky,
  Whiter than the evening cloud.
    My love is dead,
      Gone to his death-bed,
      All under the willow-tree.

Here, upon my true love's grave,
  Shall the barren flowers be laid;
Not one holy saint to save
  All the coldness of a maid.
    My love is dead,
      Gone to his death-bed,
      All under the willow-tree.

With my hands I'll fix the briars
  Round his holy corse to grow,
Elfin fairy, light your fires,
  Here, my body still shall be.
    My love is dead,
      Gone to his death-bed,
      All under the willow-tree.

Come, with acorn-cup and thorn,
  Drain my own heart's blood away;
Life and all its good I scorn,
  Dance by night, or feast by day.
    My love is dead,
      Gone to his death-bed,
      All under the willow-tree.

Water-witches, crowned with reytes,
  Bear me to your lethal tide.

I die; I come; my true love waits.
Thus the damsel spake and died.

George Crabbe (1754–1832)

From THE VILLAGE

The Oncoming Industrial Revolution

Where are the swains, who, daily labour done,
With rural games play'd down the setting sun;
Who struck with matchless force the bounding ball
Or made the pond'rous quoit obliquely fall;
While some huge Ajax, terrible and strong,
Engaged some artful stripling of the throng,
And fell beneath him, foil'd, while far around
Hoarse triumph rose, and rocks return'd the sound?
Where now are these?—Beneath yon cliff they stand
To show the freighted pinnace where to land;
To load the ready steed with guilty haste,
To fly in terror o'er the pathless waste,
Or, when detected, in their struggling course,
To foil their foes by cunning or by force;
Or, yielding part (which equal knaves demand),
To gain a lawless passport through the land.
   Here, wand'ring long, amid these frowning fields,
I sought the simple life that Nature yields;
Rapine and Wrong and Fear usurp'd her place,
And a bold, artful, surly, savage race;
Who, only skill'd to take the finny tribe,
The yearly dinner, or septennial bribe,
Wait on the shore, and, as the waves run high,
On the tost vessel bend their eager eye,
Which to their coast directs its vent'rous way;
Theirs, or the ocean's, miserable prey.
   As on their neighbouring beach yon swallows stand,

And wait for favouring winds to leave the land,
While still for flight the ready wing is spread:
So waited I the favouring hour, and fled—
Fled from these shores where guilt and famine reign,
And cried, Ah! hapless they who still remain;
Who still remain to hear the ocean roar,
Whose greedy waves devour the lessening shore;
Till some fierce tide, with more imperious sway,
Sweeps the low hut and all its holds away;
When the sad tenant weeps from door to door,
And begs a poor protection from the poor! ...

William Blake (1757–1827)

SONGS

"Hear the voice of the Bard"

Hear the voice of the Bard!
Who present, past, and future, sees;
Whose ears have heard
The Holy Word
That walk'd among the ancient trees,

Calling the lapsèd soul,
And weeping in the evening dew;
That might control
The starry pole,
And fallen, fallen light renew!

'O Earth, O Earth, return!
Arise from out the dewy grass;
Night is worn,
And in the morn
Rises from the slumberous mass.

'Turn away no more;
Why wilt thou turn away.
The starry floor,
The wat'ry shore,
Is giv'n thee till the break of day.'

The Garden of Love

I went to the Garden of Love,
And I saw what I never had seen:
A Chapel was built in the midst,
Where I used to play on the green.

And the gates of this Chapel were shut,
And 'Thou shalt not' writ over the door;
So I turn'd to the Garden of Love
That so many sweet flowers bore;

And I saw it was fillèd with graves,
And tomb-stones where flowers should be;
And priests in black gowns were walking their rounds,
And binding with briars my joys and desires.

The Little Black Boy

My mother bore me in the southern wild,
And I am black, but O! my soul is white;
White as an angel is the English child,
But I am black, as if bereav'd of light.

My mother taught me underneath a tree,
And, sitting down before the heat of day,
She took me on her lap and kissèd me,
And, pointing to the east, began to say:

'Look on the rising sun—there God does live,
And gives His light, and gives His heat away;
And flowers and trees and beasts and men receive
Comfort in morning, joy in the noonday.

'And we are put on earth a little space,
That we may learn to bear the beams of love;
And these black bodies and this sunburnt face
Is but a cloud, and like a shady grove.

'For when our souls have learn'd the heat to bear,
The cloud will vanish; we shall hear His voice,
Saying: "Come out from the grove, My love and care,
And round My golden tent like lambs rejoice." '

Thus did my mother say, and kissèd me;
And thus I say to little English boy
When I from black and he from white cloud free,
And round the tent of God like lambs we joy,

I'll shade him from the heat, till he can bear
To lean in joy upon our Father's knee;
And then I'll stand and stroke his silver hair,
And be like him, and he will then love me.

The Fly

Little Fly,
Thy summer's play
My thoughtless hand
Has brush'd away.

Am not I
A fly like thee?
Or art not thou
A man like me?

For I dance,
And drink, and sing,
Till some blind hand
Shall brush my wing.

If thought is life
And strength and breath,
And the want
Of thought is death;

Then am I
A happy fly,
If I live
Or if I die.

The Tyger

Tyger! Tyger! burning bright
In the forests of the night,

What immortal hand or eye
Could frame thy fearful symmetry?

In what distant deeps or skies
Burnt the fire of thine eyes?
On what wings dare he aspire?
What the hand dare seize the fire?

And what shoulder, and what art,
Could twist the sinews of thy heart?
And when thy heart began to beat,
What dread hand? and what dread feet?

What the hammer? what the chain?
In what furnace was thy brain?
What the anvil? what dread grasp
Dare its deadly terrors clasp?

When the stars threw down their spears,
And water'd heaven with their tears,
Did he smile his work to see?
Did he who made the Lamb make thee?

Tyger! Tyger! burning bright
In the forests of the night,
What immortal hand or eye
Dare frame thy fearful symmetry?

A Little Boy Lost

'Nought loves another as itself,
Nor venerates another so,
Nor is it possible to Thought
A greater than itself to know;

'And, Father, how can I love you
Or any of my brothers more?
I love you like the little bird
That picks up crumbs around the door.'

The Priest sat by and heard the child,
In trembling zeal he seiz'd his hair;
He led him by his little coat,
And all admir'd the priestly care.

And standing on the altar high,
'Lo! what a fiend is here,' said he,

'One who sets reason up for judge
Of our most holy Mystery.'

The weeping child could not be heard,
The weeping parents wept in vain;
They stripp'd him to his little shirt,
And bound him in an iron chain;

And burn'd him in a holy place,
Where many had been burn'd before:
The weeping parents wept in vain.
Are such things done on Albion's shore?

London

I wander thro' each charter'd street,
Near where the charter'd Thames does flow,
And mark in every face I meet
Marks of weakness, marks of woe.

In every cry of every Man,
In every Infant's cry of fear,
In every voice, in every ban,
The mind-forg'd manacles I hear.

How the chimney-sweeper's cry
Every black'ning church appals;
And the hapless soldier's sigh
Runs in blood down palace walls.

But most thro' midnight streets I hear
How the youthful harlot's curse
Blasts the new-born infant's tear,
And blights with plagues the marriage hearse.

"Never seek to tell thy love"

Never seek to tell thy love,
Love that never told can be;
For the gentle wind does move
Silently, invisibly.

I told my love, I told my love,
I told her all my heart;
Trembling, cold, in ghastly fears,
Ah! she doth depart.

Soon as she was gone from me,
A traveller came by,
Silently, invisibly:
He took her with a sigh.

From Milton

And did those feet in ancient time
Walk upon England's mountains green?
And was the holy Lamb of God
On England's pleasant pastures seen?

And did the Countenance Divine
Shine forth upon our clouded hills?
And was Jerusalem builded here
Among these dark Satanic Mills?

Bring me my Bow of burning gold!
Bring me my Arrows of desire!
Bring me my Spear! O clouds unfold!
Bring me my Chariot of fire!

I will not cease from Mental Fight,
Nor shall my Sword sleep in my hand,
Till we have built Jerusalem
In England's green and pleasant Land.

AUGURIES OF INNOCENCE

To see a World in a Grain of Sand,
And Heaven in a Wild Flower,
Hold Infinity in the palm of your hand,
And Eternity in an hour.
A Robin Redbreast in a Cage
Puts all Heaven in a Rage.
A dove-house fill'd with Doves and Pigeons
Shudders Hell thro' all its regions.
A dog starv'd at his Master's Gate
Predicts the ruin of the State.
A Horse misus'd upon the Road
Calls to Heaven for Human blood.
Each outcry of the hunted Hare
A fibre from the Brain does tear.
A Skylark wounded in the wing,

A Cherubim does cease to sing.
The Game Cock clip'd and arm'd for fight
Does the Rising Sun affright.
Every Wolf's and Lion's howl
Raises from Hell a Human Soul.
The wild Deer, wand'ring here and there,
Keeps the Human Soul from Care.
The Lamb misus'd breeds Public Strife
And yet forgives the Butcher's knife.
The Bat that flits at close of Eve
Has left the Brain that won't Believe.
The Owl that calls upon the Night
Speaks the Unbeliever's fright.
He who shall hurt the little Wren
Shall never be belov'd by Men.
He who the Ox to wrath hath mov'd
Shall never be by Woman lov'd.
The wanton Boy that kills the Fly
Shall feel the Spider's enmity.
He who torments the Chafer's Sprite
Weaves a Bower in endless Night.
The Caterpiller on the Leaf
Repeats to thee thy Mother's grief.
Kill not the Moth nor Butterfly,
For the Last Judgement draweth nigh.
He who shall train the Horse to war
Shall never pass the Polar Bar.
The Beggar's Dog and Widow's Cat,
Feed them and thou wilt grow fat.
The Gnat that sings his Summer's Song
Poison gets from Slander's tongue.
The poison of the Snake and Newt
Is the sweat of Envy's Foot.
The poison of the Honey Bee
Is the Artist's Jealousy.
The Prince's Robes and Beggar's Rags
Are Toadstools on the Miser's Bags.
A Truth that's told with bad intent
Beats all the Lies you can invent.
It is right it should be so;
Man was made for Joy and Woe
And when this we rightly know,
Thro' the World we safely go,
Joy and Woe are woven fine,
A Clothing for the soul divine.
Under every grief and pine

Runs a joy with silken twine.
The Babe is more than Swaddling Bands;
Throughout all these Human Lands
Tools were made, and Born were hands.
Every Farmer Understands.
Every Tear from Every Eye
Becomes a Babe in Eternity;
This is caught by Females bright
And return'd to its own delight.
The Bleat, the Bark, Bellow and Roar,
Are waves that beat on Heaven's Shore.
The Babe that weeps the Rod beneath
Writes Revenge in realms of Death.
The Beggar's Rags, fluttering in Air,
Does to Rags the Heavens tear.
The Soldier, arm'd with Sword and Gun,
Palsied strikes the Summer's Sun.
The poor man's Farthing is worth more
Than all the Gold on Afric's Shore.
One Mite wrung from the Lab'rer's hands
Shall buy and sell the Miser's Lands;
Or, if protected from on high,
Does that whole Nation sell and buy.
He who mocks the Infant's Faith
Shall be mock'd in Age and Death.
He who shall teach the Child to Doubt
The rotting Grave shall ne'er get out.
He who respects the Infant's faith
Triumphs over Hell and Death.
The Child's Toys and the Old Man's Reasons
Are the Fruits of the Two seasons.
The Questioner, who sits so sly,
Shall never know how to Reply.
He who replies to words of Doubt
Doth put the Light of Knowledge out.
The Strongest Poison ever known
Came from Caesar's Laurel Crown.
Naught can deform the Human Race
Like the Armour's iron brace.
When Gold and Gems adorn the Plow
To Peaceful Arts shall Envy Bow.
A Riddle, or the Cricket's Cry,
Is to Doubt a fit Reply.
The Emmet's Inch and Eagle's Mile
Make Lame Philosophy to smile.
He who Doubts from what he sees

Will ne'er Believe, do what you Please.
If the Sun and Moon should Doubt
They'd immediately Go Out.
To be in a Passion you Good may do,
But no Good if a Passion is in you.
The Whore and Gambler, by the State
Licensed, build that Nation's Fate.
The Harlot's cry from Street to Street
Shall weave Old England's winding Sheet.
The Winner's Shout, the Loser's Curse,
Dance before dead England's Hearse.
Every Night and every Morn
Some to Misery are Born.
Every Morn and every Night
Some are Born to Sweet Delight.
Some are Born to Sweet Delight,
Some are born to Endless Night.
We are led to Believe a Lie
When we see not Thro' the Eye,
Which was Born in a Night to perish in a Night,
When the Soul Slept in Beams of Light.
God Appears, and God is Light,
To those poor souls who dwell in Night;
But does a Human Form Display
To those who Dwell in Realms of Day.

TO THE ACCUSER WHO IS THE
GOD OF THIS WORLD

Truly, My Satan, thou art but a Dunce,
And dost not know the Garment from the Man;
Every Harlot was a Virgin once,
Nor can'st thou ever change Kate into Nan.

Tho' thou art Worship'd by the Names Divine
Of Jesus and Jehovah, thou art still
The Son of Morn in weary Night's decline,
The lost Traveller's Dream under the Hill.

Robert Burns (1759–1796)

SONGS

Corn Rigs Are Bonie

It was upon a Lammas night,
　When corn rigs[1] are bonie,
Beneath the moon's unclouded light,
　I held awa to Annie;
The time flew by, wi' tentless[2] heed;
　Till, 'tween the late and early,
Wi' sma' persuasion she agreed
　To see me thro' the barley.
　　　Corn rigs, an' barley rigs,
　　　　An' corn rigs are bonie:
　　　I'll ne'er forget that happy night,
　　　　Amang the rigs wi' Annie.

The sky was blue, the wind was still,
　The moon was shining clearly;
I set her down, wi' right good will,
　Amang the rigs O' barley:
I ken't[3] her heart was a' my ain;
　I lov'd her most sincerely;
I kiss'd her owre and owre again,
　Amang the rigs o' barley.

I lock'd her in my fond embrace;
　Her heart was beating rarely:

[1] ridges or rows
[2] careless
[3] knew

My blessings on that happy place,
    Amang the rigs o' barley.
But by the moon and stars so bright,
    That shone that hour so clearly!
She ay shall bless that happy night
    Amang the rigs o' barley.

I had been blythe wi' comrades dear;
    I hae been merry drinking;
I had been joyfu' gath'rin gear;[4]
    I hae been happy thinking:
But a' the pleasures e'er I saw,
    Tho' three times doubled fairly—
That happy night was worth them a',
    Amang the rigs o' barley.

Ode to Spring

When maukin bucks,[1] at early fucks
    In dewy grass are seen, Sir,
And birds, on boughs, take off their mows[2]
    Amang the leaves sae green, Sir;
Latona's sun looks liquorish on
    Dame Nature's grand impètus
Till his prick go rise, then westward flies
    To roger Madame Thetis.

Yon wandering rill that marks the hill,
    And glances o'er the brae, Sir,
Slides by a bower where many a flower
    Sheds fragrance on the day, Sir;
There Damon lay, with Sylvia gay,
    To love they thought no crime, Sir;
The wild-birds sang, the echoes rang,
    While Damon's arse beat time, Sir.—

First, wi' the thrush, his thrust & push
    Had compass large & long, Sir;
The blackbird next, his tuneful text,
    Was bolder, clear & strong, Sir:
The linnet's lay then came in play,
    And the lark that soar'd aboon,[3] Sir;

4 making money
1 hares
2 coits
3 above

Till Damon fierce, mistimed his arse,
    And fucked quite out of tune, Sir.

A Red, Red Rose

O, my luve's like a red, red rose,
    That's newly sprung in June.
O, my luve's like the melodie
    That's sweetly play'd in tune.

As fair art thou, my bonie lass,
    So deep in luve am I,
And I will luve thee still, my Dear,
    Till a' the seas gang[1] dry.

Till a' the seas gang dry, my Dear,
    And the rocks melt wi' the sun!
O I will luve thee still, my Dear,
    While the sands o' life shall run.

And fare thee weel, my only Luve,
    And fare thee weel a while!
And I will come again, my Luve,
    Tho' it were ten thousand mile!

"I murder hate by field or flood"

I murder hate by field or flood,
    Tho' Glory's name may Screen us.
In wars at hame I'll spend my blood—
    Life-giving wars of Venus.
The deities that I adore
    Are Social Peace and Plenty:
I'm better pleas'd to make one more
    Than be the death of twenty.

I would not die like Socrates,
    For all the fuss of Plato;
Nor would I with Leonidas,
    Nor yet would I with Cato;
The zealots of the Church and State
    Shall ne'er my mortal foes be;
But let me have bold Zimri's fate
    Within the arms of Cozbi.

[1] go

The Lass that Made the Bed to Me

When Januar' wind was blawin cauld,
　As to the North I took my way,
The mirksome[1] night did me enfauld,
　I knew na where to lodge till day.
By my guid luck a maid I met
　Just in the middle o' my care,
And kindly did she me invite
　To walk into a chamber fair.

I bow'd fu' low unto this maid,
　And thank'd her for her courtesie;
I bow'd fu' low unto this maid,
　And bade her mak a bed to me.
She made the bed baith large and wide,
　Wi' twa white hands she spread it down,
She put the cup to her rosy lips,
　And drank:—'Young man, now sleep ye soun'.'

She snatch'd the candle in her hand,
　And frae my chamber went wi' speed,
But I call'd her quickly back again
　To lay some mair[2] below my head:
A cod[3] she laid below my head,
　And servèd me with due respeck,
And, to salute her wi' a kiss,
　I put my arms about her neck.

'Haud[4] aff your hands, young man,' she said,
　'And dinna[5] sae uncivil be;
Gif ye hae onie luve for me,
　O, wrang na my virginitie!'
Her hair was like the links o' gowd,[6]
　Her teeth were like the ivorie,
Her cheeks like lilies dipt in wine,
　The lass that made the bed to me!

Her bosom was the driven snaw,
　Twa drifted heaps sae fair to see;

---

[1] darksome
[2] more
[3] pillow
[4] hold
[5] do not
[6] gold

Her limbs the polish'd marble stane,
　　The lass that made the bed to me!
I kiss'd her o'er and o'er again,
　　And ay she wist na what to say,
I laid her 'tween me an' the wa'—
　　The lassie thocht na lang[7] till day.

Upon the morrow, when we raise,[8]
　　I thank't her for her courtesie,
But ay she blush'd, and ay she sigh'd,
　　And said:—'Alas, ye've ruin'd me!'
I clasp'd her waist, and kiss'd her syne,[9]
　　While the tear stood twinklin in her e'e.[10]
I said:—'My lassie, dinna cry,
　　For ye ay shall mak the bed to me.'

She took her mither's holland sheets,
　　An' made them a' in sarks[11] to me.
Blythe and merry may she be,
　　The lass that made the bed to me!
The bonie lass made the bed to me,
　　The braw[12] lass made the bed to me!
I'll ne'er forget till the day I die
　　The lass that made the bed to me.

"Is there for honest poverty"

Is there for honest poverty
　　That *hings*[1] his head, an' a that?
The coward slave, we pass him by—
　　We dare be poor for a' that!
For a' that, an' a' that,
　　Our toils obscure, an' a' that,
The rank is but the guinea's stamp,
　　The man's the *gowd*[2] for a' that.

[7] deemed it not long
[8] rose
[9] then
[10] eye
[11] shirts
[12] handsome
[1] hangs
[2] gold

young through great books that never grow old. These books include Utopia by Thomas More; the complete works of Shakespeare; Benjamin Franklin's Autobiography; Omar Khayyam's Rubaiyat; Walden by Thoreau; and other fresh, spontaneous, even outspoken works that stretch your mind and sweep away the mental cobwebs that hold back most men.

You never have to buy any of these books. (To force you to buy a classic would be barbaric.) As a member, take only those books you really want to own. And, at any time, you may cancel your membership, without penalty or hurt feelings.

(Continued on other side) →

LET THESE 3 WISE MEN INTO YOUR HOME. LATER, YOU MIGHT LIKE TO INVITE THEIR FRIENDS.

Do you have room in your home for three wise men? They are Plato, Aristotle, and Marcus Aurelius . . . three of the wisest, wittiest, most stimulating minds that ever lived.

They still live . . . in the Five Great Dialogues of Plato, the Meditations of Marcus Aurelius, and Aristotle's On Man in the Universe.

All three books (regularly $11.67) can be yours for only $1.00 as your introduction to the Classics Club.

The Classics Club is quite unlike any other book club.

The Club does not offer best sellers that come and go. Instead, it offers its members a chance to stay

What though on hamely fare we dine,
  Wear *hoddin grey,*[3] an' a' that?
Gie fools their silks, and knaves their wine—
  A man's a man for a' that.
For a' that, an' a' that,
  Their tinsel show, an' a' that,
The honest man, tho' e'er sae poor,
  Is king o' men for a' that.

Ye see yon *birkie ca'd*[4] 'a lord,'
  Wha struts, an' stares, an a' that?
Tho' hundreds worship at his word,
  He's but a *cuif*[5] for a' that.
For a' that, an' a' that,
  His ribband, star, an' a' that,
The man o' independent mind
  He looks an' laughs at a' that.

A prince can mak a belted knight,
  A marquis, duke, and a' that!
But an honest man's aboon[6] his might—
  Guid faith, he mauna[7] fa' that!
For a' that, an' a' that,
  Their dignities, an' a' that,
The pith o' sense an' pride o' worth
  Are higher rank than a' that.

Then let us pray that come it may
  (As come it will for a' that)
That Sense and Worth o'er a' the earth
  Shall bear the gree[8] an' a' that!
For a' that, an' a' that,
  It's comin yet for a' that,
That man to man the world o'er
  Shall brithers be for a' that.

Ae Fond Kiss

Ae fond kiss, and then we sever!

---

[3] coarse grey woolen
[4] fellow called
[5] dolt
[6] above
[7] must not
[8] have the first place

[163]

Ae farewell, and then forever!
Deep in heart-wrung tears I'll pledge thee,
Warring sighs and groans I'll wage thee.

Who shall say that Fortune grieves him,
While the star of hope she leaves him?
Me, nae cheerfu' twinckle lights me,
Dark despair around benights me.

I'll ne'er blame my partial fancy:
Naething could resist my Nancy!
But to see her was to love her,
Love but her and love for ever.

Had we never lov'd sae kindly,
Had we never lov'd sae blindly,
Never met—or never parted—
We had ne'er been broken-hearted.

Fare-thee-weel, thou first and fairest!
Fare-thee-weel, thou best and dearest!
Thine be ilka[1] joy and treasure,
Peace, Enjoyment, Love and Pleasure!

Ae fond kiss, and then we sever!
Ae fareweel, alas, for ever!
Deep in heart-wrung tears I'll pledge thee,
Warring sighs and groans I'll wage thee.

Seventh Song

from LOVE AND LIBERTY
(THE JOLLY BEGGARS)

CHORUS

A fig for those by law protected!
  Liberty's a glorious feast,
Courts for cowards were erected,
  Churches built to please the priest!

See the smoking bowl before us!
  Mark our jovial, ragged ring!

[1] every

Round and round take up the chorus,
  And in raptures let us sing:

What is title, what is treasure,
  What is reputation's care?
If we lead a life of pleasure,
  'Tis no matter how or where!

With the ready trick and fable
  Round we wander all the day;
And at night in barn or stable
  Hug our doxies on the hay.

Does the train-attended carriage
  Thro' the country lighter rove?
Does the sober bed of marriage
  Witness brighter scenes of love?

Life is all a variorum,
  We regard not how it goes;
Let them prate about decorum,
  Who have character to lose.

Here's no budgets, bags and wallets!
  Here's to all the wandering train!
Here's our ragged brats and callets!
  One and all, cry out, Amen!

HOLY WILLIE'S PRAYER

And send the godly in a pet to pray.
                                    POPE

O Thou that in the Heavens does dwell,
Wha, as it pleases best Thysel,
Sends ane to Heaven an' ten to Hell
                A' for Thy glory,
And no for onie guid or ill
                They've done before Thee!

I bless and praise Thy matchless might,
When thousands Thou hast left in night,
That I am here before Thy sight,
                For gifts an' grace

A burning and a shining light
                To a' this place.

What was I, or my generation,
That I should get sic[1] exaltation?
I, wha deserv'd most just damnation
                For broken laws
Sax[2] thousand years ere my creation,
                Thro' Adam's cause!

When from my mither's womb I fell,
Thou might hae plung'd me dee in hell
To gnash my gooms,[3] and weep, and wail
                In burning lakes,
Whare damnèd devils roar and yell,
                Chain'd to their stakes.

Yet I am here, a chosen sample,
To show Thy grace is great and ample:
I'm here a pillar o' Thy temple,
                Strong as a rock,
A guide, a buckler, and example
                To a' Thy flock!

But yet, O Lord! confess I must:
At times I'm fash'd[4] wi' fleshy lust;
An' sometimes, too, in warldly trust,
                Vile self gets in;
But Thou remembers we are dust,
                Defiled wi' sin.

O Lord! yestreen,[5] Thou kens,[6] wi' Meg—
Thy pardon I sincerely beg—
O, may't ne'er be a living plague
                To my dishonor!
An' I'll ne'er lift a lawless leg
                Again upon her.

Besides, I farther maun[7] avow—
Wi' Leezie's lass, three times, I trow—

[1] such
[2] six
[3] gums
[4] irked
[5] last night
[6] knowest
[7] must

But, Lord, that Friday I was fou,[8]
          When I cam near her,
Or else, Thou kens, Thy servant true
          Wad never steer[9] her.

Maybe Thou lets this fleshly thorn
Buffet Thy servant e'en and morn,
Lest he owre proud and high should turn
          That he's sae[10] gifted:
If Sae, Thy han' maun e'en be borne
          Until Thou lift it.

Lord, bless Thy chosen in this place,
For here Thou has a chosen race!
But God confound their stubborn face
          An' blast their name,
Wha bring Thy elders to disgrace
          An' open shame!

Lord, mind Gau'n Hamilton's deserts:
He drinks, an' swears, an' plays at cartes,[11]
Yet has sae monie takin arts
          Wi' great and sma',
Frae God's ain Priest the people's hearts
          He steals awa.

And when we chasten'd him therefore,
Thou kens how he bred sic a splore,[12]
And set the warld in a roar
          O' laughin at us:
Curse Thou his basket and his store,
          Kail an' potatoes!

Lord, hear my earnest cry and pray'r
Against that Presbyt'ry of Ayr!
Thy strong right hand, Lord, mak it bare
          Upo' their heads!
Lord, visit them, an' dinna[13] spare,
          For their misdeeds!

[8] drunk
[9] meddle with
[10] too
[11] cards
[12] such a row
[13] do not

O Lord, my God! that glib-tongu'd Aiken,
My vera heart and flesh are quakin,
To think how we stood sweatin, shakin,
      An' pish'd wi' dread,
While he, wi' hingin lip an' snakin,[14]
      Held up his head.

Lord, in Thy day o' vengeance try him!
Lord, visit him wha did employ him!
And pass not in Thy mercy by them,
      Nor hear their pray'r,
But for Thy people's sake destroy them,
      An' dinna spare!

But, Lord, remember me and mine
Wi' mercies temporal and divine,
That I for grace an' gear[15] may shine
      Excell'd by nane;
And a' the glory shall be Thine—
      Amen, amen!

William Wordsworth (1770–1850)

ODE: INTIMATIONS OF IMMORTALITY FROM RECOLLECTIONS OF EARLY CHILDHOOD

The Child is Father of the Man;
And I could wish my days to be
Bound each to each by natural piety.

1

There was a time when meadow, grove, and stream,
The earth, and every common sight,
      To me did seem

14 sneering
15 wealth

Apparelled in celestial light,
The glory and the freshness of a dream.
It is not now as it hath been of yore;—
　　Turn wheresoe'er I may,
　　　By night or day,
The things which I have seen I now can see no more.

2

　　The Rainbow comes and goes,
　　And lovely is the Rose,
　　The Moon doth with delight
Look round her when the heavens are bare,
　　Waters on a starry night
　　Are beautiful and fair;
　The sunshine is a glorious birth;
　But yet I know, where'er I go,
That there hath past away a glory from the earth.

3

Now, while the birds thus sing a glorious song,
　And while the young lambs bound
　　As to the tabor's sound,
To me alone there came a thought of grief:
A timely utterance gave that thought relief,
　　And I again am strong:
The cataracts blow their trumpets from the steep;
No more shall grief of mine the season wrong;
I hear the Echoes through the mountains throng,
The Winds come to me from the fields of sleep,
　　　And all the earth is gay;
　　　　Land and sea
　　Give themselves up to jollity,
　　　And with the heart of May
　Doth every Beast keep holiday;—
　　　Thou Child of Joy,
Shout round me, let me hear thy shouts, thou happy
　　　　Shepherd-boy!

4

Ye blessèd Creatures, I have heard the call
　Ye to each other make; I see
The heavens laugh with you in your jubilee;
　My heart is at your festival,

My head hath its coronal,
The fullness of your bliss, I feel—I feel it all.
Oh evil day! if I were sullen
    While Earth herself is adorning,
        This sweet May-morning,
    And the Children are culling
        On every side,
    In a thousand valleys far and wide,
    Fresh flowers; while the sun shines warm,
And the Babe leaps up on his Mother's arm:—
    I hear, I hear, with joy I hear!
    —But there's a Tree, of many, one,
A single Field which I have looked upon,
Both of them speak of something that is gone:
        The Pansy at my feet
        Doth the same tale repeat:
Whither is fled the visionary gleam?
Where is it now, the glory and the dream?

5

Our birth is but a sleep and a forgetting:
The Soul that rises with us, our life's Star,
        Hath had elsewhere its setting,
            And cometh from afar:
        Not in entire forgetfulness,
        And not in utter nakedness,
But trailing clouds of glory do we come
        From God, who is our home:
Heaven lies about us in our infancy!
Shades of the prison-house begin to close
        Upon the growing Boy,
But He beholds the light, and whence it flows,
        He sees it in his joy;
The Youth, who daily farther from the east
        Must travel, still is Nature's Priest,
            And by the vision splendid
            Is on his way attended;
At length the Man perceives it die away,
And fade into the light of common day.

6

Earth fills her lap with pleasures of her own;
Yearnings she hath in her own natural kind,

And, even with something of a Mother's mind,
And no unworthy aim,
The homely Nurse doth all she can
To make her Foster-child, her Inmate Man,
Forget the glories he hath known,
And that imperial palace whence he came.

7

Behold the Child among his new-born blisses,
A six years' Darling of a pigmy size!
See, where 'mid work of his own hand he lies,
Fretted by sallies of his mother's kisses,
With light upon him from his father's eyes!
See, at his feet, some little plan or chart,
Some fragment from his dream of human life,
Shaped by himself with newly-learnèd art;
A wedding or a festival,
A mourning or a funeral;
And this hath now his heart,
And unto this he frames his song:
Then will he fit his tongue
To dialogues of business, love, or strife;
But it will not be long
Ere this be thrown aside,
And with new joy and pride
The little Actor cons another part;
Filling from time to time his "humorous stage"
With all the Persons, down to palsied Age,
That Life brings with her in her equipage;
As if his whole vocation
Were endless imitation.

8

Thou, whose exterior semblance doth belie
Thy Soul's immensity;
Thou best Philosopher, who yet dost keep
Thy heritage, thou Eye among the blind,
That, deaf and silent, read'st the eternal deep,
Haunted forever by the eternal mind,—
Mighty Prophet! Seer blest!
On whom those truths do rest,
Which we are toiling all our lives to find,
In darkness lost, the darkness of the grave;
Thou, over whom thy Immortality

Broods like the Day, a Master o'er a Slave,
A Presence which is not to be put by;
Thou little Child, yet glorious in the might
Of heaven-born freedom on thy Being's height
Why with such earnest pains dost thou provoke
The years to bring the inevitable yoke,
Thus blindly with thy blessedness at strife?
Full soon thy Soul shall have her earthly freight,
And custom lie upon thee with a weight,
Heavy as frost, and deep almost as life!

9

O joy! that in our embers
Is something that doth live,
That nature yet remembers
What was so fugitive!
The thought of our past years in me doth breed
Perpetual benediction: not indeed
For that which is most worthy to be blest;
Delight and liberty, the simple creed
Of Childhood, whether busy or at rest,
With new-fledged hope still fluttering in his breast:—
Not for these I raise
The song of thanks and praise;
But for those obstinate questionings
Of sense and outward things,
Fallings from us, vanishings;
Blank misgivings of a Creature
Moving about in worlds not realised,
High instincts before which our mortal Nature
Did tremble like a guilty Thing surprised:
But for those first affections,
Those shadowy recollections,
Which, be they what they may,
Are yet the fountain-light of all our day,
Are yet a master-light of all our seeing;
Uphold us, cherish, and have power to make
Our noisy years seem moments in the being
Of the eternal Silence; truths that wake,
To perish never:
Which neither listlessness, nor mad endeavour,
Nor Man nor Boy,
Nor all that is at enmity with joy,

Can utterly abolish or destroy.
 Hence in a season of calm weather
  Though inland far we be,
Our souls have sight of that immortal sea
  Which brought us hither,
  Can in a moment travel thither,
And see the Children sport upon the shore,
And hear the mighty waters rolling evermore.

10

Then sing, ye Birds, sing, sing a joyous song!
  And let the young Lambs bound
  As to the tabor's sound!
We in thought will join your throng,
  Ye that pipe and yet that play,
  Ye that through your hearts to-day
  Feel the gladness of the May!
What though the radiance which was once so bright
Be now for ever taken from my sight,
 Though nothing can bring back the hour
Of splendour in the grass, of glory in the flower;
  We will grieve not, rather find
  Strength in what remains behind;
  In the primal sympathy
  Which having been must ever be;
  In the soothing thoughts that spring
  Out of human suffering;
  In the faith that looks through death,
In years that bring the philosophic mind.

11

And O, ye Fountains, Meadows, Hills, and Groves,
Forebode not any severing of our loves!
Yet in my heart of hearts I feel your might;
I only have relinquished one delight
To live beneath your more habitual sway.
I love the Brooks which down their channels fret,
Even more than when I tripped lightly as they;
The innocent brightness of a new-born Day
   Is lovely yet;
The Clouds that gather round the setting sun
Do take a sober colouring from an eye
That hath kept watch o'er man's mortality;
Another race hath been, and other palms are won.

Thanks to the human heart by which we live,
Thanks to its tenderness, its joys, and fears,
To me the meanest flower that blows can give
Thoughts that too often lie too deep for tears.

SONNETS

"Nuns fret not at their convent's narrow room"

Nuns fret not at their convent's narrow room;
And hermits are contented with their cells;
And students with their pensive citadels;
Maids at the wheel, the weaver at his loom,
Sit blithe and happy; bees that soar for bloom
High as the highest Peak of Furness-fells,
Will murmur by the hour in foxglove bells:
In truth the prison, unto which we doom
Ourselves, no prison is: and hence for me,
In sundry moods, 'twas pastime to be bound
Within the Sonnet's scanty plot of ground;
Pleased if some Souls (for such there needs must be)
Who have felt the weight of too much liberty,
Should find brief solace there, as I have found.

"Surprised by joy—impatient as the Wind"

Surprised by joy—impatient as the Wind
I turned to share the transport—Oh! with whom
But Thee, deep buried in the silent tomb,
That spot which no vicissitude can find?
Love, faithful love, recalled thee to my mind—
But how could I forget thee? Through that power
Even for the least division of an hour,
Have I been so beguiled as to be blind
To my most grievous loss!—That thought's return
Was the worst pang that sorrow ever bore,
Save one, one only, when I stood forlorn,
Knowing my heart's best treasure was no more;
That neither present time, nor years unborn
Could to my sight that heavenly face restore.

Composed upon Westminster Bridge

September 3, 1802

Earth has not anything to show more fair:
Dull would he be of soul who could pass by
A sight so touching in its majesty:
This City now doth, like a garment, wear
The beauty of the morning; silent, bare,
Ships, towers, domes, theatres, and temples lie
Open unto the fields, and to the sky;
All bright and glittering in the smokeless air.
Never did sun more beautifully steep
In his first splendour, valley, rock, or hill;
Ne'er saw I, never felt, a calm so deep!
The river glideth at his own sweet will:
Dear God! the very houses seem asleep;
And all that mighty heart is lying still!

"The World is too much with us; late and soon"

The world is too much with us; late and soon,
Getting and spending, we lay waste our powers:
Little we see in Nature that is ours;
We have given our hearts away, a sordid boon!
This Sea that bares her bosom to the moon;
The winds that will be howling at all hours,
And are upgathered now like sleeping flowers;
For this, for every thing, we are out of tune;
It moves us not.—Great God! I'd rather be
A Pagan suckled in a creed outworn;
So might I, standing on this pleasant lea,
Have glimpses that would make me less forlorn;
Have sight of Proteus rising from the sea;
Or hear old Triton blow his wreathèd horn.

On the Extinction of the Venetian Republic

Once did she hold the gorgeous east in fee;
And was the safeguard of the west: the worth
Of Venice did not fall below her birth,
Venice, the eldest Child of Liberty,
She was a maiden City, bright and free;
No guile seduced, no force could violate;
And, when she took unto herself a Mate,
She must espouse the everlasting Sea.

And what if she had seen those glories fade,
Those titles vanish, and that strength decay;
Yet shall some tribute of regret be paid
When her long life has reached its final day:
Men are we, and must grieve when even the Shade
Of that which once was great, is passed away.

To Toussaint L'Ouverture

Toussaint, the most unhappy man of men!
Whether the whistling Rustic tend his plough
Within thy hearing, or thy head be now
Pillow'd in some deep dungeon's earless den;—
O miserable Chieftain! where and when
Wilt thou find patience? Yet die not; do thou
Wear rather in thy bonds a cheerful brow:
Though fallen thyself, never to rise again,
Live, and take comfort. Thou hast left behind
Powers that will work for thee; air, earth, and skies;
There's not a breathing of the common wind
That will forget thee; thou hast great allies;
Thy friends are exultations, agonies,
And love, and man's unconquerable mind.

London, 1802

Milton! thou shouldst be living at this hour:
England hath need of thee: she is a fen
Of stagnant waters: altar, sword, and pen,
Fireside, the heroic wealth of hall and bower,
Have forfeited their ancient English dower
Of inward happiness. We are selfish men;
Oh! raise us up, return to us again;
And give us manners, virtue, freedom, power.
Thy soul was like a Star, and dwelt apart;
Thou hadst a voice whose sound was like the sea:
Pure as the naked heavens, majestic, free,
So didst thou travel on life's common way,
In cheerful godliness; and yet thy heart
The lowliest duties on herself did lay.

"Scorn not the Sonnet; Critic, you have frowned"

Scorn not the Sonnet; Critic, you have frowned,
Mindless of its just honours; with this key

Shakespeare unlocked his heart; the melody
Of this small lute gave ease to Petrarch's wound;
A thousand times this pipe did Tasso sound;
With it Camöens soothed an exile's grief;
The Sonnet glittered a gay myrtle leaf
Amid the cypress with which Dante crowned
His visionary brow: a glow-worm lamp,
It cheered mild Spenser, called from Faery-land
To struggle through dark ways; and, when a damp
Fell round the path of Milton, in his hand
The Thing became a trumpet; whence he blew
Soul-animating strains—alas, too few!

From THE PRELUDE

From Book 1: *One Summer Evening*

One summer evening (led by her) I found
A little boat tied to a willow tree
Within a rocky cove, its usual home.
Straight I unloosed her chain, and stepping in
Pushed from the shore. It was an act of stealth
And troubled pleasure, nor without the voice
Of mountain-echoes did my boat move on;
Leaving behind her still, on either side,
Small circles glittering idly in the moon,
Until they melted all into one track
Of sparkling light. But now, like one who rows,
Proud of his skill, to reach a chosen point
With an unswerving line, I fixed my view
Upon the summit of a craggy ridge,
The horizon's utmost boundary; far above
Was nothing but the stars and the grey sky.
She was an elfin pinnace; lustily
I dipped my oars into the silent lake,
And, as I rose upon the stroke, my boat
Went heaving through the water like a swan;
When, from behind that craggy steep till then
The horizon's bound, a huge peak, black and huge,
As if with voluntary power instinct
Upreared its head. I struck and struck again,
And growing still in stature the grim shape
Towered between me and the stars, and still,
For so it seemed, with purpose of its own

And measured motion like a living thing,
Strode after me. With trembling oars I turned,
And through the silent water stole my way
Back to the covert of the willow tree;
There in her mooring-place I left my bark,—
And through the meadows homeward went, in grave
And serious mood; but after I had seen
That spectacle, for many days, my brain
Worked with a dim and undetermined sense
Of unknown modes of being; O'er my thoughts
There hung a darkness, call it solitude
Or blank desertion. No familiar shapes
Remained, no pleasant images of trees,
Of sea or sky, no colours of green fields;
But huge and mighty forms, that do not live
Like living men, moved slowly through the mind
By day, and were a trouble to my dreams.

Samuel Taylor Coleridge (1772–1834)

PHILOSOPHIC POEMS

Constancy to an Ideal Object

Since all that beat about in Nature's range,
Or veer or vanish; why should'st thou remain
The only constant in a world of change,
O yearning Thought! that liv'st but in the brain?
Call to the Hours, that in the distance play,
The faery people of the future day—
Fond Thought! not one of all that shining swarm
Will breathe on thee with life-enkindling breath,
Till when, like strangers shelt'ring from a storm,
Hope and Despair meet in the porch of Death!
Yet still thou haunt'st me; and though well I see,
She is not thou, and only thou art she,
Still, still as though some dear embodied Good,
Some living Love before my eyes there stood
With answering look a ready ear to lend,
I mourn to thee and say—"Ah! loveliest friend!
That this the meed of all my toils might be,

To have a home, an English home, and thee!"
Vain repetition! Home and Thou are one.
The peacefull'st cot the moon shall shine upon,
Lulled by the thrush and wakened by the lark,
Without thee were but a becalmèd bark,
Whose Helmsman on an ocean waste and wide
Sits mute and pale his mouldering helm beside.

And art thou nothing? Such thou art, as when
The woodman winding westward up the glen
At wintry dawn, where o'er the sheep-track's maze
The viewless snow-mist weaves a glist'ning haze,
Sees full before him, gliding without tread,
An image with a glory round its head;
The enamoured rustic worships its fair hues,
Nor knows he makes the shadow he pursues!

Limbo

. . . .
The sole true Something—This! In Limbo's Den
It frightens Ghosts, as here Ghosts frighten men.
Thence cross's unseiz'd—and shall some fated hour
Be pulveriz'd by Demogorgon's power,
And given as poison to annihilate souls—
Even now it shrinks them—they shrink in as Moles
(Nature's mute monks, live mandrakes of the ground)
Creep back from Light—then listen for its sound;—
See but to dread, and dread they know not why—
The natural alien of their negative eye.

'Tis a strange place, this Limbo!—not a Place,
Yet name it so;—where Time and weary Space
Fettered from flight, with night-mare sense of fleeing,
Strive for their last crepuscular half-being;—
Lank Space, and scytheless Time with branny hands
Barren and soundless as the measuring sands,
Not mark'd by flit of Shades,—unmeaning they
As moonlight on the dial of the day!
But that is lovely—looks like Human Time,
An Old Man with a steady look sublime,
That stops his earthly task to watch the skies;
But he is blind—a Statue hath such eyes;—
Yet having moonward turn'd his face by chance,
Gazes the orb with moonlike countenance,
With scant white hairs, with foretop bald and high,

He gazes still,—his eyeless face all eye;—
As 'twere an organ full of silent sight,
His whole face seemeth to rejoice in light!
Lip touching lip, all moveless, bust and limb—
He seems to gaze at that which seems to gaze on him!
    No such sweet sights doth Limbo den immure,
Wall'd round, and made a spirit-jail secure,
By the mere horror of blank Naught-at-all,
Whose circumambience doth these ghosts enthral.
A lurid thought is growthless, dull Privation,
Yet that is but a Purgatory curse;
Hell knows a fear far worse,
A fear—a future state;—'tis positive Negation!

MAGICAL POEMS

From *Christabel*

PART 1

'Tis the middle of night by the castle clock,
And the owls have awakened the crowing cock;
Tu—whit!—Tu—whoo!
And hark, again! the crowing cock,
How drowsily it crew.

Sir Leoline, the Baron rich,
Hath a toothless mastiff bitch;
From her kennel beneath the rock
She maketh answer to the clock,
Four for the quarters, and twelve for the hour;
Ever and aye, by shine and shower,
Sixteen short howls, not over loud;
Some say, she sees my lady's shroud.

Is the night chilly and dark?
The night is chilly, but not dark.
The thin gray cloud is spread on high,
It covers but not hides the sky.
The moon is behind, and at the full;
And yet she looks both small and dull.
The night is chill, the cloud is gray:
'Tis a month before the month of May,
And the Spring comes slowly up this way.

The lovely lady, Christabel,
Whom her father loves so well,
What makes her in the wood so late,
A furlong from the castle gate?
She had dreams all yesternight
Of her own betrothèd knight;
And she in the midnight wood will pray
For the weal of her lover that's far away.

She stole along, she nothing spoke,
The sighs she heaved were soft and low,
And naught was green upon the oak
But moss and rarest mistletoe:
She kneels beneath the huge oak tree,
And in silence prayeth she.

The lady sprang up suddenly,
The lovely lady, Christabel!
It moaned as near, as near can be,
But what it is she cannot tell.—
On the other side it seems to be,
Of the huge, broad-breasted, old oak tree.

The night is chill; the forest bare;
Is it the wind that moaneth bleak?
There is not wind enough in the air
To move away the ringlet curl
From the lovely lady's cheek—
There is not wind enough to twirl
The one red leaf, the last of its clan,
That dances as often as dance it can,
Hanging so light, and hanging so high,
On the topmost twig that looks up at the sky . . .

From The Rime of the Ancient Mariner

PART 2

The Sun now rose upon the right:
Out of the sea came he,
Still hid in mist, and on the left
Went down into the sea.

And the good south wind still blew behind,
But no sweet bird did follow,

Nor any day for food or play
Came to the mariners' hollo!

His shipmates cry out against the ancient Mariner, for killing the bird of good luck.

And I had done a hellish thing,
And it would work 'em woe:
For all averred, I had killed the bird
That made the breeze to blow.
Ah wretch! said they, the bird to slay,
That made the breeze to blow!

But when the fog cleared off, they justify the same, and thus make themselves accomplices in the crime.

Nor dim nor red, like God's own head,
The glorious Sun uprist:
Then all averred, I had killed the bird
That brought the fog and mist.
'Twas right, said they, such birds to slay,
That bring the fog and mist.

The fair breeze continues; the ship enters the Pacific Ocean, and sails northward, even till it reaches the Line.

The fair breeze blew, the white foam flew,
The furrow followed free;
We were the first that ever burst
Into that silent sea.

Down dropt the breeze, the sails dropt down,
'Twas sad as sad could be;
And we did speak only to break
The silence of the sea!

The ship hath been suddenly becalmed.

All in a hot and copper sky,
The bloody Sun, at noon,
Right up above the mast did stand,
No bigger than the Moon.

Day after day, day after day,
We stuck, nor breath nor motion;
As idle as a painted ship
Upon a painted ocean.

And the Albatross begins to be avenged.

Water, water, every where,
And all the boards did shrink;
Water, water, every where
Nor any drop to drink.

The very deep did rot: O Christ!
That ever this should be!
Yea, slimy things did crawl with legs
Upon the slimy sea.

About, about, in reel and rout
The death-fires danced at night;
The water, like a witch's oils,
Burnt green, and blue and white.

A Spirit had
followed them;
one of the
invisible
inhabitants of

And some in dreams assurèd were
Of the Spirit that plagued us so;
Nine fathom deep he had followed us
From the land of mist and snow.

this planet, neither departed souls nor angels; concerning whom the learned
Jew, Josephus, and the Platonic Constantinopolitan, Michael Psellus, may
be consulted. They are very numerous, and there is no climate or element
without one or more.

And every tongue, through utter drought,
Was withered at the root;
We could not speak, no more than if
We had been choked with soot.

The shipmates,
in their sore
distress,
would fain
throw the whole

Ah! well a-day! what evil looks
Had I from old and young!
Instead of the Cross, the Albatross
About my neck was hung.

guilt on the ancient Mariner: in sign whereof they hang the dead sea-bird
round his neck.

Kubla Khan

OR, A VISION IN A DREAM. A FRAGMENT.

In Xanadu did Kubla Khan
A stately pleasure-dome decree:
Where Alph, the sacred river, ran
Through caverns measureless to man
 Down to a sunless sea.
So twice five miles of fertile ground
With walls and towers were girdled round;
And there were gardens bright with sinuous rills,
Where blossomed many an incense-bearing tree;
And here were forests ancient as the hills,
Enfolding sunny spots of greenery.

But oh! that deep romantic chasm which slanted
Down the green hill athwart a cedarn cover!
A savage place! as holy and enchanted

[183]

As e'er beneath a waning moon was haunted
By woman wailing for her demon-lover!
And from this chasm, with ceaseless turmoil seething,
As if this earth in fast thick pants were breathing,
A mighty fountain momently was forced:
Amid whose swift half-intermitted burst
Huge fragments vaulted like rebounding hail,
Or chaffy grain beneath the thresher's flail:
And 'mid these dancing rocks at once and ever
It flung up momently the sacred river.
Five miles meandering with a mazy motion
Through wood and dale the sacred river ran,
Then reached the caverns measureless to man,
And sank in tumult to a lifeless ocean:
And 'mid this tumult Kubla heard from far
Ancestral voices prophesying war!
    The shadow of the dome of pleasure
    Floated midway on the waves;
    Where was heard the mingled measure
    From the fountain and the caves.
It was a miracle of rare device,
A sunny pleasure-dome with caves of ice!

    A damsel with a dulcimer
    In a vision once I saw:
    It was an Abyssinian maid,
    And on her dulcimer she played,
    Singing of Mount Abora.
    Could I revive within me
    Her symphony and song,
    To such a deep delight 'twould win me,
That with music loud and long,
I would build that dome in air,
That sunny dome! those caves of ice!
And all who heard should see them there,
And all should cry, Beware! Beware!
His flashing eyes, his floating hair!
Weave a circle round him thrice,
And close your eyes with holy dread,
For he on honey-dew hath fed,
And drunk the milk of Paradise.

Walter Savage Landor (1775–1864)

TO OUR HOUSE-DOG CAPTAIN

Captain! we often heretofore
Have boxt behind the coach-house door,
When thy strong paws were rear'd against
My ribs and bosom, badly fenc'd:
None other dared to try thy strength,
And hurl thee side-long at full length,
But we well knew each other's mind,
And paid our little debts in kind.
I have often braved with boyish fist
The vanquisht bull's antagonist,
And saw unsheath'd thy tiny teeth
And the dark cell that oped beneath.
Thou wert like others of the strong,
But only more averse from wrong;
Reserved and proud perhaps, but just,
And strict and constant to thy trust,
Somewhat inclement to the poor,
Suspecting each for evil-doer,
But hearing reason when I spoke,
And letting go the ragged cloak.
Thee dared I; but I never dar'd
To drive the pauper from the yard.

George Gordon, Lord Byron (1788–1824)

From DON JUAN

Fragment, on the back of the MS.

I would to Heaven that I were so much clay,
　　As I am blood, bone, marrow, passion, feeling—
Because at least the past were pass'd away—
　　And for the future—(but I write this reeling,
Having got drunk exceedingly to-day,
　　So that I seem to stand upon the ceiling)
I say—the future is a serious matter—
And so—for God's sake—hock and soda-water!

The Seduction of Juan
(CANTO I, 90–92, 108–117, 122–127)

90

Young Juan wandered by the glassy brooks,
　　Thinking unutterable things; he threw
Himself at length within the leafy nooks
　　Where the wild branch of the cork forest grew;
There poets find materials for their books,
　　And every now and then we read them through,
So that their plan and prosody are eligible,
Unless, like Wordsworth, they prove unintelligible.

91

He, Juan (and not Wordsworth), so pursued
　　His self-communion with his own high soul,
Until his mighty heart, in its great mood,

Had mitigated part, though not the whole
Of its disease; he did the best he could
With things not very subject to control,
And turned, without perceiving his condition,
Like Coleridge, into a metaphysician.

92

He thought about himself, and the whole earth,
Of man the wonderful, and of the stars,
And how the deuce they ever could have birth;
And then he thought of earthquakes, and of wars,
How many miles the moon might have in girth,
Of air-balloons, and of the many bars
To perfect knowledge of the boundless skies;—
And then he thought of Donna Julia's eyes . . .

108

When people say, "I've told you *fifty* times,"
They mean to scold, and very often do;
When poets say, "I've written *fifty* rhymes,"
They make you dread that they'll recite them too;
In gangs of *fifty*, thieves commit their crimes;
At *fifty* love for love is rare, 't is true,
But then, no doubt, it equally as true is,
A good deal may be bought for *fifty* Louis.

109

Julia had honour, virtue, truth, and love
For Don Alfonso; and she inly swore,
By all the vows below to Powers above,
She never would disgrace the ring she wore,
Nor leave a wish which wisdom might reprove;
And while she pondered this, besides much more,
One hand on Juan's carelessly was thrown,
Quite by mistake—she thought it was her own;

110

Unconsciously she leaned upon the other,
Which played within the tangles of her hair;
And to contend with thoughts she could not smother
She seemed by the distraction of her air.
'Twas surely very wrong in Juan's mother

To leave together this imprudent pair,
She who for many years had watched her son so—
I'm very certain *mine* would not have done so.

111

The hand which still held Juan's, by degrees
    Gently, but palpably confirmed its grasp,
As if it said, "Detain me, if you please";
    Yet there's no doubt she only meant to clasp
His fingers with a pure Platonic squeeze;
    She would have shrunk as from a toad, or asp,
Had she imagined such a thing could rouse
A feeling dangerous to a prudent spouse.

112

I cannot know what Juan thought of this,
    But what he did, is much what you would do;
His young lip thanked it with a grateful kiss,
    And then, abashed at its own joy, withdrew
In deep despair, lest he had done amiss—
    Love is so very timid when 't is new:
She blushed, and frowned not, but she strove to speak,
And held her tongue, her voice was grown so weak.

113

The sun set, and up rose the yellow moon:
    The devil's in the moon for mischief; they
Who called her CHASTE, methinks, began too soon
    Their nomenclature; there is not a day,
The longest, not the twenty-first of June,
    Sees half the business in a wicked way,
On which three single hours of moonshine smile—
And then she looks so modest all the while!

114

There is a dangerous silence in that hour,
    A stillness, which leaves room for the full soul
To open all itself, without the power
    Of calling wholly back its self-control;
The silver light which, hallowing tree and tower,
    Sheds beauty and deep softness o'er the whole,

Breathes also to the heart, and o'er it throws
A loving languor, which is not repose.

115

And Julia sate with Juan, half embraced
   And half retiring from the glowing arm,
Which trembled like the bosom where 't was placed;
   Yet still she must have thought there was no harm,
Or else 't were easy to withdraw her waist;
   But then the situation had its charm,
And then—God knows what next—I can't go on;
I'm almost sorry that I e'er begun.

116

Oh Plato! Plato! you have paved the way,
   With your confounded fantasies, to more
Immoral conduct by the fancied sway
   Your system feigns o'er the controlless core
Of human hearts, than all the long array
   Of poets and romancers:—You're a bore,
A charlatan, a coxcomb—and have been,
At best, no better than a go-between.

117

And Julia's voice was lost, except in sighs,
   Until too late for useful conversation;
The tears were gushing from her gentle eyes,
   I wish, indeed, they had not had occasion;
But who, alas! can love, and then be wise?
   Not that Remorse did not oppose Temptation;
A little still she strove, and much repented,
And whispering "I will ne'er consent"—consented. ...

122

We'll talk of that anon.—'Tis sweet to hear
   At midnight on the blue and moonlit deep
The song and oar of Adria's gondolier,
   By distance mellowed, o'er the waters sweep;
'Tis sweet to see the evening star appear;
   'Tis sweet to listen as the night-winds creep

From leaf to leaf; 'tis sweet to view on high
The rainbow, based on ocean, span the sky.

123

'Tis sweet to hear the watch-dog's honest bark
    Bay deep-mouthed welcome as we draw near home;
'Tis sweet to know there is an eye will mark
    Our coming, and look brighter when we come;
'Tis sweet to be awakened by the lark,
    Or lulled by falling waters; sweet the hum
Of bees, the voice of girls, the song of birds,
The lisp of children, and their earliest words.

124

Sweet is the vintage, when the showering grapes
    In Bacchanal profusion reel to earth,
Purple and gushing; sweet are our escapes
    From civic revelry to rural mirth;
Sweet to the miser are his glittering heaps,
    Sweet to the father is his first-born's birth,
Sweet is revenge—especially to women—
Pillage to soldiers, prize-money to seamen.

125

Sweet is a legacy, and passing sweet
    The unexpected death of some old lady,
Or gentleman of seventy years complete,
    Who've made "us youth" wait too—too long already,
For an estate, or cash, or country seat,
    Still breaking, but with stamina so steady
That all the Israelites are fit to mob its
Next owner for their double-damned post-obits.

126

'Tis sweet to win, no matter how, one's laurels,
    By blood or ink; 'tis sweet to put an end
To strife; 'tis sometimes sweet to have our quarrels,
    Particularly with a tiresome friend:
Sweet is old wine in bottles, all in barrels;
    Dear is the helpless creature we defend

Against the world; and dear the schoolboy spot
We ne'er forget, though there we are forgot.

127

But sweeter still than this, than these, than all,
    Is first and passionate Love—it stands alone,
Like Adam's recollection of his fall;
    The Tree of Knowledge has been plucked—all's known—
And Life yields nothing further to recall
    Worthy of this ambrosial sin, so shown,
No doubt in fable, as the unforgiven
Fire which Prometheus filched for us from Heaven. ...

Modern Discoveries
(CANTO I, 129–132)

129

What opposite discoveries we have seen!
    (Signs of true genius, and of empty pockets.)
One makes new noses, one a guillotine,
    One breaks your bones, one sets them in their sockets;
But Vaccination certainly has been
    A kind antithesis to Congreve's rockets,
With which the Doctor paid off an old pox
By borrowing a new one from an ox.

130

Bread has been made (indifferent) from potatoes:
    And Galvanism has set some corpses grinning,
But has not answered like the apparatus
    Of the Humane Society's beginning,
By which men are unsuffocated gratis:
    What wondrous new machines have late been spinning!
I said the small-pox has gone out of late;
Perhaps it may be followed by the great.

131

'Tis said the great came from America;
    Perhaps it may set out on its return—
The population there so spreads, they say
    'Tis grown high time to thin it in its turn,

With war, or plague, or famine—any way,
    So that civilization they may learn;
And which in ravage the more loathsome evil is—
Their real lues, or our pseudo-syphilis?

132

This is the patent age of new inventions
    For killing bodies, and for saving souls,
All propagated with the best intentions;
    Sir Humphrey Davy's lantern, by which coals
Are safely mined for in the mode he mentions,
    Tombuctoo travels, voyages to the poles
Are ways to benefit mankind, as true,
Perhaps, as shooting them at Waterloo.

Moon Shot
(CANTO X, 1–2)

1

When Newton saw an apple fall, he found
    In that slight startle from his contemplation—
'Tis *said* (for I'll not answer above ground
    For any sage's creed or calculation)—
A mode of proving that the Earth turned round
    In a most natural whirl, called "gravitation";
And this is the sole mortal who could grapple,
Since Adam—with a fall—or with an apple.

2

Man fell with apples, and with apples rose,
    If this be true; for we must deem the mode
In which Sir Isaac Newton could disclose
    Through the then unpaved stars the turnpike road,
A thing to counterbalance human woes:
    For, ever since, immortal man hath glowed
With all kinds of mechanics, and full soon
Steam-engines will conduct him to the moon.

Race
(CANTO XIV, 82)

O Wilberforce! thou man of black renown,
    Whose merit none enough can sing or say,

Thou hast struck one immense Colossus down,
  Thou moral Washington of Africa!
But there's another little thing, I own,
  Which you should perpetrate some summer's day,
And set the other half of Earth to rights;
You have freed the *blacks*—now pray shut up the whites.

Percy Bysshe Shelley (1792–1822)

POLITICAL POEMS

From The Mask of Anarchy
Written on the Occasion of
The Massacre at Manchester

I met Murder on the way—
He had a mask like Castlereagh—
Very smooth he looked, yet grim;
Seven blood-hounds followed him:

All were fat; and well they might
Be in admirable plight,
For one by one, and two by two,
He tossed them human hearts to chew
Which from his wide cloak he drew.

Next came Fraud, and he had on,
Like Eldon, an erminèd gown;
His big tears, for he wept well,
Turned to mill-stones as they fell.

And the little children, who
Round his feet played to and fro,
Thinking every tear a gem,
Had their brains knocked out by them.

Clothed with the Bible, as with light,
And the shadows of the night,

Like Sidmouth, next, Hypocrisy
On a crocodile rode by.

And many more Destructions played
In this ghastly masquerade,
All disguised, even to the eyes,
Like Bishops, lawyers, peers, or spies.

Last came Anarchy; he rode
On a white horse, splashed with blood;
He was pale, even to the lips,
Like Death in the Apocalypse.

And he wore a kingly crown;
And in his grasp a sceptre shone;
And on his brow this mark I saw—
"I AM GOD, AND KING, AND LAW!"

From Peter Bell the Third

Hell is a city much like London—
  A populous and a smoky city;
There are all sorts of people undone,
And there is little or no fun done;
  Small justice shown, and still less pity.

There is a Castle, and a Canning,
  A Cobbett, and a Castlereagh;
All sorts of caitiff corpses planning
All sorts of cozening for trepanning
  Corpses less corrupt than they.

There is a ——— ———, who has lost
  His wits, or sold them, none knows which;
He walks about a double ghost,
And though as thin as Fraud almost—
  Ever grows more grim and rich.

There is a Chancery Court; a King;
  A manufacturing mob; a set
Of thieves who by themselves are sent
Similar thieves to represent;
  An army; and a public debt.

Which last is a scheme of paper money,
  And means—being interpreted—
"Bees, keep your wax—give us the honey,
And we will plant, while skies are sunny,
  Flowers, which in winter serve instead."

There is a great talk of revolution—
  And a great chance of despotism—
German soldiers—camps—confusion—
Tumults—lotteries—rage—delusion—
  Gin—suicide—and methodism.

Taxes, too, on wine and bread,
  And meat, and beer, and tea, and cheese,
From which those patriots pure are fed,
Who gorge before they reel to bed
  The tenfold essence of all these ...

And this is Hell—and in this smother
  All are damnable and damned;
Each one damning, damns the other
They are damned by one another,
  By none other are they damned.

Sonnet: Political Greatness

Nor happiness, nor majesty, nor fame,
Nor peace nor strength, nor skill in arms or arts,
Shepherd those herds whom tyranny makes tame;
Verse echoes not one beating of their hearts,
History is but the shadow of their shame.
Art veils her glass, or from the pageant starts
As to oblivion their blind millions fleet,
Staining that Heaven with obscene imagery
Of their own likeness. What are numbers knit
By force or custom? Man who man would be,
Must rule the empire of himself; in it
Must be supreme, establishing his throne
On vanquished will, quelling the anarchy
Of hopes and fears, being himself alone.

Ozymandias

I met a traveller from an antique land,
Who said: Two vast and trunkless legs of stone

Stand in the desert. Near them, on the sand,
Half sunk, a shattered visage lies, whose frown
And wrinkled lip and sneer of cold command
Tell that its sculptor well those passions read,
Which yet survive stamped on these lifeless things
The hand that mocked them, and the heart that fed:
And on the pedestal these words appear:
'My name is Ozymandias, King of Kings:
Look on my works, ye Mighty, and despair!'
Nothing beside remains. Round the decay
Of that colossal wreck, boundless and bare
The lone and level sands stretch far away.

ODE TO THE WEST WIND

1

O Wild West Wind, thou breath of Autumn's being,
Thou, from whose unseen presence the leaves dead
Are driven, like ghosts from an enchanter fleeing,

Yellow, and black, and pale, and hectic red,
Pestilence-stricken multitudes: O thou,
Who chariotest to their dark wintry bed

The wingèd seeds, where they lie cold and low,
Each like a corpse within its grave, until
Thine azure sister of the Spring shall blow

Her clarion o'er the dreaming earth, and fill
(Driving sweet buds like flocks to feed in air)
With living hues and odours plain and hill:

Wild Spirit, which art moving everywhere;
Destroyer and preserver; hear, oh, hear!

2

Thou on whose stream, 'mid the steep sky's commotion,
Loose clouds like earth's decaying leaves are shed,
Shook from the tangled boughs of Heaven and Ocean,

Angels of rain and lightning: there are spread
On the blue surface of thine aery surge,

Like the bright hair uplifted from the head
Of some fierce Maenad, even from the dim verge
Of the horizon to the zenith's height,
The locks of the approaching storm. Thou dirge

Of the dying year, to which this closing night
Will be the dome of a vast sepulchre,
Vaulted with all thy congregated might

Of vapours, from whose solid atmosphere
Black rain, and fire, and hail will burst: oh, hear!

3

Thou who didst waken from his summer dreams
The blue Mediterranean, where he lay,
Lulled by the coil of his crystalline streams,

Beside a pumice isle in Baiae's bay,
And saw in sleep old palaces and towers
Quivering within the wave's intenser day,

All overgrown with azure moss and flowers
So sweet, the sense faints picturing them! Thou
For whose path the Atlantic's level powers

Cleave themselves into chasms, while far below
The sea-blooms and the oozy woods which wear
The sapless foliage of the ocean, know

Thy voice, and suddenly grow gray with fear,
And tremble and despoil themselves: oh hear!

4

If I were a dead leaf thou mightest bear;
If I were a swift cloud to fly with thee;
A wave to pant beneath thy power, and share

The impulse of thy strength, only less free
Than thou, O uncontrollable! If even
I were as in my boyhood, and could be

The comrade of thy wanderings over Heaven,
As then, when to outstrip thy skiey speed
Scarce seemed a vision; I would ne'er have striven

As thus with thee in prayer in my sore need.
Oh, lift me as a wave, a leaf, a cloud!
I fall upon the thorns of life! I bleed!

A heavy weight of hours has chained and bowed
One too like thee: tameless, and swift, and proud.

5

Make me thy lyre, even as the forest is:
What if my leaves are falling like its own!
The tumult of thy mighty harmonies

Will take from both a deep, autumnal tone,
Sweet though in sadness. Be thou, Spirit fierce,
My spirit! Be thou me, impetuous one!

Drive my dead thoughts over the universe
Like withered leaves to quicken a new birth!
And, by the incantation of this verse,

Scatter, as from an unextinguished hearth
Ashes and sparks, my words among mankind!
Be through my lips to unawakened earth

The trumpet of a prophecy! O, Wind,
If Winter comes, can Spring be far behind?

John Clare (1793–1864)

GIPSIES

The snow falls deep; the forest lies alone;
The boy goes hasty for his load of brakes,
Then thinks upon the fire and hurries back;
The gipsy knocks his hands and tucks them up,

And seeks his squalid camp, half hid in snow,
Beneath the oak which breaks away the wind,
And bushes close in snow like hovel warm;
There tainted mutton wastes upon the coals,
And the half-wasted dog squats close and rubs,
Then feels the heat too strong, and goes aloof;
He watches well, but none a bit can spare,
And vainly waits the morsel thrown away.
'Tis thus they live—a picture to the place,
A quiet, pilfering, unprotected race.

CLOCK-A-CLAY (THE LADYBIRD)

In the cowslip pips I lie
Hidden from the buzzing fly,
While green grass beneath me lies
Pearled wi' dew like fishes' eyes.
Here I lie, a clock-a-clay,
Waiting for the time o' day.

While grassy forests quake surprise,
And the wild wind sobs and sighs,
My gold home rocks as like to fall
On its pillar green and tall;
When the parting rain drives by
Clock-a-clay keeps warm and dry.

Day by day and night by night
All the week I hide from sight.
In the cowslip pips I lie
In rain and dew still warm and dry.
Day and night, and night and day,
Red, black-spotted clock-a-clay.

My home it shakes in wind and showers,
Pale green pillar topped wi' flowers,
Bending at the wild wind's breath
Till I touch the grass beneath.
Here I live, lone clock-a-clay,
Watching for the time of day.

AUTUMN

The thistle down's flying, though the winds are all still,
On the green grass now lying, now mounting the hill,
The spring from the fountain now boils like a pot;
Through stones past the counting it bubbles red-hot.

The ground parched and cracked is like overbaked bread,
The greensward all wracked is, bents dried up and dead.
The fallow fields glitter like water indeed,
And gossamers twitter, flung from weed unto weed.

Hill tops like hot iron glitter bright in the sun,
And the rivers we're eying burn to gold as they run;
Burning hot is the ground, liquid gold is the air;
Whoever looks round sees Eternity there.

John Keats (1795–1821)

SONNETS

On First Looking into Chapman's Homer

Much have I travell'd in the realms of gold,
  And many goodly states and kingdoms seen;
  Round many western islands have I been
Which bards in fealty to Apollo hold.
Oft of one wide expanse had I been told
  That deep-brow'd Homer ruled as his demesne;
  Yet did I never breathe its pure serene
Till I heard Chapman speak out loud and bold:
Then felt I like some watcher of the skies
  When a new planet swims into his ken;

Or like stout Cortez when with eagle eyes
  He star'd at the Pacific—and all his men
Look'd at each other with a wild surmise—
  Silent, upon a peak in Darien.

On the Grasshopper and Cricket

The poetry of earth is never dead:
  When all the birds are faint with the hot sun,
  And hide in cooling trees, a voice will run
From hedge to hedge about the new-mown mead;
That is the Grasshopper's—he takes the lead
  In summer luxury,—he has never done
  With his delights; for when tired out with fun
He rests at ease beneath some pleasant weed.
The poetry of earth is ceasing never:
  On a lone winter evening, when the frost
    Has wrought a silence, from the stove there shrills
The Cricket's song, in warmth increasing ever,
  And seems to one in drowsiness half lost,
    The Grasshopper's among some grassy hills.

What the Thrush Said

O thou whose face hath felt the Winter's wind,
  Whose eye has seen the snow-clouds hung in mist,
  And the black elm tops 'mong the freezing stars,
  To thee the spring will be a harvest-time.
O thou, whose only book has been the light
  Of supreme darkness which thou feddest on
  Night after night when Phœbus was away,
  To thee the Spring shall be a triple morn.
O fret not after knowledge—I have none,
  And yet my song comes native with the warmth.
O fret not after knowledge—I have none,
  And yet the evening listens. He who saddens
At thought of idleness cannot be idle,
And he's awake who thinks himself asleep.

To Sleep

O soft embalmer of the still midnight,
  Shutting with careful fingers and benign,
Our gloom-pleas'd eyes, embower'd from the light,
  Enshaded in forgetfulness divine:

O soothest Sleep! if so it please thee, close
  In midst of this thine hymn my willing eyes,
Or wait the 'Amen,' ere thy poppy throws
  Around my bed its lulling charities.
Then save me, or the passèd day will shine
Upon my pillow, breeding many woes,—
  Save me from curious Conscience, that still lords
Its strength for darkness, burrowing like a mole;
  Turn the key deftly in the oilèd wards,
And seal the hushèd Casket of my soul.

"Why did I laugh to-night? No voice will tell"

Why did I laugh to-night? No voice will tell:
  No God, no Demon of severe response,
Deigns to reply from Heaven or from Hell.
  Then to my human heart I turn at once.
Heart! Thou and I are here sad and alone;
  I say, why did I laugh? O mortal pain!
O Darkness! Darkness! ever must I moan,
  To question Heaven and Hell and Heart in vain.
Why did I laugh? I know this Being's lease,
  My fancy to its utmost blisses spreads;
Yet would I on this very midnight cease,
  And the world's gaudy ensigns see in shreds;
Verse, Fame, and Beauty are intense indeed,
But Death intenser—Death is Life's high meed.

"When I have fears that I may cease to be"

When I have fears that I may cease to be
  Before my pen has glean'd my teeming brain,
Before high-pilèd books, in charactery,
  Hold like rich garners the full ripen'd grain;
When I behold, upon the night's starr'd face,
  Huge cloudy symbols of a high romance,
And think that I may never live to trace
  Their shadows, with the magic hand of chance;
And when I feel, fair creature of an hour,
  That I shall never look upon thee more,
Never have relish in the faery power
  Of unreflecting love;—then on the shore
Of the wide world I stand alone, and think
Till love and fame to nothingness do sink.

Bright star, would I were steadfast as thou art—
　Not in lone splendour hung aloft the night
And watching, with eternal lids apart,
　Like nature's patient, sleepless Eremite,
The moving waters at their priestlike task
　Of pure ablution round earth's human shores,
Or gazing on the new soft-fallen mask
　Of snow upon the mountains and the moors—
No—yet still stedfast, still unchangeable,
　Pillow'd upon my fair love's ripening breast,
　To feel for ever its soft fall and swell,
　Awake for ever in a sweet unrest,
Still, still to hear her tender-taken breath,
And so live ever—or else swoon to death.

ODES

Fragment of an Ode to Maia

Mother of Hermes! and still youthful Maia!
　　　May I sing to thee
As thou wast hymnèd on the shores of Baiae?
　　　Or may I woo thee
In earlier Sicilian? or thy smiles
Seek as they once were sought, in Grecian isles,
By bards who died content on pleasant sward,
Leaving great verse unto a little clan?
O, give me their old vigour, and unheard
Save of the quiet Primrose, and the span
　　　Of heaven and few ears,
Rounded by thee, my song should die away
　　　Content as theirs,
Rich in the simple worship of a day.

Ode to a Nightingale

My heart aches, and a drowsy numbness pains
　My sense, as though of hemlock I had drunk,
Or emptied some dull opiate to the drains
　One minute past, and Lethe-wards had sunk:
'Tis not through envy of thy happy lot,
　But being too happy in thine happiness,—

That thou, light-wingèd Dryad of the trees,
        In some melodious plot
Of beechen green, and shadows numberless,
    Singest of summer in full-throated ease.

O, for a draught of vintage! that hath been
    Cool'd a long age in the deep-delvèd earth,
Tasting of Flora and the country green,
    Dance, and Provençal song, and sunburnt mirth!
O for a beaker full of the warm South,
    Full of the true, the blushful Hippocrene,
        With beaded bubbles winking at the brim,
            And purple-stainèd mouth;
    That I might drink, and leave the world unseen,
        And with thee fade away into the forest dim:

Fade far away, dissolve, and quite forget
    What thou among the leaves hast never known,
The weariness, the fever, and the fret
    Here, where men sit and hear each other groan;
Where palsy shakes a few, sad, last gray hairs,
    Where youth grows pale, and spectre-thin, and dies;
        Where but to think is to be full of sorrow
            And leaden-eyed despairs,
    Where Beauty cannot keep her lustrous eyes,
        Or new Love pine at them beyond tomorrow.

Away! away! for I will fly to thee
    Not charioted by Bacchus and his pards,
But on the viewless wings of Poesy,
    Though the dull brain perplexes and retards:
Already with thee! tender is the night,
    And haply the Queen-Moon is on her throne,
        Cluster'd around by all her starry Fays;
            But here there is no light,
    Save what from heaven is with the breezes blown
        Through verdurous glooms and winding mossy ways.

I cannot see what flowers are at my feet,
    Nor what soft incense hangs upon the boughs,
But, in embalmèd darkness, guess each sweet
    Wherewith the seasonable month endows
The grass, the thicket, and the fruit-tree wild;
    White hawthorn, and the pastoral eglantine;
        Fast fading violets cover'd up in leaves;
            And mid-May's eldest child,

The coming musk-rose, full of dewy wine,
　　The murmurous haunt of flies on summer eves.

Darkling I listen; and for many a time
　　I have been half in love with easeful Death,
Call'd him soft names in many a musèd rhyme,
　　To take into the air my quiet breath;
Now more than ever it seems rich to die,
　　To cease upon the midnight with no pain,
　　　　While thou art pouring forth thy soul abroad
　　　　　　In such an ecstasy!
Still wouldst thou sing, and I have ears in vain—
　　To thy high requiem become a sod.

Thou wast not born for death, immortal Bird!
　　No hungry generations tread thee down;
The voice I hear this passing night was heard
　　In ancient days by emperor and clown:
Perhaps the self-same song that found a path
　　Through the sad heart of Ruth, when, sick for home,
　　　She stood in tears amid the alien corn;
　　　　　The same that oft-times hath
Charm'd magic casements, opening on the foam
　　Of perilous seas, in faery lands forlorn.

Forlorn! the very word is like a bell
　　To toll me back from thee to my sole self!
Adieu! the fancy cannot cheat so well
　　As she is fam'd to do, deceiving elf.
Adieu adieu! thy plaintive anthem fades
　　Past the near meadows, over the still stream,
　　　Up the hill-side; and now 'tis buried deep
　　　　　In the next valley-glades:
Was it a vision, or a waking dream?
　　Fled is that music:—Do I wake or sleep?

Ode on a Grecian Urn

Thou still unravish'd bride of quietness,
　　Thou foster-child of silence and slow time,
Sylvan historian, who canst thus express
　　A flowery tale more sweetly than our rhyme:
What leaf-fring'd legend haunts about thy shape
　　Of deities or mortals, or of both,
　　　In Tempe or the dales of Arcady?
What men or gods are these? What maidens loth?

What mad pursuit? What struggle to escape?
  What pipes and timbrels? What wild ecstasy?

Heard melodies are sweet, but those unheard
  Are sweeter; therefore, ye soft pipes, play on;
Not to the sensual ear, but, more endear'd,
  Pipe to the spirit ditties of no tone:
Fair youth, beneath the trees, thou canst not leave
  Thy song, nor ever can those trees be bare;
    Bold Lover, never, never canst thou kiss,
Though winning near the goal—yet, do not grieve;
  She cannot fade, though thou hast not thy bliss,
    For ever wilt thou love, and she be fair!

Ah, happy, happy boughs! that cannot shed
  Your leaves, nor ever bid the Spring adieu;
And, happy melodist, unwearièd,
  For ever piping songs, for ever new;
More happy love! more happy, happy love!
  For ever warm and still to be enjoy'd,
    For ever panting, and for ever young;
All breathing human passion far above,
  That leaves a heart high-sorrowful and cloy'd,
    A burning forehead, and a parching tongue.

Who are these coming to the sacrifice?
  To what green altar, O mysterious priest,
Lead'st thou that heifer lowing at the skies,
  And all her silken flanks with garlands drest?
What little town by river or sea shore,
  Or mountain-built with peaceful citadel,
    Is emptied of this folk, this pious morn?
And little town, thy streets for evermore
  Will silent be; and not a soul to tell
    Why thou art desolate, can e'er return.

O Attic shape! Fair attitude! with brede
  Of marble men and maidens overwrought,
With forest branches and the trodden weed;
  Thou, silent form, dost tease us out of thought
As doth eternity: Cold Pastoral!
  When old age shall this generation waste,
    Thou shalt remain, in midst of other woe
Than ours, a friend to man, to whom thou say'st,
  'Beauty is truth, truth beauty,' that is all
    Ye know on earth, and all ye need to know.

Ode on Melancholy

No, no, go not to Lethe, neither twist
  Wolf's-bane, tight-rooted, for its poisonous wine;
Nor suffer thy pale forehead to be kiss'd
  By nightshade, ruby grape of Proserpine;
Make not your rosary of yew-berries,
  Nor let the beetle, nor the death-moth be
    Your mournful Psyche, nor the downy owl
A partner in your sorrow's mysteries;
  For shade to shade will come too drowsily,
    And drown the wakeful anguish of the soul.

But when the melancholy fit shall fall
  Sudden from heaven like a weeping cloud,
That fosters the droop-headed flowers all,
  And hides the green hill in an April shroud;
Then glut thy sorrow on a mourning rose,
  Or on the rainbow of the salt sand-wave,
    Or on the wealth of globèd peonies;
Or if thy mistress some rich anger shows,
  Emprison her soft hand, and let her rave,
    And feed deep, deep upon her peerless eyes.

She dwells with Beauty—Beauty that must die;
  And Joy, whose hand is ever at his lips
Bidding adieu; and aching Pleasure nigh,
  Turning to Poison while the bee-mouth sips:
Ay, in the very temple of delight
  Veil'd Melancholy has her sovran shrine,
    Though seen of none save him whose strenuous tongue
Can burst Joy's grape against his palate fine;
His soul shall taste the sadness of her might,
  And be among her cloudy trophies hung.

To Autumn

Season of mists and mellow fruitfulness,
  Close bosom-friend of the maturing sun;
Conspiring with him how to load and bless
  With fruit the vines that round the thatch-eves run;
To bend with apples the moss'd cottage-trees,
  And fill all fruit with ripeness to the core;
    To swell the gourd, and plump the hazel shells
With a sweet kernel; to set budding more,

And still more, later flowers for the bees,
Until they think warm days will never cease,
   For summer has o'er-brimm'd their clammy cells

Who hath not seen thee oft amid thy store?
   Sometimes whoever seeks abroad may find
Thee sitting careless on a granary floor,
   Thy hair soft-lifted by the winnowing wind;
Or on a half-reap'd furrow sound asleep,
   Drows'd with the fume of poppies, while thy hook
     Spares the next swath and all its twinèd flowers:
And sometimes like a gleaner thou dost keep
   Steady thy laden head across a brook;
   Or by a cyder-press, with patient look,
     Thou watchest the last oozings hours by hours.

Where are the songs of Spring? Ay, where are they?
   Think not of them, thou hast thy music too,—
While barrèd clouds bloom the soft-dying day,
   And touch the stubble-plains with rosy hue;
Then in a wailful choir the small gnats mourn
   Among the river shallows, borne aloft
     Or sinking as the light wind lives or dies;
And full-grown lambs loud bleat from hilly bourn;
   Hedge-crickets sing; and now with treble soft
   The red-breast whistles from a garden croft;
     And gathering swallows twitter in the skies.

From THE FALL OF HYPERION: A DREAM

Death

Slow, heavy, deadly was my pace: the cold
Grew stifling, suffocating, at the heart;
And when I clasp'd my hands I felt them not.
One minute before death, my iced foot touch'd
The lowest stair; and as it touch'd, life seem'd
To pour in at the toes: I mounted up,
As once fair angels on a ladder flew
From the green turf to Heaven—'Holy Power,'
Cried I, approaching near the hornèd shrine,
'What am I that should so be saved from death?
'What am I that another death come not
'To choke my utterance sacrilegious, here?'

Then said the veilèd shadow—'thou hast felt
'What 'tis to die and live again before
'Thy fated hour, that thou hast power to do so
'Is thy own safety, thou hast dated on
'Thy doom,'—'High Prophetess,' said I, 'purge off,
'Benign, if so it please thee, my mind's film.'
'None can usurp this height,' returned that shade,
'But those to whom the miseries of the world
'Are misery, and will not let them rest.
'All else who find a heaven in the world,
'Where they may thoughtless sleep away their days,
'If by a chance into this fane they come,
'Rot on the pavement where thou rottedst half.—'

Thomas Lovell Beddoes (1803–1849)

SONG

Old Adam, the carrion crow,
    The old crow of Cairo;
He sat in the shower, and let it flow
    Under his tail and over his crest;
      And through every feather
      Leaked the wet weather;
    And the bough swung under his nest;
For his beak it was heavy with marrow.
    Is that the wind dying? O no;
    It's only two devils, that blow
      Through a murderer's bones, to and fro
      In the ghosts' moonshine.

Ho! Eve, my grey carrion wife,
    When we have supped on king's marrow,
Where shall we drink and make merry our life?
    Our nest it is queen Cleopatra's skull,
      'Tis cloven and cracked,
      And battered and hacked,

But with tears of blue eyes it is full:
Let us drink then, my raven of Cairo.
   Is that the wind dying? O no;
   It's only two devils, that blow
     Through a murderer's bones, to and fro
     In the ghosts' moonshine.

Elizabeth Barrett Browning (1806-1861)

A MUSICAL INSTRUMENT

What was he doing, the great god Pan,
   Down in the reeds by the river?
Spreading ruin and scattering ban,
Splashing and paddling with hoofs of a goat,
And breaking the golden lilies afloat
   With the dragon-fly on the river.

He tore out a reed, the great god Pan,
   From the deep cool bed of the river;
The limpid water turbidly ran,
And the broken lilies a-dying lay,
And the dragon-fly had fled away,
   Ere he brought it out of the river.

High on the shore sat the great god Pan,
   While turbidly flow'd the river;
And hack'd and hew'd as a great god can,
With his hard bleak steel at the patient reed,
Till there was not a sign of the leaf indeed
   To prove it fresh from the river.

He cut it short, did the great god Pan
   (How tall it stood in the river!),
Then drew the pith, like the heart of a man,
Steadily from the outside ring,

And notch'd the poor dry empty thing
   In holes, as he sat by the river.

'This is the way,' laugh'd the great god Pan
   (Laugh'd while he sat by the river),
'The only way, since gods began
To make sweet music, they could succeed.'
Then dropping his mouth to a hole in the reed,
   He blew in power by the river.

Sweet, sweet, sweet, O Pan!
   Piercing sweet by the river!
Blinding sweet, O great god Pan!
The sun on the hill forgot to die,
And the lilies revived, and the dragon-fly
   Came back to dream on the river.

Yet half a beast is the great god Pan,
   To laugh as he sits by the river,
Making a poet out of a man:
The true god's sigh for the cost and pain—
For the reed which grows nevermore again
   As a reed with the reeds of the river.

Edward FitzGerald (1809–1883)

From RUBAIYAT OF OMAR KHAYYAM
OF NAISHAPUR

Opening Stanzas

1

Wake! For the Sun, who scattered into flight
The Stars before him for the Field of Night,
   Drives Night along with them from Heav'n, and strikes
The Sultan's Turret with a Shaft of Light.

Before the phantom of False morning died,
Methought a Voice within the Tavern cried
  "When all the Temple is prepared within,
Why nods the drowsy Worshipper outside?"

3

And, as the Cock crew, those who stood before
The Tavern shouted—"Open, then, the door!
  You know how little while we have to stay,
And, once departed, may return no more."

Now the New Year reviving old Desires,
The thoughtful Soul to Solitude retires,
  Where the White Hand of Moses on the Bough
Puts out, and Jesus from the Ground suspires.

Iram indeed is gone with all his Rose,
And Jamshyd's Sev'n-ringed Cup where no one knows;
  But still a Ruby kindles in the Vine,
And many a Garden by the Water blows.

And David's lips are lockt; but in divine
High-piping Pehlevi, with "Wine! Wine! Wine!
  Red Wine!"—the Nightingale cries to the Rose
That sallow cheek of hers to incarnadine.

Come, fill the Cup, and in the fire of Spring
Your Winter-garment of Repentance fling:
  The Bird of Time has but a little way
To flutter—and the Bird is on the Wing.

Whether at Naishapur or Babylon,
Whether the Cup with sweet or bitter run,

The Wine of Life keeps oozing drop by drop,
The Leaves of Life keep falling one by one.

9

Each Morn a thousand Roses brings, you say;
Yes, but where leaves the Rose of Yesterday?
　　And this first Summer month that brings the Rose
Shall take Jamshyd and Kaikobad away.

10

Well, let it take them! What have we to do
With Kaikobad the Great, or Kaikhosru?
　　Let Zal and Rostum bluster as they will,
Or Hatim call to Supper—heed not you.

11

With me along the strip of Herbage strown
That just divides the desert from the sown,
　　Where name of Slave and Sultan is forgot—
And Peace to Mahmud on his golden Throne!

12

A Book of Verses underneath the Bough
A Jug of Wine, a Loaf of Bread—and Thou
　　Beside me singing in the Wilderness—
Oh, Wilderness were Paradise enow!

13

Some for the Glories of this World; and some
Sigh for the Prophet's Paradise to come;
　　Ah, take the Cash, and let the Credit go,
Nor heed the rumble of a distant Drum!

Alfred, Lord Tennyson (1809–1892)

TITHONUS

The woods decay, the woods decay and fall,
The vapours weep their burthen to the ground,
Man comes and tills the fields and lies beneath,
And after many a summer dies the swan.
Me only cruel immortality
Consumes: I wither slowly in thine arms,
Here at the quiet limit of the world,
A white-hair'd shadow roaming like a dream
The ever-silent spaces of the East,
Far-folded mists, and gleaming halls of morn.

Alas! for this gray shadow, once a man—
So glorious in his beauty and thy choice,
Who madest him thy chosen that he seem'd
To his great heart none other than a God!
I ask'd thee, "Give me immortality."
Then didst thou grant mine asking with a smile,
Like wealthy men who care not how they give.
But thy strong Hours indignant work's their wills
And beat me down and marr'd and wasted me,
And tho' they could not end me, left me maimed
To dwell in presence of immortal youth,
Immortal age beside immortal youth,
And all I was in ashes. Can thy love,
Thy beauty, make amends, tho' even now,
Close over us, the silver star, thy guide,
Shines in those tremulous eyes that fill with tears
To hear me? Let me go: take back thy gift:
Why should a man desire in any way
To vary from the kindly race of men,

Or pass beyond the goal of ordinance
When all should pause, as is most meet for all?

A soft air fans the cloud apart; there comes
A glimpse of that dark world where I was born.
Once more the old mysterious glimmer steals
From thy pure brows, and from thy shoulders pure,
And bosom beating with a heart renew'd.
Thy cheek begins to redden through the gloom,
Thy sweet eyes brighten slowly close to mine,
Ere yet they blind the stars, and the wild team
Which love thee, yearning for thy yoke, arise,
And shake the darkness from their loosen'd manes,
And beat the twilight into flakes of fire.

Lo! ever thus thou growest beautiful
In silence, then before thine answer given
Departest, and thy tears are on my cheek.

Why wilt thou ever scare me with thy tears,
And make me tremble lest a saying learnt
In days far-off, on that dark earth, be true?
"The Gods themselves cannot recall their gifts."

Ay me! Ay me! with what another heart
In days far-off, and with what other eyes
I used to watch—if I be he that watch'd—
The lucid outline forming round thee; saw
The dim curls kindle into sunny rings;
Changed with thy mystic change, and felt my blood
Glow with the glow that slowly crimson'd all
Thy presence and thy portals, while I lay,
Mouth, forehead, eyelids, growing dewy-warm
With kisses balmier than half-opening buds
Of April, and could hear the lips that kiss'd
Whispering I knew not what of wild and sweet,
Like that strange song I heard Apollo sing
While Ilion like a mist rose into towers.

Yet hold me not for ever in thine East:
How can my nature longer mix with thine?
Coldly thy rosy shadows bathe me, cold
Are all thy lights, and cold my wrinkled feet
Upon thy glimmering thresholds, when the steam
Floats up from those dim fields about the homes
Of happy men that have the power to die,

And grassy barrows of the happier dead.
Release me, and restore me to the ground;
Thou seëst all things, thou wilt see my grave;
Thou wilt renew thy beauty morn by morn;
I earth in earth forget these empty courts,
And thee returning on thy silver wheels.

THE EAGLE

He clasps the crag with crooked hands:
Close to the sun in lonely lands,
Ringed with the azure world, he stands.

The wrinkled sea beneath him crawls;
He watches from his mountain walls,
And like a thunderbolt he falls.

Robert Browning (1812–1889)

SIBRANDUS SCHAFNABURGENSIS

1

Plague take all your pedants, say I!
   He who wrote what I hold in my hand,
Centuries back was so good as to die,
   Leaving this rubbish to cumber the land;
This, that was a book in its time,
   Printed on paper and bound in leather,
Last month in the white of a matin-prime
   Just when the birds sang all together.

2

Into the garden I brought it to read,
   And under the arbute and laurustine

[216]

Read it, so help me grace in my need,
　From the title-page to closing line.
Chapter on chapter did I count,
　As a curious traveller counts Stone-henge;
Added up the mortal account;
　And then proceeded to my revenge.

3

Yonder's a plum-tree with a crevice
　An owl would build in, were he but sage;
For a lap of moss, like a fine pont-levis
　In a castle of the middle age,
Joins to a lip of gum, pure amber;
　When he'd be private, there might he spend
Hours alone in his lady's chamber:
　Into this crevice I dropped our friend.

4

Splash, went he, as under he ducked,
　—I knew at the bottom rain-drippings stagnate;
Next a handful of blossoms I plucked
　To bury him with, my bookshelf's magnate;
Then I went indoors, brought out a loaf,
　Half a cheese, and a bottle of Chablis;
Lay on the grass and forgot the oaf
　Over a jolly chapter of Rabelais.

5

Now, this morning betwixt the moss
　And gum that locked our friend in limbo,
A spider had spun his web across,
　And sat in the midst with arms akimbo:
So I took pity, for learning's sake,
　And *de profundis, accentibus laetis,*
Cantate! quoth I, as I got a rake,
　And up I fished his delectable treatise.

6

Here you have it, dry in the sun,
　With all the binding all of a blister,
And great blue spots where the ink has run,
　And reddish streaks that wink and glister

O'er the page so beautifully yellow:
    Oh, well have the droppings played their tricks!
Did he guess how toadstools grow, this fellow?
    Here's one stuck in his chapter six!

7

How did he like it when the live creatures
    Tickled and toused and browsed him all over,
And worm, slug, eft, with serious features,
    Came in, each one, for his right of trover?
—When the water-beetle with great blind deaf face
    Made of her eggs the stately deposit,
And the newt borrowed just so much of the preface
    As tiled in the top of his black wife's closet?

8

All that life and fun and romping,
    All that frisking and twisting and coupling,
While slowly our poor friend's leaves were swamping
    And clasps were cracking and covers suppling!
As if you had carried sour John Knox
    To the play-house at Paris, Vienna, or Munich,
Fastened him into a front-row box,
    And danced off the ballet with trousers and tunic.

9

Come, old martyr! What, torment enough is it?
    Back to my room shall you take your sweet self!
Good-bye, mother-beetle; husband-eft, *sufficit!*
    See the snug niche I have made on my shelf.
A.'s book shall prop you up, B.'s shall cover you,
    Here's C. to be grave with, or D. to be gay,
And with E. on each side, and F. right over you,
    Dry-rot at ease till the Judgement-day!

THE CONFESSIONAL

(Spain)

1

It is a lie—their Priests, their Pope,
Their Saints, their . . . all they fear or hope

Are lies, and lies—there! through my door
And ceiling, there! and walls and floor,
There, lies, they lie—and still be hurled
Till spite of them I reach the world!

2

You think Priests just and holy men!
Before they put me in this one
I was a human creature too,
With flesh and blood like one of you,
A girl that laughed in beauty's pride
Like lilies in your world outside.

3

I had a lover—shame avaunt!
This poor wrenched body, grim and gaunt,
Was kissed all over till it burned,
By lips the truest, love e'er turned
His heart's own tint: one night they kissed
My soul out in a burning mist.

4

So, next day when the accustomed train
Of things grew round my sense again,
'That is a sin,' I said; and slow
With downcast eyes to church I go
And pass to the confession-chair,
And tell the old mild father there.

5

But when I falter Beltran's name,
'Ha?' quoth the father, 'much I blame
The sin; yet wherefore idly grieve?
Despair not,—strenuously retrieve!
Nay, I will turn this love of thine
To lawful love, almost divine.

6

'For he is young, and led astray,
This Beltran, and he schemes, men say,
To change the laws of church and state;

So, thine shall be an angel's fate,
Who, ere the thunder breaks, should roll
Its cloud away and save his soul.

7

'For, when he lies upon thy breast,
Thou may'st demand and be possessed
Of all his plans, and next day steal
To me, and all those plans reveal,
That I and every priest, to purge
His soul, may fast and use the scourge.'

8

That father's beard was long and white.
With love and truth his brow seemed bright;
I went back, all on fire with joy,
And, that same evening, bade the boy
Tell me, as lovers should, heart-free,
Something to prove his love of me.

9

He told me what he would not tell
For hope of Heaven or fear of Hell;
And I lay listening in such pride!
And, soon as he had left my side,
Tripped to the church by morning-light
To save his soul in his despite.

10

I told the father all his schemes,
Who were his comrades, what their dreams;
'And now make haste,' I said, 'to pray
The one spot from his soul away;
Tonight he comes, but not the same
Will look!' At night he never came.

11

Nor next night: on the after-morn,
I went forth with a strength new-born,
The church was empty; something drew
My steps into the street; I knew

It led me to the market-place—
Where, lo, on high, the father's face!

12

That horrible black scaffold dressed,
That stapled block ... God sink the rest!
That head strapped back, that blinding vest,
Those knotted hands and naked breast,
Till near one busy hangman pressed,
And, on the neck these arms caressed. ...

13

No part in aught they hope or fear!
No Heaven with them, no Hell!—and here,
No Earth, not so much space as pens
My body in their worst of dens
But shall bear God and Man my cry,
Lies—lies, again—and still, they lie!

SOLILOQUY OF THE SPANISH CLOISTER

1

Gr-r-r—there go, my heart's abhorence!
    Water your damned flower-pots, do!
If hate killed men, Brother Lawrence,
    God's blood, would not mine kill you!
What? your myrtle-bush wants trimming?
    Oh, that rose has prior claims—
Needs its leaden vase filled brimming?
    Hell dry you up with its flames!

2

At the meal we sit together:
    Salve tibi! I must hear
Wise talk of the kind of weather,
    Sort of season, time of year:
*Not a plenteous cork-crop: scarcely
    Dare we hope oak-galls, I doubt:*
What's the Latin name for 'parsley'?
    What's the Greek name for Swine's Snout?

Whew! We'll have our platter burnished,
  Laid with care on our own shelf!
With a fire-new spoon we're furnished,
  And a goblet for ourself,
Rinsed like something sacrificial
  Ere 'tis fit to touch our chaps—
Marked with L. for our initial!
  (He-he! There his lily snaps!)

4

Saint, forsooth! While brown Dolores
  Squats outside the Convent bank,
With Sanchicha, telling stories,
  Steeping tresses in the tank,
Blue-black, lustrous, thick like horse-hairs,
  —Can't I see his dead eye glow,
Bright as 'twere a Barbary corsair's?
  (That is, if he'd let it show!)

5

When he finishes refection,
  Knife and fork he never lays
Cross-wise, to my recollection,
  As do I, in Jesu's praise.
I, the Trinity illustrate,
  Drinking watered orange-pulp—
In three sips the Arian frustrate;
  While he drains his at one gulp!

6

Oh, those melons! If he's able
  We're to have a feast; so nice!
One goes to the Abbot's table,
  All of us get each a slice.
How go on your flowers? None double?
  Not one fruit-sort can you spy?
Strange!—And I, too, at such trouble,
  Keep them close-nipped on the sly!

7

There's a great text in Galatians,
  Once you trip on it, entails

Twenty-nine distinct damnations,
   One sure, if another fails:
If I trip him just a-dying,
   Sure of Heaven as sure can be,
Spin him round and send him flying
   Off to Hell, a Manichee?

8

Or, my scrofulous French novel
   On grey paper with blunt type!
Simply glance at it, you grovel
   Hand and foot in Belial's gripe:
If I double down its pages
   At the woeful sixteenth print,
When he gathers his greengages,
   Ope a sieve and slip it in't?

9

Or, there's Satan!—one might venture
   Pledge one's soul to him, yet leave
Such a flaw in the indenture
   As he'd miss till, past reprieve,
Blasted lay that rose-acacia
   We're so proud of! *Hy, Zy, Hine* ...
'St, there's Vespers! *Plena gratiá*
   Ave, Virgo! Gr-r-r—you swine!

HOME-THOUGHTS, FROM ABROAD

1

Oh, to be in England
Now that April's there,
And whoever wakes in England
Sees, some morning, unaware,
That the lowest boughs and the brush-wood sheaf
Round the elm-tree bole are in tiny leaf,
While the chaffinch sings on the orchard bough
In England—now!

2

And after April, when May follows,

And the whitethroat builds, and all the swallows!
Hark, where my blossomed pear-tree in the hedge
Leans to the field and scatters on the clover
Blossoms and dewdrops—at the bent spray's edge—
That's the wise thrush; he sings each song twice over,
Lest you should think he never could recapture
The first fine careless rapture!
And though the fields look rough with hoary dew,
All will be gay when noontide wakes anew
The buttercups, the little children's dower
Far brighter than this gaudy melon-flower!

HOME-THOUGHTS, FROM THE SEA

Nobly, nobly Cape Saint Vincent to the North-West died
    away;
Sunset ran, one glorious blood-red, reeking into Cadiz Bay;
Bluish mid the burning water, full in face Trafalgar lay;
In the dimmest North-East distance, dawned Gibraltar grand
    and gray;
'Here and here did England help me; how can I help En-
    gland?'—say,
Whoso turns as I, this evening, turn to God to praise and
    pray,
While Jove's planet rises yonder, silent over Africa.

Edward Lear (1812–1888)

INCIDENTS IN THE LIFE OF MY UNCLE ARLY

1

O my agèd Uncle Arly!
Sitting on a heap of Barley
    Thro' the silent hours of night,—

Close beside a leafy thicket:—
On his nose there was a Cricket,—
In his hat a Railway-Ticket;—
   (But his shoes were far too tight).

2

Long ago, in youth, he squander'd
All his goods away, and wander'd
   To the Tiniskoop-hills afar.
There on golden sunsets blazing,
Every evening found him gazing,—
Singing,—'Orb! you're quite amazing!
   How I wonder what you are!'

3

Like the ancient Medes and Persians,
Always by his own exertions
   He subsisted on those hills;—
Whiles—by teaching children spelling,—
Or at times by merely yelling,—
Or at intervals by selling
   'Propter's Nicodemus Pills.'

4

Later, in his morning rambles
He perceived the moving brambles
   Something square and white disclose;—
'Twas a First-class Railway-Ticket;
But, on stooping down to pick it
Off the ground,—a pea-green Cricket
   Settled on my uncle's Nose.

5

Never—never more,—oh! never,
Did that Cricket leave him ever,—
   Dawn or evening, day or night;—
Clinging as a constant treasure,—
Chirping with a cheerious measure,—
Wholly to my uncle's pleasure,—
   (Though his shoes were far too tight).

So for three-and-forty winters,
Till his shoes were worn to splinters,
 All those hills he wander'd o'er,—
Sometimes silent, sometimes yelling;—
Till he came to Borley-Melling,
Near his old ancestral dwelling;—
 (But his shoes were far too tight).

7

On a little heap of Barley
Died my agèd uncle Arly,
 And they buried him one night;—
Close beside the leafy thicket;—
There,—his hat and Railway-Ticket;—
There,—his ever-faithful Cricket;—
 (But his shoes were far too tight).

Emily Brontë (1818–1848)

REMEMBRANCE

Cold in the earth, and the deep snow piled above thee!
Far, far removed, cold in the dreary grave!
Have I forgot, my Only Love, to love thee,
Severed at last by Time's all-wearing wave?

Now, when alone, do my thoughts no longer hover
Over the mountains, on Angora's shore,
Resting their wings where heath and fern-leaves cover
That noble heart for ever, ever more?

Cold is the earth, and fifteen wild Decembers
From those brown hills, have melted into spring:

Faithful, indeed, is the spirit that remembers
After such years of change and suffering!

Sweet Love of youth, forgive if I forget thee,
While the World's tide is bearing me along;
Sterner desires and darker hopes beset me,
Hopes that obscure, but cannot do thee wrong.

No other Sun has lightened up my heaven,
No other Star has ever shone for me;
All my life's bliss from thy dear life was given,
All my life's bliss is in the grave with thee.

But, when the days of golden dreams had perished,
And even Despair was powerless to destroy;
Then did I learn how existence could be cherished,
Strengthened and fed without the aid of joy.

Then did I check the tears of useless passion,
Weaned my young soul from yearning after thine;
Sternly denied its burning wish to hasten
Down to that tomb already more than mine.

And, even yet, I dare not let it languish,
Dare not indulge in memory's rapturous pain;
   Once drinking deep of that divinest anguish,
   How could I seek the empty world again?

LAST LINES

   No coward soul is mine,
No trembler in the world's storm-troubled sphere:
   I see Heaven's glories shine.
And faith shines equal, arming me from fear.

   O God within my breast,
Almighty, ever-present Deity!
   Life—that in me has rest,
As I, undying Life, have power in thee!

   Vain are the thousand creeds
That move men's hearts, unalterably vain;
   Worthless as withered weeds,
Or idlest froth amid the boundless main,

To waken doubt in one
Holding so fast by thine infinity;
   So surely anchored on
The steadfast rock of immortality.

   With wide-embracing love
Thy spirit animates eternal years,
   Pervades and broods above,
Changes, sustains, dissolves, creates, and rears.

   Though earth and moon were gone,
And suns and universes ceased to be,
   And Thou wert left alone,
Every existence would exist in Thee.

   There is not room for Death,
Nor atom that his might could render void:
   Thou—Thou art Being and Breath,
And what Thou art may never be destroyed.

Arthur Hugh Clough (1819–1861)

From AMOURS DE VOYAGE

Canto II, 2

Dulce it is, and *decorum,* no doubt, for the country to fall,—to
Offer one's blood an oblation to Freedom, and die for the Cause; yet
Still, individual culture is also something, and no man
Finds quite distinct the assurance that he of all others is called on,
Or would be justified, even, in taking away from the world that
Precious creature, himself. Nature sent him here to abide here,

Else why sent him at all? Nature wants him still, it is likely.
On the whole, we are meant to look after ourselves; it is certain
Each has to eat for himself, digest for himself, and in general
Care for his own dear life, and see to his own preservation;
Nature's intentions, in most things uncertain, in this are decisive;
Which, on the whole, I conjecture the Romans will follow, and I shall.
    So we cling to our rocks like limpets; Ocean may bluster,
Over and under and round us; we open our shells to imbibe our
Nourishment, close them again, and are safe, fulfilling the purpose
Nature intended,—a wise one, of course, and a noble, we doubt not.
Sweet it may be and decorous, perhaps, for the country to die; but,
On the whole, we conclude the Romans won't do it, and I shan't.

4

Now supposing the French or the Neapolitian soldier
Should by some evil chance come exploring the Maison Serny
(Where the family English are all to assemble for safety),
Am I prepared to lay down my life for the British female?
Really, who knows? One has bowed and talked, till, little by little,
All the natural heat has escaped of the chivalrous spirit.
Oh, one conformed, of course; but one doesn't die for good manners,
Stab or shoot, or be shot, by way of a graceful attention.
No, if it should be at all, it should be on the barricades there;
Should I incarnadine ever this inky pacifical finger,
Sooner far should it be for this vapour of Italy's freedom,
Sooner far by the side of the d———d and dirty plebeians.
Ah, for a child in the street I could strike; for the full-blown lady—
Somehow, Eustace, alas! I have not felt the vocation.
Yet these people of course will expect, as of course, my protection,
Vernon in radiant arms stand forth for the lovely Georgina,
And to appear, I suppose, were but common civility. Yes, and
Truly I do not desire they should either be killed or offended.

Oh, and of course you will say, 'When the time comes, you
    will be ready.'
Ah, but before it comes, am I to presume it will be so?
What I cannot feel now, am I to suppose that I shall feel?
Am I not free to attend for the ripe and indubious instinct?
Am I forbidden to wait for the clear and lawful perception?
Is it the calling of man to surrender his knowledge and in-
    sight
For the mere venture of what may, perhaps, be the virtuous
    action?
Must we, walking on earth, discerning a little, and hoping
Some plain visible task shall yet for our hands be assigned
    us,—
Must we abandon the future for fear of omitting the present,
Quit our own fireside hopes at the alien call of a neighbour,
To the mere possible shadow of Deity offer the victim?
And is all this, my friend, but a weak and ignoble refining,
Wholly unworthy the head or the heart of Your Own Corre-
    spondent?

11

There are two different kinds, I believe, of human attraction:
One which simply disturbs, unsettles, and makes you uneasy,
And another that poises, retains, and fixes and holds you.
I have no doubt, for myself, in giving my voice for the latter.
I do not wish to be moved, but growing where I was
    growing,
There more truly to grow, to live where as yet I had lan-
    guished.
I do not like being moved: for the will is excited; and action
Is a most dangerous thing; I tremble for something factitious,
Some malpractice of heart and illegitimate process;
We are so prone to these things with our terrible notions of
    duty.

Canto III, 2

Tell me, my friend, do you think that the grain would sprout
    in the furrow,
Did it not truly accept as its *summum* and *ultimum bonum*
That mere and maybe indifferent soil it is set in?
Would it have force to develop and open its young coty-
    ledons,
Could it compare, and reflect, and examine one thing with
    another?

Would it endure to accomplish the round of its natural func-
    tions,
Were it endowed with a sense of the general scheme of exis-
    tence? ...

Canto V, 5

... There was a time, methought it was but lately departed,
When, if a thing was denied me, I felt I was bound to
    attempt it;
Choice alone should take, and choice alone should surrender.
There was a time, indeed, when I had not retired thus early,
Languidly thus, from pursuit of a purpose I once had
    adopted.
But it is over, all that! I have slunk from the perilous field in
Whose wild struggle of forces the prizes of life are contested.
It is over, all that! I am a coward, and know it.
Courage in me could be only factitious, unnatural, useless ...

Matthew Arnold (1822–1888)

DOVER BEACH

The sea is calm to-night.
The tide is full, the moon lies fair
Upon the straits;—on the French coast, the light
Gleams, and is gone; the cliffs of England stand,
Glimmering and vast, out in the tranquil bay.
Come to the window, sweet is the night-air!
Only, from the long line of spray
Where the sea meets the moon-blanch'd sand,
Listen! you hear the grating roar
Of pebbles which the waves draw back, and fling,
At their return, up the high strand,
Begin, and cease, and then again begin,

With tremulous cadence slow, and bring
The eternal note of sadness in.

Sophocles long ago
Heard it on the Ægean, and it brought
Into his mind the turbid ebb and flow
Of human misery; we
Find also in the sound a thought,
Hearing it by this distant northern sea.

The Sea of Faith
Was once, too, at the full, and round earth's shore
Lay like the folds of a bright girdle furl'd.
But now I only hear
Its melancholy, long, withdrawing roar,
Retreating, to the breath
Of the night-wind down the vast edges drear
And naked shingles of the world.

Ah, love, let us be true
To one another! for the world, which seems
To lie before us like a land of dreams,
So various, so beautiful, so new,
Hath really neither joy, nor love, nor light,
Nor certitude, nor peace, nor help for pain;
And we are here as on a darkling plain
Swept with confused alarms of struggle and flight,
Where ignorant armies clash by night.

Dante Gabriel Rossetti (1828–1882)

From THE HOUSE OF LIFE

Silent Noon

Your hands lie open in the long fresh grass,—
    Your finger-points look through like rosy blooms:

Your eyes smile peace. The pasture gleams and glooms
'Neath billowing skies that scatter and amass.
All round our nest, far as the eye can pass,
    Are golden kingcup-fields with silver edge
    Where the cow-parsley skirts the hawthorn-hedge.
'Tis visibile silence, still as the hour-glass.

Deep in the sun-searched growths the dragon-fly
Hangs like a blue thread loosened from the sky:—
    So this wing'd hour is dropt to us from above.
Oh! clasp we to our hearts, for deathless dower,
This close-companioned inarticulate hour
    When two-fold silence was the song of love.

George Meredith (1828–1909)

From MODERN LOVE

43

Mark where the pressing wind shoots javelin-like
Its skeleton shadow on the broad-backed wave!
Here is a fitting shot to dig love's grave;
Here where the ponderous breakers plunge and strike,
And dart their hissing tongues high up the sand:
In hearing of the ocean, and in sight
Of those ribbed wind-streaks running into white.
If I the death of Love had deeply planned,
I never could have made it half so sure,
As by the unblest kisses which upbraid
The full-waked sense; or, failing that, degrade!
'Tis morning: but no morning can restore
What we have forfeited. I see no sin:
The wrong is mixed. In tragic life, God wot,
No villain need be! Passions spin the plot:
We are betrayed by what is false within.

LUCIFER IN STARLIGHT

On a starred night Prince Lucifer uprose.
Tired of his dark dominion swung the fiend
Above the rolling ball, in cloud part screened,
Where sinners hugged their spectre of repose.
Poor prey to his hot fit of pride were those.
And now upon his western wing he leaned,
Now his huge bulk o'er Afric's sands careened,
Now the black planet shadowed Arctic snows.
Soaring through wider zones that pricked his scars
With memory of the old revolt from Awe,
He reached a middle height, and at the stars,
Which are the brain of heaven, he looked, and sank.
Around the ancient track marched, rank on rank,
The army of unalterable law.

Christina Rossetti (1830–1894)

IN AN ARTIST'S STUDIO

One face looks out from all his canvases,
    One selfsame figure sits or walks or leans:
    We found her hidden just behind those screens,
That mirror gave back all her loveliness.
A queen in opal or in ruby dress,
    A nameless girl in freshest summer-greens,
    A saint, an angel—every canvas means
The same one meaning, neither more nor less.
He feeds upon her face by day and night,
    And she with true kind eyes looks back on him,
Fair as the moon and joyful as the light:
    Not wan with waiting, not with sorrow dim;
Not as she is, but was when hope shone bright;
    Not as she is, but as she fills his dream.

Lewis Carroll (1832–1898)

JABBERWOCKY

'Twas brillig, and the slithy toves
   Did gyre and gimble in the wabe;
All mimsy were the borogoves,
   And the mome raths outgrabe.

"Beware the Jabberwock, my son!
   The jaws that bite, the claws that catch!
Beware the Jubjub bird, and shun
   The frumious Bandersnatch!"

He took his vorpal sword in hand:
   Long time the manxome foe he sought—
So rested he by the Tumtum tree,
   And stood awhile in thought.

And as in uffish thought he stood,
   The Jabberwock with eyes of flame,
Came whiffling through the tulgey wood,
   And burbled as it came!

One, two! One, two! And through and through
   The vorpal blade went snicker-snack!
He left it dead, and with its head
   He went galumphing back.

"And hast thou slain the Jabberwock?
   Come to my arms, my beamish boy!
O frabjous day, Callooh! Callay!"
   He chortled in his joy.

'Twas brillig, and the slithy toves
   Did gyre and gimble in the wabe;

All mimsy were the borogoves,
    And the mome raths outgrabe.

THE WHITE KNIGHT'S SONG

I'll tell thee everything I can:
    There's little to relate.
I saw an agèd agèd man
    A-sitting on a gate.
"Who are you, agèd man?" I said.
    "And how is it you live?"
And his answer trickled through my head
    Like water through a sieve.

He said "I look for butterflies
    That sleep among the wheat.
I make them into mutton-pies
    And sell them in the street.
I sell them unto men," he said,
    "Who sail on stormy seas;
And that's the way I get my bread—
    A trifle, if you please."

But I was thinking of a plan
    To die one's whiskers green,
And always use so large a fan
    That they could not be seen.
So, having no reply to give
    To what the old man said,
I cried "Come tell me how you live!"
    And thumped him on the head.

His accents mild took up the tale:
    He said "I go my ways,
And when I find a mountain rill,
    I set it in a blaze;
And thence they make a stuff they call
    Rowland's Macassar Oil—
Yet twopence-halfpenny is all
    They give me for my toil."

But I was thinking of a way
    To feed oneself on batter,

And so go on from day to day
    Getting a little fatter.
I shook him well from side to side,
    Until his face was blue:
"Come, tell me how you live," I cried,
    "And what it is you do!"

He said "I hunt for haddocks' eyes
    Among the heather bright,
And work them into waistcoat buttons
    In the silent night.
And these I do not sell for gold
    Or coin of silvery shine,
But for a copper halfpenny,
    And that will purchase nine.

I sometimes dig for buttered rolls,
    Or set limed twigs for crabs:
I sometimes search the grassy knolls
    For wheels of Hansom-cabs.
And that's the way" (he gave a wink)
    "By which I get my wealth—
And very gladly will I drink
    Your Honor's noble health."

I heard him then, for I had just
    Completed my design
To keep the Menai bridge from rust
    By boiling it in wine.
I thanked him much for telling me
    The way he got his wealth,
But chiefly for his wish that he
    Might drink my noble health.

And now, if e'er by chance I put
    My fingers into glue,
Or madly freeze a right-hand foot
    Into a left-hand shoe,
Or if I drop upon my toe
    A very heavy weight,
I weep for it reminds me so
    Of that old man I used to know—
Whose look was mild, whose speech was slow,
Whose hair was whiter than the snow,
Whose face was very like a crow,
With eyes, like cinders, all aglow,

Who seemed distracted with his woe,
Who rocked his body to and fro,
And muttered mumblingly and low,
As if his mouth were full of dough,
Who snorted like a buffalo—
That summer evening long ago,
    A-sitting on a gate.

William Morris (1834–1896)

THE HAYSTACK IN THE FLOODS

Had she come all the way for this,
To part at last without a kiss?
Yea, had she borne the dirt and rain
That her own eyes might see him slain
Beside the haystack in the floods?

Along the dripping leafless woods,
The stirrup touching either shoe,
She rode astride as troopers do;
With kirtle kilted to her knee,
To which the mud splash'd wretchedly;
And the wet dripp'd from every tree
Upon her head and heavy hair,
And on her eyelids broad and fair;
The tears and rain ran down her face.

By fits and starts they rode apace,
And very often was his place
Far off from her; he had to ride
Ahead, to see what might betide
When the roads cross'd; and sometimes, when
There rose a murmuring from his men,
Had to turn back with promises;
Ah me! she had but little ease;
And often for pure doubt and dread

She sobb'd, made giddy in the head
By the swift riding; while, for cold,
Her slender fingers scarce could hold
The wet reins; yea, and scarcely, too,
She felt the foot within her shoe
Against the stirrup: all for this,
To part at last without a kiss
Beside the haystack in the floods.

For when they near'd that old soak'd hay,
They saw across the only way
That Judas, Godmar, and the three
Red running lions dismally
Grinn'd from his pennon, under which,
In one straight line along the ditch,
They counted thirty heads.

                So then,
While Robert turn'd round to his men,
She saw at once the wretched end,
And, stooping down, tried hard to rend
Her coif the wrong way from her head,
And hid her eyes; while Robert said:
"Nay, love, 'tis scarcely two to one,
At Poictiers where we made them run
So fast—why, sweet my love, good cheer,
The Gascon frontier is so near,
Nought after this."

              But, "O," she said,
"My God! my God! I have to tread
The long way back without you; then
The court at Paris; those six men;
The gratings of the Chatelet;
The swift Seine on some rainy day
Like this, and people standing by,
And laughing, while my weak hands try
To recollect how strong men swim.
All this, or else a life with him,
For which I should be damned at last;
Would God that this next hour were past!"

He answer'd not, but cried his cry,
"St. George for Marny!" cheerily;
And laid his hand upon her rein.
Alas! no man of all his train
Gave back that cheery cry again;
And, while for rage his thumb beat fast

Upon his sword-hilt, someone cast
About his neck a kerchief long,
And bound him.

           Then they went along
To Godmar; who said: "Now, Jehane,
Your lover's life is on the wane
So fast, that, if this very hour
You yield not as my paramour,
He will not see the rain leave off—
Nay, keep your tongue from gibe and scoff,
Sir Robert, or I slay you now."

She laid her hand upon her brow,
Then gazed upon the palm, as though
She thought her forehead bled, and—"No!"
She said, and turn'd her head away,
As there were nothing else to say,
And everything were settled: red
Grew Godmar's face from chin to head:
"Jehane, on yonder hill there stands
My castle, guarding well my lands:
What hinders me from taking you,
And doing that I list to do
To your fair wilful body, while
Your knight lies dead?"

           A wicked smile
Wrinkled her face, her lips grew thin,
A long way out she thrust her chin:
"You know that I should strangle you
While you were sleeping; or bite through
Your throat, by God's help-ah!" she said,
"Lord Jesus, pity your poor maid!
For in such wise they hem me in,
I cannot choose but sin and sin,
Whatever happens: yet I think
They could not make me eat or drink,
And so should I just reach my rest."

"Nay, if you do not my behest,
O Jehane! though I love you well,"
Said Godmar, "would I fail to tell
All that I know?" "Foul lies," she said.
"Eh? lies my Jehane? by God's head,
At Paris folks would deem them true!
Do you know, Jehane, they cry for you:
'Jehane the brown! Jehane the brown!

Give us Jehane to burn or drown!'—
Eh—gag me Robert—sweet my friend,
This were indeed a piteous end
For those long fingers, and long feet
And long neck, and smooth shoulders sweet:
An end that few men would forget
That saw it—So, an hour yet—
Consider, Jehane, which to take
Of life or death!"

                    So, scarce awake,
Dismounting, did she leave that place,
And totter some yards: with her face
Turn'd upward to the sky she lay,
Her head on a wet heap of hay,
And fell asleep: and while she slept
And did not dream, the minutes crept
Round to the twelve again; but she,
Being waked at last, sigh'd quietly,
And strangely childlike came, and said:
"I will not." Straightway Godmar's head,
As though it hung on strong wires, turn'd
Most sharply round, and his face burn'd.

For Robert—both his eyes were dry,
He could not weep, but gloomily
He seem'd to watch the rain; yea, too,
His lips were firm; he tried once more
To touch her lips; she reach'd out, sore
And vain desire so tortured them,
The poor grey lips, and now the hem
Of his sleeve brush'd them.

                    With a start
Up Godmar rose, thrust them apart;
From Robert's throat he loosed the bands
Of silk and mail; with empty hands
Held out, she stood and gazed, and saw,
The long bright blade without a flaw
Glide out from Godmar's sheath, his hand
In Robert's hair; she saw him bend
Back Robert's head; she saw him send
The thin steel down; the blow told well,
Right backward the knight Robert fell,
And moan'd as dogs do, being half dead,
Unwitting, as I deem; so then
Godmar turn'd grinning to his men,

Who ran, some five or six, and beat
His head to pieces at their feet.

Then Godmar turn'd again and said:
"So, Jehane, the first fitte is read!
Take note, my lady, that your way
Lies backward to the Chatelet!"
She shook her head and gazed awhile
At her cold hands with a rueful smile,
As though this thing had made her mad.

This was the parting that they had
Beside the haystack in the floods.

Algernon Charles Swinburne (1837–1909)

BEFORE PARTING

A month or twain to live on honeycomb
Is pleasant; but one tires of scented time,
Cold sweet recurrence of accepted rhyme,
And that strong purple under juice and foam
Where the wine's heart has burst;
Nor feel the latter kisses like the first.

Once yet, this poor one time; I will not pray
Even to change the bitterness of it,
The bitter taste ensuing on the sweet,
To make your tears fall where your soft hair lay
All blurred and heavy in some perfumed wise
Over my face and eyes.

And yet who knows what end the scythed wheat
Makes of its foolish poppies' mouths of red?
These were not sown, these are not harvested,
They grow a month and are cast under feet

And none has cared thereof,
As none has care of a divided love.

I know each shadow of your lips by rote,
Each change of love in eyelids and eyebrows;
The fashion of fair temples tremulous
With tender blood, and colour of your throat;
I know not how love is gone out of this,
Seeing that all was his.

Love's likeness there endures upon all these:
But out of these one shall not gather love.
Day hath not strength nor the night shade enough
To make love whole and fill his lips with ease,
As some bee-builded cell
Feels at filled lips the heavy honey swell.

I know not how this last month leaves your hair
Less full of purple colour and hid spice,
And that luxurious trouble of closed eyes
Is mixed with meaner shadow and waste care;
And love, kissed out by pleasure, seems not yet
Worth patience to regret.

Thomas Hardy (1840–1928)

THE LEVELLED CHURCHYARD

"O Passenger, pray list and catch
    Our sighs and piteous groans,
Half stifled in this jumbled patch
    Of wrenched memorial stones!

"We late-lamented, resting here,
    Are mixed to human jam,
And each to each exclaims in fear,
    'I know not which I am!'

"The wicked people have annexed
        The verses on the good;
A roaring drunkard sports the text
        Teetotal Tommy should!

"Where we are huddled none can trace,
        And if our names remain,
They pave some path or porch or place
        Where we have never lain!

"Here's not a modest maiden elf
        But dreads the final Trumpet,
Lest half of her should rise herself,
        And half some sturdy strumpet!

"From restorations of Thy fane,
        From smoothings of Thy sward,
From zealous Churchmen's pick and plane
        Deliver us O Lord! Amen!"

THE RUINED MAID

"O 'Melia, my dear, this does everything crown!
Who could have supposed I should meet you in Town?
And whence such fair garments, such prosperi-ty?"—
"O didn't you know I'd been ruined?" said she.

—"You left us in tatters, without shoes or socks,
Tired of digging potatoes, and spudding up docks;
And now you've gay bracelets and bright feathers three!"—
"Yes: that's how we dress when we're ruined," said she.

—"At home in the barton you said 'thee' and 'thou,'
And 'thik oon,' and 'theäs oon,' and 't'other'; but now
Your talking quite fits 'ee for high compa-ny!"—
"Some polish is gained with one's ruin," said she.

—"Your hands were like paws then, your face blue and bleak
But now I'm bewitched by your delicate cheek,
And your little gloves fit as on any la-dy!"—
"We never do work when we're ruined," said she.

—"You used to call home-life a hag-ridden dream,
And you'd sigh, and you'd sock; but at present you seem

To know not of megrims or melancho-ly!"—
"True. One's pretty lively when ruined," said she.

—"I wish I had feathers, a fine sweeping gown,
And a delicate face, and could strut about Town!"—
"My dear—a raw country girl, such as you be,
Cannot quite expect that. You ain't ruined," said she.

GOD'S EDUCATION

I saw him steal the light away
    That haunted in her eye;
It went so gently none could say
More than that it was there one day
    And missing by-and-by.

I watched her longer, and he stole
    Her lily tincts and rose;
All her young sprightliness of soul
Next fell beneath his cold control,
    And disappeared like those.

I asked: "Why do you serve her so?
    Do you, for some glad day,
Hoard these her sweets—?" He said, "O no,
They charm not me; I bid Time throw
    Them carelessly away."

Said I: "We call that cruelty—
    We, your poor mortal kind."
He mused. "The thought is new to me.
Forsooth, though I men's master be,
    Theirs is the teaching mind!"

THE NIGHT OF THE DANCE

The cold moon hangs to the sky by its horn,
    And centres its gaze on me;
The stars, like eyes in reverie,
Their westering as for a while forborne,
    Quiz downward curiously.

[245]

Old Robert draws the backbrand in,
    The green logs steam and spit;
The half-awakened sparrows flit
From the riddled thatch; and owls begin
    To whoo from the gable-slit.

Yes; far and nigh things seem to know
    Sweet scenes are impending here;
That all is prepared; that the hour is near
For welcomes, fellowships, and flow
    Of sally, song, and cheer;

That spigots are pulled and viols strung;
    That soon will arise the sound
Of measures trod to tunes renowned;
That she will return in Love's low tongue
    My vows as we wheel around.

CHANNEL FIRING

That night your great guns, unawares,
Shook all our coffins as we lay,
And broke the chancel window-squares,
We thought it was the Judgment-day

And sat upright. While drearisome
Arose the howl of wakened hounds:
The mouse let fall the altar-crumb,
The worms drew back into the mounds,

The glebe cow drooled. Till God called, "No;
It's gunnery practice out at sea
Just as before you went below;
The world is as it used to be:

"All nations striving strong to make
Red war yet redder. Mad as hatters
They do no more for Christès sake
Than you who are helpless in such matters.

"That this is not the judgment-hour
For some of them's a blessèd thing,
For if it were they'd have to scour
Hell's floor for so much threatening. . . .

"Ha, ha. It will be warmer when
I blow the trumpet (if indeed
I ever do; for you are men,
And rest eternal sorely need)."

So down we lay again. "I wonder,
Will the world ever saner be,"
Said one, "than when He sent us under
In our indifferent century!"

And many a skeleton shook his head.
"Instead of preaching forty year,"
My neighbour Parson Thirdly said,
"I wish I had stuck to pipes and beer."

Again the guns disturbed the hour,
Roaring their readiness to avenge,
As far inland as Stourton Tower,
And Camelot, and starlit Stonehenge.

April 1914

THE SCHRECKHORN

(With thoughts of Leslie Stephen)

Aloof, as if a thing of mood and whim;
Now that its spare and desolate figure gleams
Upon my nearing vision, less it seems
A looming Alp-height than a guise of him
Who scaled its horn with ventured life and limb,
Drawn on by vague imaginings, maybe,
Of semblance to his personality
In its quaint glooms, keen lights, and rugged trim.
At his last change, when Life's dull coils unwind,
Will he, in old love, hitherward escape,
And the eternal essence of his mind
Enter this silent adamantine shape,
And his low voicing haunt its slipping snows
When dawn that calls the climber dyes them rose?

COPYING ARCHITECTURE IN AN OLD MINSTER

(Wimborne)

How smartly the quarters of the hour march by
    That the jack-o'-clock never forgets;
Ding-dong; and before I have traced a cusp's eye
Or got the true twist of the ogee over,
    A double ding-dong ricochetts.

Just so did he clang here before I came,
    And so will he clang when I'm gone
Through the Minster's cavernous hollows—the same
Tale of hours never more to be will he deliver
    To the speechless midnight and dawn!

I grow to conceive it a call to ghosts,
    Whose mould lies below and around.
Yes; the next "Come, come," draws them out from their
    posts,
And they gather, and one shade appears, and another,
    As the eve-damps creep from the ground.

See—a Courtenay stands by his quatre-foiled tomb,
    And a Duke and a Duchess near;
And one Sir Edmund in columned gloom,
And a Saxon king by the presbytery chamber;
    And shapes unknown in the rear.

Maybe they have met for a parle on some plan
    To better all-stricken mankind;
I catch their cheepings, though thinner than
The overhead creak of a passager's pinion
    When leaving land behind.

Or perhaps they speak to the yet unborn,
    And caution them not to come
To a world so ancient and trouble-torn,
Of foiled intents, vain lovingkindness,
    And ardours chilled and numb.

They waste to fog as I stir and stand,
  And move from the arched recess,
And pick up the drawing that slipped from my hand,
And feel for the pencil I dropped in the cranny
  In a moment's forgetfulness.

MIDNIGHT ON THE GREAT WESTERN

In the third-class seat sat the journeying boy,
  And the roof-lamp's oily flame
Played down on his listless form and face,
Bewrapt past knowing to what he was going
  Or whence he came.

In the band of his hat the journeying boy
  Had a ticket stuck; and a string
Around his neck bore the key of his box
That twinkled gleams of the lamp's sad beams
  Like a living thing.

What past can be yours, O journeying boy,
  Towards a world unknown,
Who calmly, as if incurious quite
On all at stake, can undertake
  This plunge alone?

Knows your soul a sphere, O journeying boy,
  Our rude realms far above,
Whence with spacious vision you mark and mete
This region of sin that you find you in
  But are not of?

AFTERWARDS

When the Present has latched its postern behind my tremulous
    stay,
  And the May month flaps its glad green leaves like wings,
Delicate-filmed as new-spun silk, will the neighbours say,
  "He was a man who used to notice such things"?

If it be in the dusk when, like an eyelid's soundless blink,
  The dewfall-hawk comes crossing the shades to alight

Upon the wind-warped upland thorn, a gazer may think,
  "To him this must have been a familiar sight."

If I pass during some nocturnal blackness, mothy and warm,
  When the hedgehog travels furtively over the lawn,
One may say, "He strove that such innocent creatures should
    come to no harm,
  But he could do little for them; and now he is gone."

If, when hearing that I have been stilled at last, they stand at
    the door,
  Watching the full-starred heavens that winter sees,
Will this thought rise on those who will meet my face no
    more,
  "He was one who had an eye for such mysteries"?

And will any say when my bell of quittance is heard in the
    gloom,
  And a crossing breeze cuts a pause in its outrollings,
Till they rise again, as they were a new bell's boom,
  "He hears it not now, but used to notice such things?"

LAST LOOK ROUND ST. MARTIN'S FAIR

The sun is like an open furnace door,
Whose round revealed retort contains the roar
        Of fires beyond terrene;
The moon presents the lustre-lacking face
        Of a brass dial gone green,
        Whose hours no eye can trace.
The unsold heathcroppers are driven home
To the shades of the Great Forest whence they come
By men with long cord-waistcoats in brown monochrome.
        The stars break out, and flicker in the breeze,
            It seems, that twitches the trees.—
            From its hot idol soon
The fickle unresting earth has turned to a fresh patroon—
            The cold, now brigher, moon.
        The woman in red, at the nut-stall with the gun,
            Lights up, and still goes on:
        She's redder in the flare-lamp than the sun
            Showed it ere it was gone.
        Her hands are black with loading all the day,
        And yet she treats her labour as 'twere play,

Tosses her ear-rings, and talks ribaldry
To the young men around as natural gaiety,
        And not a weary work she'd readily stay
        And never again nut-shooting see,
            Though crying, "Fire away!"

Gerard Manley Hopkins (1844–1889)

GOD'S GRANDEUR

The world is charged with the grandeur of God.
    It will flame out, like shining from shook foil;
    It gathers to a greatness, like the ooze of oil
Crushed. Why do men then now not reck his rod?
Generations have trod, have trod, have trod;
    And all is seared with trade; bleared, smeared with toil;
    And wears man's smudge and shares man's smell: the soil
Is bare now, nor can foot feel, being shod.

And for all this, nature is never spent;
    There lives the dearest freshness deep down things;
And though the last lights off the black West went
    Oh, morning, at the brown brink eastward, springs—
Because the Holy Ghost over the bent
    World broods with warm breast and with ah! bright wings.

SPRING

Nothing is so beautiful as spring—
    When weeds, in wheels, shoot long and lovely and lush;
    Thrush's eggs look like low heavens, and thrush
Through the echoing timber does so rinse and wring
The ear, it strikes like lightnings to hear him sing;
    The glassy peartree leaves and blooms, they brush

The descending blue; that blue is all in a rush
With richness; the racing lambs too have fair their fling.

What is all this juice and all this joy?
   A strain of the earth's sweet being in the beginning
In Eden garden.—Have, get, before it cloy,
   Before it cloud, Christ, lord, and sour with sinning,
Innocent mind and Mayday in girl and boy,
   Most, O maid's child, thy choice and worthy the winning.

HURRAHING IN HARVEST

Summer ends now; now, barbarous in beauty, the stooks
      arise
   Around; up above, what wind-walks! what lovely behaviour
   Of silk-sack clouds! has wilder, wilful-wavier
Meal-drift moulded ever and melted across skies?
I walk, I lift up, I lift up heart, eyes,
   Down all that glory in the heavens to glean our Saviour;
   And, éyes, heárt, what looks, what lips yet gave you a
Rapturous love's greeting of realer, of rounder replies?

And the azurous hung hills are his world-wielding shoulder
   Majestic—as a stallion stalwart, very-violet-sweet!—
These things, these things were here and but the beholder
   Wanting; which two when they once meet,
The heart réars wíngs bold and bolder
   And hurls for him, O half hurls earth for him off under his
      feet.

DUNS SCOTUS'S OXFORD

Towery city and branchy between towers;
Cuckoo-echoing, bell-swarmèd, lark-charmèd, rook-racked,
      river-rounded;
The dapple-eared lily below thee; that country and town did
Once encounter in, here coped and poisèd powers;

Thou hast a base and brickish skirt there, sours
That neighbour-nature thy grey beauty is grounded
Best in; graceless growth, thou hast confounded
Rural rural keeping—folk, flocks, and flowers.

Yet ah! this air I gather and I release
He lived on; these weeds and waters, these walls are what
He haunted who of all men most sways my spirits to peace;

Of realty the rarest-veinèd unraveller; a not
Rivalled insight, be rival Italy or Greece;
Who fired France for Mary without spot.

FELIX RANDAL

Felix Randal the farrier, O he is dead then? my duty all
    ended,
Who have watched his mould of man, big-boned and hardy-
    handsome
Pining, pining, till time when reason rambled in it and some
Fatal four disorders, fleshed there, all contended?
Sickness broke him. Impatient he cursed at first, but mended
Being anointed and all; though a heavenlier heart began some
Months earlier, since I had our sweet reprieve and ransom
Tendered to him. Ah well, God rest him all road ever he
    offended!

This seeing the sick endears them to us, us too it endears.
My tongue had taught thee comfort, touch had quenched thy
    tears,
Thy tears that touched my heart, child, Felix, poor Felix
    Randal;
How far from then forethought of, all thy more boisterous
    years,
When thou at the random grim forge, powerful amidst peers,
Didst fettle for the great grey drayhorse his bright and
    battering sandal!

FRAGMENT

Strike, churl; hurl, cheerless wind, then; heltering hail
May's beauty massacre and wispèd wild clouds grow
Out on the giant air; tell Summer No,
Bid joy back, have at the harvest, keep Hope pale.

SONNET

No worst, there is none. Pitched past pitch of grief,
More pangs will, schooled at forepangs, wilder wring.
Comforter, where, where is your comforting?
Mary, mother of us all, where is your relief?
My cries heave, herds-long; huddle in a main, a chief
Woe, world-sorrow; on an age-old anvil wince and sing—
Then lull, then leave off. Fury had shrieked 'No lingering! Let me be fell: force I must be brief.'

O the mind, mind has mountains; cliffs of fall
Frightful, sheer, no-man-fathomed. Hold them cheap
May who ne'er hung there. Nor does long our small
Durance deal with that steep or deep. Here! creep,
Wretch, under a comfort serves in a whirlwind: all
Life death does end and each day dies with sleep.

Robert Bridges (1844–1930)

THE PHILOSOPHER TO HIS MISTRESS

Because thou canst not see,
Because thou canst not know
The black and hopeless woe
That hath encompassed me:
Because, should I confess
The thought of my despair,
My words would wound thee less
Than swords can hurt the air:

Because with thee I seem
As one invited near
To taste the fairy cheer

Of spirits in a dream;
Of whom he knoweth nought
Save that they vie to make
All motion, voice and thought
A pleasure for his sake:

Therefore more sweet and strange
Has been the mystery
Of thy long love to me,
That doth not quit nor change,
Nor tax my solemn heart,
That kisseth in a gloom,
Knowing not who thou art
That givest, nor to whom.

Therefore the tender touch
Is more; more dear the smile:
And thy light words beguile
My wisdom overmuch:
And O with swiftness fly
The fancies of my song
To happy worlds, where I
Still in thy love belong.

JOHANNES MILTON, SENEX

Scazons

Since I believe in God the Father Almighty,
Man's Maker and Judge, Overruler of Fortune,
'Twere strange should I praise anything and refuse Him
    praise,
Should love the creature forgetting the Crēator,
Nor unto Him in suff'ring and sorrow turn me:
Nay how could I withdraw from His embracing?

But since that I have seen not, and cannot know Him,
Nor in my earthly temple apprehend rightly
His wisdom and the heav'nly purpose ēternal;
Therefore will I be bound to no studied system
Nor argument, nor with delusion enslave me,
Nor seek to pleáse Him in any foolish invention,
Which my spirit within me, that loveth beauty
And hateth evil, hath reprov'd as unworthy:

[255]

But I cherish my freedom in loving service,
Gratefully adoring for delight beyond asking
Or thinking, and in hours of anguish and darkness
Confiding always on His excellent greatness.

John Davidson (1857–1909)

THIRTY BOB A WEEK

I couldn't touch a stop and turn a screw,
  And set the blooming world a-work for me,
Like such as cut their teeth—I hope, like you—
  On the handle of a skeleton gold key;
I cut mine on a leek, which I eat it every week:
  I'm a clerk at thirty bob as you can see.

But I don't allow it's luck and all a toss;
  There's no such thing as being starred and crossed;
It's just the power of some to be a boss,
  And the bally power of others to be bossed:
I face the music, sir; you bet I ain't a cur;
  Strike me lucky if I don't believe I'm lost!

For like a mole I journey in the dark,
  A-travelling along the underground
From my Pillared Halls and broad Suburban Park,
  To come the daily dull official round;
And home again at night with my pipe all alight,
  A-scheming how to count ten bob a pound.

And it's often very cold and very wet,
  And my missis stitches towels for a hunks;
And the Pillared Halls is half of it to let—
  Three rooms about the size of travelling trunks.
And we cough, my wife and I, to dislocate a sigh,
  When the noisy little kids are in their bunks.

But you never hear her do a growl or whine,
    For she's made of flint and roses, very odd;
And I've got to cut my meaning rather fine,
    Or I'd blubber, for I'm made of greens and sod:
So p'r'aps we are in Hell for all that I can tell.
    And lost and damned and served up hot to God.

I ain't blaspheming, Mr. Silver-tongue;
    I'm saying things a bit beyond your art:
Of all the rummy starts you ever sprung,
    Thirty bob a week's the rummiest start!
With your science and your books and your the'ries about
        spooks,
    Did you ever hear of looking in your heart?

I didn't mean your pocket, Mr., no:
    I mean that having children and a wife,
With thirty bob on which to come and go,
    Isn't dancing to the tabor and the fife:
When it doesn't make you drink, by Heaven! it makes you
        Think,
    And notice curious items about life.

I step into my heart and there I meet
    A god-almighty devil singing small
Who would like to shout and whistle in the street,
    And squelch the passers flat against the wall;
If the whole world was a cake he had the power to take,
    He would take it, ask for more, and eat it all.

And I meet a sort of simpleton beside,
    The kind that life is always giving beans;
With thirty bob a week to keep a bride
    He fell in love and married in his teens:
At thirty bob he stuck; but he knows it isn't luck:
    He knows the seas are deeper than tureens.

And the god-almighty devil and the fool
    That meet me in the High Street on the strike,
When I walk about my heart a-gathering wool,
    Are my good and evil angels if you like.
And both of them together in every kind of weather
    Ride me like a double-seated bike.

That's rough a bit and needs its meaning curled.
    But I have a high old hot un in my mind—

A most engrugious notion of the world,
  That leaves your lightning 'rithmetic behind:
I give it at a glance when I say, 'There ain't no chance,
  Nor nothing of the lucky-lottery kind.'

And it's this way I make it out to be:
  No fathers, mothers, countries, climates—none;
Not Adam was responsible for me.
  Nor society, nor systems, nary one:
A little sleeping seed, I woke—I did, indeed—
  A million years before the blooming sun.

I woke because I thought the time had come;
  Beyond my will there was no other cause;
And every where I found myself at home,
  Because I chose to be the thing I was;
And in whatever shape of mollusc or of ape
  I always went according to the laws.

I was the love that chose my mother out;
  I joined two lives and from the union burst;
My weakness and my strength without a doubt
  Are mine alone for ever from the first:
It's just the very same with a difference in the name
  As 'Thy will be done.' You say it if you durst!

They say it daily up and down the land
  As easy as you take a drink, it's true;
But the difficultest go to understand,
  And the difficultest job a man can do,
Is to come it brave and meek with thirty bob a week,
  And feel that that's the proper thing for you.

It's a naked child against a hungry wolf;
  It's playing bowls upon a splitting wreck;
It's walking on a string across a gulf
  With millstones fore-and-aft about your neck;
But the thing is daily done by many and many a one;
  And we fall, face forward, fighting, on the deck.

A. E. Housman (1859–1936)

"THE LAWS OF GOD, THE LAWS OF MAN"

The laws of God, the laws of man,
He may keep that will and can;
Not I: let God and man decree
Laws for themselves and not for me;
And if my ways are not as theirs
Let them mind their own affairs.
Their deeds I judge and much condemn,
Yet when did I make laws for them?
Please yourselves, say I, and they
Need only look the other way.
But no, they will not; they must still
Wrest their neighbour to their will,
And make me dance as they desire
With jail and gallows and hell-fire.
And how am I to face the odds
Of man's bedevilment and God's?
I, a stranger and afraid
In a world I never made.
They will be master, right or wrong;
Though both are foolish, both are strong.
And since, my soul, we cannot fly
To Saturn nor to Mercury,
Keep we must, if keep we can,
These foreign laws of God and man.

"OTHERS, I AM NOT THE FIRST"

Others, I am not the first,
Have willed more mischief than they durst:

If in the breathless night I too
Shiver now, 'tis nothing new.

More than I, if truth were told,
Have stood and sweated hot and cold,
And through their reins in ice and fire
Fear contended with desire.

Agued once like me were they,
But I like them shall win my way
Lastly to the bed of mould
Where there's neither heat nor cold.

But from my grave across my brow
Plays no wind of healing now,
And fire and ice within me fight
Beneath the suffocating night.

EPITAPH ON AN ARMY OF MERCENARIES

These, in the day when heaven was falling,
   The hour when earth's foundations fled,
Followed their mercenary calling
   And took their wages and are dead.

Their shoulders held the sky suspended;
   They stood, and earth's foundations stay;
What God abandoned, these defended,
   And saved the sum of things for pay.

Rudyard Kipling (1865–1936)

SONG OF THE GALLEY-SLAVES

We pulled for you when the wind was against us and the sails were low.
  Will you never let us go?
We ate bread and onions when you took towns, or ran aboard quickly when you were beaten back by the foe.
The Captains walked up and down the deck in fair weather singing songs, but we were below.
We fainted with our chins on the oars and you did not see that we were idle, for we still swung to and fro.
  Will you never let us go?
The salt made the oar-handles like shark-skin; our knees were cut to the bone with salt-cracks; our hair was stuck to our foreheads; and our lips were cut to the gums, and you whipped us because we could not row.
  Will you never let us go?
But, in a little time, we shall run out of the port-holes as the water runs along the oar-blades, and though you tell the others to row after us you will never catch us till you catch the oar-thresh and tie up the winds in the belly of the sail. Aho!
  Will you never let us go?

THE SEA AND THE HILLS

Who hath desired the Sea?—the sight of salt water unbounded—
The heave and the halt and the hurl and the crash of the comber wind-hounded?
The sleek-barrelled swell before storm, grey, foamless, enormous, and growing—

Stark calm on the lap of the Line or the crazy-eyed hurricane
  blowing—
His Sea in no showing the same—his Sea and the same 'neath
  each showing:
> His Sea as she slackens or thrills?
So and no otherwise—so and no otherwise—hillmen desire
  their Hills!

Who hath desired the Sea?—the immense and contemptuous
  surges?
The shudder, the stumble, the swerve, as the star-stabbing
  bowsprit emerges?
The orderly clouds of the Trades, the ridged, roaring sap-
  phire thereunder—
Unheralded cliff-haunting flaws and the headsail's low-volley-
  ing thunder—
His Sea in no wonder the same—his Sea and the same
  through each wonder:
> His Sea as she rages or stills?
So and no otherwise—so and no otherwise—hillmen desire
  their Hills.

Who hath desired the Sea? Her menaces swift as her mercies?
The in-rolling walls of the fog and the silver-winged breeze
  that disperses?
The unstable mined berg going South and the calvings and
  groans that declare it—
White water half-guessed overside and the moon breaking
  timely to bare it—
His Sea as his fathers have dared—his Sea as his children
  shall dare it:
> His Sea as she serves him or kills?
So and no otherwise—so and no otherwise—hillmen desire
  their hills.

Who hath desired the Sea? Her excellent loneliness rather
Than forecourts of kings, and her outermost pits than the
  streets where men gather
Inland, among dust, under trees—inland where the slayer
  may slay him—
Inland, out of reach of her arms, and the bosom whereon he
  must lay him—
His Sea from the first that betrayed—at the last that shall
  never betray him:
> His Sea that his being fulfils?

So and no otherwise—so and no otherwise—hillmen desire
 their Hills.

THE GODS OF THE COPYBOOK HEADINGS
(1919)

As I pass through my incarnations in every age and race,
I make my proper prostrations to the Gods of the Market-
 Place.
Peering through reverent fingers I watch them flourish and
 fall,
And the Gods of the Copybook Headings, I notice, outlast
 them all.

We were living in trees when they met us. They showed us
 each in turn
That Water would certainly wet us, as Fire would certainly
 burn:
But we found them lacking in Uplift, Vision and Breadth of
 Mind,
So we left them to teach the Gorillas while we followed the
 March of Mankind.

We moved as the spirit listed. *They* never altered their pace
Being neither cloud nor wind-borne like the Gods of the
 Market-Place;
But they always caught up with our progress, and presently
 word would come
That a tribe had been wiped off its icefield, or the lights had
 gone out in Rome.

With the Hopes that our World is built on they were utterly
 out of touch.
They denied that the Moon was Stilton; they denied she was
 even Dutch.
They denied that Wishes were Horses; they denied that a Pig
 had Wings.
So we worshipped the Gods of the Market Who promised
 these beautiful things.

When the Cambrian measures were forming, They promised
 perpetual peace.
They swore, if we gave them our weapons, that the wars of
 the tribes would cease.

[263]

But when we disarmed They told us and delivered us bound
to our foe,
And the Gods of the Copybook Headings said: *"Stick to the
Devil you know."*

On the first Feminian Sandstones we were promised the Fuller
Life
(Which started by loving our neighbour and ended by loving
his wife)
Till our women had no more children and the men lost rea-
son and faith,
And the Gods of the Copybook Headings said: *"The Wages
of Sin is Death."*

In the Carboniferous Epoch we were promised abundance
for all,
By robbing selected Peter to pay for collective Paul;
But, though we had plenty of money, there was nothing our
money could buy,
And the Gods of the Copybook Headings said: *"If you don't
work you die."*

Then the Gods of the Market tumbled, and their smooth-
tongued wizards withdrew,
And the hearts of the meanest were humbled and began to
believe it was true
That All is not Gold that Glitters, and Two and Two make
Four—
And the Gods of the Copybook Headings limped up to ex-
plain it once more.

As it will be in the future, it was at the birth of Man—
There are only four things certain since Social Progress be-
gan:—
That the Dog returns to his Vomit and the Sow returns to
her Mire,
And the burnt Fool's bandaged finger goes wabbling back to
the Fire;
And that after this is accomplished, and the brave new world
begins
When all men are paid for existing and no man must pay for
his sins,
As surely as Water will wet us, and surely as Fire will burn,
The Gods of the Copybook Headings with terror and slaugh-
ter return!

W. B. Yeats (1865–1939)

THE SORROW OF LOVE

The brawling of a sparrow in the eaves,
The brilliant moon and all the milky sky,
And all that famous harmony of leaves,
Had blotted out man's image and his cry.

A girl arose that had red mournful lips
And seemed the greatness of the world in tears,
Doomed like Odysseus and the labouring ships
And proud as Priam murdered with his peers;

Arose, and on the instant clamorous eaves,
A climbing moon upon an empty sky,
And all that lamentation of the leaves,
Could but compose man's image and his cry.

THE DEDICATION TO A BOOK OF STORIES SELECTED FROM THE IRISH NOVELISTS

There was a green branch hung with many a bell
When her own people ruled this tragic Eire;
And from its murmuring greenness, calm of Faery,
A Druid kindness, on all hearers fell.

It charmed away the merchant from his guile,
And turned the farmer's memory from his cattle,
And hushed in sleep the roaring ranks of battle:
And all grew friendly for a little while.

Ah, Exiles wandering over lands and seas,
And planning, plotting always that some morrow

May set a stone upon ancestral Sorrow!
I also bear a bell-branch full of ease.

I tore it from green boughs winds tore and tossed
Until the sap of summer had grown weary!
I tore it from the barren boughs of Eire,
That country where a man can be so crossed;

Can be so battered, badgered and destroyed
That he's a loveless man: gay bells bring laughter
That shakes a mouldering cobweb from the rafter;
And yet the saddest chimes are best enjoyed.

Gay bells or sad, they bring you memories
Of half-forgotten innocent old places:
We and our bitterness have left no traces
On Munster grass and Connemara skies.

THE SONG OF WANDERING AENGUS

I went out to the hazel wood,
Because a fire was in my head,
And cut and peeled a hazel wand,
And hooked a berry to a thread;
And when white moths were on the wing,
And moth-like stars were flickering out,
I dropped the berry in a stream
And caught a little silver trout.

When I had laid it on the floor
I went to blow the fire a-flame,
But something rustled on the floor,
And some one called me by my name:
It had become a glimmering girl
With apple blossom in her hair
Who called me by my name and ran
And faded through the brightening air.

Though I am old with wandering
Through hollow lands and hilly lands,
I will find out where she has gone,
And kiss her lips and take her hands;
And walk among long dappled grass,
And pluck till time and times are done

The silver apples of the moon,
The golden apples of the sun.

EASTER 1916

I have met them at close of day
Coming with vivid faces
From counter or desk among grey
Eighteenth-century houses.
I have passed with a nod of the head
Or polite meaningless words,
Or have lingered awhile and said
Polite meaningless words,
And thought before I had done
Of a mocking tale or a gibe
To please a companion
Around the fire at the club,
Being certain that they and I
But lived where motley is worn:
All changed, changed utterly:
A terrible beauty is born.

That woman's days were spent
In ignorant good-will,
Her nights in argument
Until her voice grew shrill.
What voice more sweet than hers
When, young and beautiful,
She rode to harriers?
This man had kept a school
And rode our wingèd horse;
This other his helper and friend
Was coming into his force;
He might have won fame in the end,
So sensitive his nature seemed,
So daring and sweet his thought.
This other man I had dreamed
A drunken, vainglorious lout.
He had done most bitter wrong
To some who are near my heart,
Yet I number him in the song;
He, too, has resigned his part
In the casual comedy;
He, too, has been changed in his turn,

Transformed utterly:
A terrible beauty is born.

Hearts with one purpose alone
Through summer and winter seem
Enchanted to a stone
To trouble the living stream.
The horse that comes from the road,
The rider, the birds that range
From cloud to tumbling cloud,
Minute by minute they change;
A shadow of cloud on the stream
Changes minute by minute;
A horse-hoof slides on the brim,
And a horse plashes within it;
The long-legged moor-hens dive,
And hens to moor-cocks call;
Minute by minute they live:
The stone's in the midst of all.

Too long a sacrifice
Can make a stone of the heart.
O when may it suffice?
That is Heaven's part, our part
To murmur name upon name,
As a mother names her child
When sleep at last has come
On limbs that had run wild.
What is it but nightfall?
No, no, not night but death;
Was it needless death after all?
For England may keep faith
For all that is done and said.
We know their dream; enough
To know they dreamed and are dead;
And what if excess of love
Bewildered them till they died?
I write it out in a verse—
MacDonagh and MacBride
And Connolly and Pearse
New and in time to be,
Wherever green is worn,
Are changed, changed utterly:
A terrible beauty is born.

September 25, 1916

[268]

THE SECOND COMING

Turning and turning in the widening gyre
The falcon cannot hear the falconer;
Things fall apart; the centre cannot hold;
Mere anarchy is loosed upon the world,
The blood-dimmed tide is loosed, and everywhere
The ceremony of innocence is drowned;
The best lack all conviction, while the worst
Are full of passionate intensity.

Surely some revelation is at hand;
Surely the Second Coming is at hand.
The Second Coming! Hardly are those words out
When a vast image out of *Spiritus Mundi*
Troubles my sight: somewhere in sands of the desert
A shape with lion body and the head of a man,
A gaze blank and pitiless as the sun,
Is moving its slow thighs, while all about it
Reel shadows of the indignant desert birds.
The darkness drops again; but now I know
That twenty centuries of stony sleep
Were vexed to nightmare by a rocking cradle,
And what rough beast, its hour come round at last,
Slouches towards Bethlehem to be born?

TWO SONGS FROM A PLAY

1

I saw a staring virgin stand
Where holy Dionysus died,
And tear the heart out of his side,
And lay the heart upon her hand
And bear that beating heart away;
And then did all the Muses sing
Of Magnus Annus at the spring,
As though God's death were but a play.

Another Troy must rise and set,
Another lineage feed the crow,
Another Argo's painted prow
Drive to a flashier bauble yet.

The Roman Empire stood appalled:
It dropped the reins of peace and war
When that fierce virgin and her Star
Out of the fabulous darkness called.

2

In pity for man's darkening thought
He walked that room and issued thence
In Galilean turbulence;
The Babylonian starlight brought
A fabulous, formless darkness in;
Odour of blood when Christ was slain
Made all Platonic tolerance vain
And vain all Doric discipline.

Everything that man esteems
Endures a moment or a day.
Love's pleasure drives his love away,
The painter's brush consumes his dreams;
The herald's cry, the soldier's tread
Exhaust his glory and his night:
Whatever flames upon the night
Man's own resinous heart has fed.

LEDA AND THE SWAN

A sudden blow: the great wings beating still
Above the staggering girl, her thighs caressed
By the dark webs, her nape caught in his bill,
He holds her helpless breast upon his breast.

How can those terrified vague fingers push
The feathered glory from her loosening thighs?
And how can body, laid in that white rush,
But feel the strange heart beating where it lies?

A shudder in the loins engenders there
The broken wall, the burning roof and tower
And Agamemnon dead.
                    Being so caught up,
So mastered by the brute blood of the air,
Did she put on his knowledge with his power
Before the indifferent beak could let her drop?

1923

POLITICS

'In our time the destiny of man presents its meaning in political terms.'—THOMAS MANN

How can I, that girl standing there,
My attention fix
On Roman or on Russian
Or on Spanish politics?
Yet here's a travelled man that knows
What he talks about,
And there's a politician
That has read and thought,
And maybe what they say is true
Of war and war's alarms,
But O that I were young again
And held her in my arms!

LAPIS LAZULI

(For Harry Clifton)

I have heard that hysterical women say
They are sick of the palette and fiddle-bow,
Of poets that are always gay,
For everybody knows or else should know
That if nothing drastic is done
Aeroplane and Zeppelin will come out,
Pitch like King Billy bomb-balls in
Until the town lie beaten flat.

All perform their tragic play,
There struts Hamlet, there is Lear,
That's Ophelia, that Cordelia;
Yet they, should the last scene be there,
The great stage curtain about to drop,
If worthy their prominent part in the play,
Do not break up their lines to weep.
They know that Hamlet and Lear are gay;
Gaiety transfiguring all that dread.
All men have aimed at, found and lost;
Black out; Heaven blazing into the head:

Tragedy wrought to its uttermost.
Though Hamlet rambles and Lear rages,
And all the drop-scenes drop at once
Upon a hundred thousand stages,
It cannot grow by an inch or an ounce.

On their own feet they came, or on shipboard,
Camel-back, horse-back, ass-back, mule-back,
Old civilizations put to the sword.
Then they and their wisdom went to rack:
No handiwork of Callimachus,
Who handled marble as if it were bronze,
Made draperies that seemed to rise
When sea-wind swept the corner, stands;
His long lamp-chimney shaped like the stem
Of a slender palm, stood but a day;
All things fall and are built again,
And those that build them again are gay.

Two Chinamen, behind them a third,
Are carved in lapis lazuli,
Over them flies a long-legged bird,
A symbol of longevity;
The third, doubtless a serving-man,
Carries a musical instrument.

Every discoloration of the stone,
Every accidental crack or dent,
Seems a water-course or an avalanche,
Or lofty slope where it still snows
Though doubtless plum or cherry-branch
Sweetens the little half-way house
Those Chinamen climb towards, and I
Delight to imagine them seated there;
There, on the mountain and the sky,
On all the tragic scene they stare.
One asks for mournful melodies;
Accomplished fingers begin to play.
Their eyes mid many wrinkles, their eyes,
Their ancient, glittering eyes, are gay.

AN ACRE OF GRASS

Picture and book remain,
An acre of green grass

For air and exercise,
New strength of body goes;
Midnight, and old house
Where nothing stirs but a mouse.

My temptation is quiet.
Here at life's end
Neither loose imagination,
Nor the mill of the mind
Consuming its rag and bone,
Can make the truth known.

Grant me an old man's frenzy,
Myself must I remake
Till I am Timon and Lear
Or that William Blake
Who beat upon the wall
Till Truth obeyed his call;

A mind Michael Angelo knew
That can pierce the clouds,
Or inspired by frenzy
Shake the dead in their shrouds;
Forgotten else by mankind,
An old man's eagle mind.

Hilaire Belloc (1870–1953)

LORD LUNDY

Lord Lundy from his earliest years
Was far too freely moved to Tears.
For instance, if his Mother said,
"Lundy! It's time to go to Bed!"
He bellowed like a Little Turk.
Or if his father, Lord Dunquerque
Said, "Hi!" in a Commanding Tone,

"Hi, Lundy! Leave the Cat alone!"
Lord Lundy, letting go its tail,
Would raise so terrible a wail
As moved
His Grandpapa the Duke
To utter the severe rebuke:
"When I, Sir! was a little Boy,
An Animal was not a Toy!"
His father's Elder Sister, who
Was married to a Parvenoo,
Confided to Her Husband, "Drat!
The Miserable, Peevish Brat!
Why don't they drown the Little Beast?"
Suggestions which, to say the least,
Are not what we expect to hear
From Daughters of an English Peer.
His grandmamma, His Mother's Mother,
Who had some dignity or other,
The Garter, or no matter what,
I can't remember all the Lot!
Said, "Oh! that I were Brisk and Spry
To give him that for which to cry!"
(An empty wish, alas! for she
Was Blind and nearly ninety-three).
The Dear old Butler thought—but there!
I really neither know nor care
For what the Dear Old Butler thought!
In my opinion, Butlers ought
To know their place, and not to play
The Old Retainer night and day
I'm getting tired and so are you,
Let's cut the Poem into two!

It happened to Lord Lundy then,
As happens to so many men:
Towards the age of twenty-six,
They shoved him into politics;
In which profession he commanded
The income that his rank demanded
In turn as Secretary for
India, the Colonies, and War.
But very soon his friends began
To doubt if he were quite the man:
Thus, if a member rose to say
(As members do from day to day),
"Arising out of that reply . . . !"

Lord Lundy would begin to cry.
A Hint at harmless little jobs
Would shake him with convulsive sobs.
While as for Revelations, these
Would simply bring him to his knees,
And leave him whimpering like a child.
It drove his Colleagues raving wild!
They let him sink from Post to Post,
From fifteen hundred at the most
To eight, and barely six—and then
To be Curator of Big Ben! . . .
And finally there came a Threat
To oust him from the Cabinet!

The Duke—his aged grand-sire—bore
The shame till he could bear no more.
He rallied his declining powers,
Summoned the youth to Brackley Towers,
And bitterly addressed him thus—
"Sir! you have disappointed us!
We had intended you to be
The next Prime Minister but three:
The stocks were sold; the press was squared;
The Middle Class was quite prepared.
But as it is! . . . My language fails!
Go out and govern New South Wales!"

. . . . .

The Aged Patriot groaned and died:
And gracious! how Lord Lundy cried!

John Masefield (1878–1967)

From REYNARD THE FOX

"From the Gallows Hill to the Tineton Copse"

From the Gallows Hill to the Tineton Copse
There were ten ploughed fields, like ten full-stops,

All wet red clay where a horse's foot
Would be swathed; feet thick, like an ash-tree root.
The fox raced on, on the headlands firm,
Where his swift feet scared the coupling worm,
The rooks rose raving to curse him raw,
He snarled a sneer at their swoop and caw.
Then on, then on, down a half-ploughed field
Where a ship-like plough drove glitter-keeled,
With a bay horse near and a white horse leading,
And a man saying "Zook," and the red earth bleeding.
He gasped as he saw the ploughman drop
The stilts and swear at the team to stop.
The ploughman ran in his red clay clogs,
Crying "Zick un, Tower; zick, good dogs."
A couple of wire-haired lurchers lean
Arose from his wallet, nosing keen;
With a rushing swoop they were on his track,
Putting chest to stubble to bite his back.
He swerved from his line with the curs at heel,
The teeth as they missed him clicked like steel,
With a worrying snarl, they quartered on him,
While the ploughman shouted, "Zick; upon him."

. . . . . .

The fox raced on, up the Barton Balks,
With a crackle of kex in the nettle stalks,
Over Hammond's grass to the dark green line
Of the larch-wood smelling of turpentine.
Scratch Steven Larches, black to the sky,
A sadness breathing with one long sigh,
Grey ghosts of trees under funeral plumes,
A mist of twig over soft brown glooms.
As he entered the wood he heard the smacks,
Chip-jar, of the fir-pole feller's axe,
He swerved to the left to a broad green ride,
Where a boy made him rush for the farther side.
He swerved to the left, to the Barton Road,
But there were the timberers come to load.
Two timber-carts and a couple of carters
With straps round their knees instead of garters.
He swerved to the right, straight down the wood,
The carters watched him, the boy hallooed.
He leaped from the larch-wood into tillage,
The cobbler's garden of Barton village.

The cobbler bent at his wooden foot,

Beating sprigs in a broken boot;
He wore old glasses with thick horn rim,
He scowled at his work, for his sight was dim.
His face was dingy, his lips were grey,
From primming sparrowbills day by day;
As he turned his boot he heard a noise
At his garden-end and he thought, "It's boys."

. . . . . .

Like a rocket shot to a ship ashore,
The lean red bolt of his body tore,
Like a ripple of wind running swift on grass,
Like a shadow on wheat when a cloud blows past,
Like a turn at the buoy in a cutter sailing
When the bright green gleam lips white at the railing,
Like the April snake whipping back to sheath,
Like the gannet's hurtle on fish beneath,
Like a kestrel chasing, like a sickle reaping,
Like all things swooping, like all things sweeping,
Like a hound for stay, like a stag for swift,
With his shadow beside like spinning drift.

Past the gibbet-stock all stuck with nails,
Where they hanged in chains what had hung in jails,
Past Ashmundshowe where Ashmund sleeps,
And none but the tumbling peewit weeps,
Past Curlew Calling, the gaunt grey corner
Where the curlew comes as a summer mourner,
Past Blowbury Beacon, shaking his fleece,
Where all winds hurry and none brings peace;
Then down on the mile-long green decline,
Where the turf's like spring and the air's like wine,
Where the sweeping spurs of the downland spill
Into Wan Brook Valley and Wan Dyke Hill.

On he went with a galloping rally
Past Maesbury Clump for Wan Brook Valley,
The blood in his veins went romping high
"Get on, on, on, to the earth or die."
The air of the downs went purely past
Till he felt the glory of going fast,
Till the terror of death, though there indeed,
Was lulled for a while by his pride of speed.
He was romping away from hounds and hunt,
He had Wan Dyke Hill and his earth in front,
In a one mile more when his point was made

He would rest in safety from dog or spade;
Nose between paws he would hear the shout
Of the "Gone to earth!" to the hounds without,
The whine of the hounds, and their cat-feet gadding
Scratching the earth, and their breath pad-padding;
He would hear the horn call hounds away
And rest in peace till another day. . . .

"I HEAR AN ARMY
CHARGING UPON THE LAND"

James Joyce (1882–1941)

I hear an army charging upon the land,
  And the thunder of horses plunging, foam about their
    knees:
Arrogant, in black armour, behind them stand,
  Disdaining the reins, with fluttering whips, the charioteers.

They cry unto the night their battle-name:
  I moan in sleep when I hear afar their whirling laughter.
They cleave the gloom of dreams, a blinding flame,
  Clanging, clanging upon the heart as upon an anvil.

They come shaking in triumph their long, green hair:
  They come out of the sea and run shouting by the shore.
My heart, have you no wisdom thus to despair?
  My love, my love, my love, why have you left me alone?

D. H. Lawrence (1885–1930)

CHERRY ROBBERS

Under the long dark boughs, like jewels red
  In the hair of an Eastern girl
Hang strings of crimson cherries, as if had bled
  Blood-drops beneath each curl.

Under the glistening cherries, with folded wings
  Three dead birds lie:
Pale-breasted throstles and a blackbird, robberlings
  Stained with red dye.

Against the haystack a girl stands laughing at me,
  Cherries hung round her ears,
Offers me her scarlet fruit: I will see
  If she has any tears.

KISSES IN THE TRAIN

I saw the midlands
  Revolve through her hair;
The fields of autumn
  Stretching bare,
And sheep on the pasture
  Tossed back in a scare.

And still as ever
  The world went round,
My mouth on her pulsing
  Throat was found,
And my breast to her beating
  Breast was bound.

But my heart at the centre
  Of all, in a swound

Was still as a pivot,
   As all the ground
On its prowling orbit
   Shifted round.

And still in my nostrils
   The scent of her flesh;
And still my blind face
   Sought her afresh;
And still one pulse
   Through the world did thresh.

And the world all whirling
   Round in joy
Like the dance of a dervish
   Did destroy
My sense—and reason
   Spun like a toy.

But firm at the centre
   My heart was found;
My own to her perfect
   Heartbeat bound,
Like a magnet's keeper
   Closing the round.

LOVE ON THE FARM

What large, dark hands are these at the window
Grasping in the golden light
Which weaves its way through the evening wind
   At my heart's delight?

Ah, only the leaves! But in the west
I see a redness suddenly come
Into the evening's anxious breast—
   'Tis the wound of love goes home!

The woodbine creeps abroad
Calling low to her lover;
   The sun-lit flirt who all the day
   Has poised above her lips in play
   And stolen kisses, shallow and gay
Of pollen, now has gone away—

She woos the moth with her sweet, low word;
And when above his moth-wings hover
Then her bright breast she will uncover
And yield her honey-drop to her lover.

Into the yellow, evening glow
Saunters a man from the farm below;
Leans, and looks in at the low-built shed
Where the swallow has hung her marriage-bed.
   The bird lies warm against the wall.
   She glances quick her startled eyes
   Towards him, then she turns away
   Her small head, making warm display
   Of red upon the throat. Her terrors sway
   Her out of the nest's warm, busy ball,
   Whose plaintive cry is heard as she flies
   In one blue swoop from out the sties
   Into the twilight's empty hall.

Oh, water-hen, beside the rushes,
Hide your quaintly scarlet blushes,
Still your quick tail, lie still as dead,
Till the distance folds over his ominous tread!

The rabbit presses back her ears,
Turns back her liquid, anguished eyes
And crouches low; then with wild spring
Spurts from the terror of his oncoming;
To be choked back, the wire ring
Her frantic effort throttling:
   Piteous brown ball of quivering fears!
Ah, soon in his large, hard hands she dies,
And swings all loose from the swing of his walk!
Yet calm and kindly are his eyes
And ready to open in brown surprise
Should I not answer to his talk
Or should he my tears surmise.

I hear his hand on the latch, and rise from my chair
Watching the door open; he flashes bare
His strong teeth in a smile, and flashes his eyes
In a smile like triumph upon me; then careless-wise
He flings the rabbit soft on the table board
And comes toward me: he! the uplifted sword
Of his hand against my bosom and oh, the broad
Blade of his glance that asks me to applaud

His coming! With his hand he turns my face to him
And caresses me with his fingers that still smell grim
Of rabbit's fur! God, I am caught in a snare!
I know not what fine wire is round my throat;
I only know I let him finger there
My pulse of life, and let him nose like a stoat
Who sniffs with joy before he drinks the blood.

And down his mouth comes to my mouth! and down
His bright dark eyes come over me, like a hood
Upon my mind! his lips meet mine, and a flood
Of sweet fire sweeps across me, so I drown
Against him, die, and find death good.

NOW IT'S HAPPENED

One cannot now help thinking
how much better it would have been
if Vronsky and Anna Karenin
had stood up for themselves and seen
Russia across her crisis,
instead of leaving it to Lenin.

The big flamboyant Russia
might have been saved, if a pair
of rebels like Anna and Vronsky
had blasted the sickly air
of Dostoevsky and Tchekov,
and spy-government everywhere.

But Tolstoi was a traitor
to the Russia that needed him most,
the clumsy, bewildered Russia
so worried by the Holy Ghost,
He shifted his job to the peasants
and landed them all on toast.

Dostoevsky, the Judas,
with his sham christianity
epileptically ruined
the last bit of sanity
left in the hefty bodies
of the Russian nobility.

So our goody-goody men betray us
and our sainty-saints let us down,
and a sickly people will slay us
if we touch the sob-stuff crown
of such martyrs; while Marxian tenets
naturally take hold of the town.

Too much of the humble Willy wet-leg
and the holy can't-help-it touch,
till you've ruined a nation's fibre
and they loathe all feeling as such,
and want to be cold and devilish hard
like machines—and you can't wonder much.—

TERRA INCOGNITA

There are vast realms of consciousness still undreamed of
vast ranges of experience, like the humming of unseen harps,
we know nothing of, within us.

Oh when man escaped from the barbed-wire entanglement
of his own ideas and his own mechanical devices
there is a marvellous rich world of contact and sheer fluid
        beauty
and fearless face-to-face awareness of now-naked life
and me, and you, and other men and women
and grapes, and ghouls, and ghosts and green moonlight
and ruddy-orange limbs stirring the limbo
of the unknown air, and eyes so soft
softer than the space between the stars.
And all things, and nothing, and being and not-being
alternately palpitate,
when at last we escape the barbed-wire enclosure
of *Know-Thyself*, knowing we can never know,
we can but touch, and wonder, and ponder, and make our ef-
        fort
and dangle in a last fastidious fine delight
as the fuchsia does, dangling her reckless drop
of purple after so much putting forth
and slow mounting marvel of a little tree.

WHALES WEEP NOT!

They say the sea is cold, but the sea contains
the hottest blood of all, and the wildest, the most urgent.

All the whales in the wider deeps, hot are they, as they urge
on and on, and dive beneath the ice-bergs.
The right whales, the sperm-whales, the hammer-heads, the
    killers
there they blow, there they blow, hot wild white breath out
    of the sea!

And they rock and they rock, through the sensual ageless
    ages
on the depths of the seven seas,
and through the salt they reel with drunk delight
and in the tropics tremble they with love
and roll with massive, strong desire, like gods.
Then the great bull lies up against his bride
in the blue deep of the sea
as mountain pressing on mountain, in the zest of life:
and out of the inward roaring of the inner red ocean of
    whale blood
the long tip reaches strong, intense, like a maelstrom-tip, and
    comes to rest
in the clasp and the soft, wild clutch of a she-whale's fathom-
    less body.

And over the bridge of the whale's strong phallus, linking the
    wonder of whales
the burning archangels under the sea keep passing, back and
    forth,
keep passing archangels of bliss
from him to her, from her to him, great Cherubim
that wait on whales in mid-ocean, suspended in the waves of
    the sea
great heaven of whales in the waters, old hierarchies.
And enormous mother whales lie dreaming suckling their
    whale-tender young
and dreaming with strange whale eyes wide open in the
    waters of the
        beginning and the end.

And bull-whales gather their women and whale-calves in a
ring
when danger threatens, on the surface of the ceaseless flood
and range themselves like great fierce Seraphim facing the
threat
encircling their huddled monsters of love,
and all this happiness in the sea, in the salt
where God is also love, but without words:
and Aphrodite is the wife of whales
most happy, happy she!

and Venus among the fishes skips and is a she-dolphin
she is the gay, delighted porpoise sporting with love and the
sea
she is the female tunny-fish, round and happy among the
males
and dense with happy blood, dark rainbow bliss in the sea.

Edith Sitwell (1887–1964)

SIR BEELZEBUB

WHEN—
Sir
Beelzebub called for his syllabub in the hotel in Hell
  Where Proserpine first fell,
Blue as the gendarmerie were the waves of the sea,

  (Rocking and shocking the bar-maid).

Nobody comes to give him his rum but the
Rim of the sky hippopotamus-glum
Enhances the chances to bless with a benison
Alfred Lord Tennyson crossing the bar laid
With cold vegetation from pale deputations
Of temperance workers (all signed In Memoriam)
Hoping with glory to trip up the Laureate's feet,

(Moving in classical meters). ....

Like Balaclava, the lava came down from the
Roof, and the sea's blue wooden gendarmerie
Took them in charge while Beelzebub roared for his rum.

... None of them come!

STILL FALLS THE RAIN

The Raids, 1940. Night and Dawn

Still falls the Rain—
Dark as the world of man, black as our loss—
Blind as the nineteen hundred and forty nails
Upon the Cross.

Still falls the Rain
With a sound like the pulse of the heart that is changed to
    the hammer-beat
In the Potter's Field, and the sound of the impious feet

On the Tomb:
       Still falls the Rain
In the Field of Blood where the small hopes breed and the
    human brain
Nurtures its greed, that worm with the brow of Cain.

Still falls the Rain
At the feet of the Starved Man hung upon the Cross.

Christ that each day, each night, nails there, have mercy on
    us—
On Dives and on Lazarus:
Under the rain the sore and the gold are as one.

Still falls the Rain—
Still falls the blood from the Starved Man's wounded Side:
He bears in His Heart all wounds,—those of the light that
    died.
The last faint spark
In the self-murdered heart, the wounds of the sad uncompre-
    hending dark,

The wounds of the baited bear,—
The blind and weeping bear whom the keepers beat
On his helpless flesh . . . the tears of the hunted hare.

Still falls the Rain—
Then—O Ile leape up to my God: who pulles me doune—
See, see where Christ's blood streames in the firmament:
It flows from the Brow we nailed upon the tree
Deep to the dying, to the thirsting heart
That holds the fires of the world,—dark-smirched with pain
As Caesar's laurel crown.

Then sounds the voice of One who like the heart of man
Was once a child who among beasts has lain—
"Still do I love, still shed my innocent light, my Blood, for
    thee."

Hugh MacDiarmid (1892–   )

AT THE CENOTAPH

Are the living so much use
That we need to mourn the dead?
Or would it yield better results
To reverse their roles instead?
The millions slain in the War—
Untimely, the best of our seed?—
Would the world be any the better
If they were still living indeed?
The achievements of such as are
To the notion lend no support;
The whole history of life and death
Yields no scrap of evidence for't.—
Keep going to your wars, you fools, as of yore;
I'm the civilisation you're fighting for.

HARRY SEMEN

I ken these islands each inhabited
Forever by a single man
Livin' in his separate world as only
In dreams yet maist folk can.
Mine's like the moonwhite belly o 'a hoo[1]
Seen in the water as a fisher draws in his line.
I canna land it nor can it ever brak awa'.

It never moves, yet seems a' movement in the brine;
A movin' picture o' the spasm frae which I was born,
It writhes again, and back to it I'm willy-nilly torn.
A' men are similarly fixt; and the difference twixt
   The sae-ca'd sane and insane
Is that the latter whiles ha'e glimpses o't
   And the former nane.

Particle frae particle'll brak asunder,
Ilk ane o' them mair livid than the neist.
A separate life?—incredible war o' equal lichts,
Nane o' them we' ocht in common in the least.
Nae threid o' a' the fabric o' my thocht
Is left alangside anither; a pack
O' leprous scuts o' weasels riddlin' a plaid
   Sic thrums[2] could never mak'.
Hoo mony shades o' white gaed curvin' owre
To yon blae[3] centre o' her belly's flower?
Milk-white, and dove-grey, we' harebell veins.
Ae scar in fair hair like the sun in sunlicht lay,
And pelvic experience in a thin shadow line;
Thocht canna mairry thocht as sic saft shadows dae.
Grey ghastly commentaries on my puir life,
A' the sperm that's gane for naething rises up to damn
In sick-white onanism the single seed
Frae which in sheer irrelevance I cam.
What were the odds against me? Let me coont.
What worth am I to a' that micht ha'e been?
To a' the wasted slime I'm capable o'

[1] dogfish
[2] threads
[3] blue

Appeals this lurid emission, whirlin' lint-white and green.
Am I alane richt, solidified to life,
Disjoined frae a' this searin' like a white-het knife,
And vauntin' my alien accretions here,
Boastin' sanctions, purpose, sense the endless tide
I cam frae lacks—the tide I still sae often feed?
O bitter glitter; wet sheet and flowin' sea—and what beside?
Sae the bealin'[4] continents lie upon the seas,
   Sprawlin' in shapeless shapes a' airts,[5]
Like ony splash that ony man can mak'
   Frae his nose or throat or ither pairts,
Fantastic as ink through blottin'-paper rins.
But this is white, white like a flooerin' gean,[6]
Passin' frae white to purer shades o' white,
Ivory, crystal, diamond, till nae difference is seen
Between its fairest blossoms and the stars
Or the clear sun they melt into,
And the wind mixes them amang each ither
Forever, hue upon still mair dazzlin' hue.

Sae Joseph may ha'e pondered; sae a snawstorm
Comes whirlin' in grey sheets frae the shadowy sky
And only in a sma' circle are the separate flakes seen.
White, whiter, they cross and recross as capricious they fly,
Mak' patterns on the grund and weave into wreaths,
Load the bare boughs, and find lodgements in corners frae
The scourin' wind that sends a snawstorm up frae the earth
To meet that frae the sky, till which is which nae man can
   say.
They melt in the waters. They fill the valleys. They scale the
   peaks.
There's a tinkle o' icicles. The topmaist summit shines oot.
Sae Joseph may ha'e pondered on the coiled fire in his seed,
The transformation in Mary, and seen Jesus tak' root.

[4] festering
[5] all directions
[6] wild cherry

Wilfred Owen (1893–1918)

THE PARABLE OF THE OLD MAN
AND THE YOUNG

So Abram rose, and clave the wood, and went,
And took the fire with him, and a knife.
And as they sojourned, both of them together,
Isaac the first-born spake, and said, My Father,
Behold the preparations, fire and iron,
But where the lamb for this burnt-offering?
Then Abram bound the youth with belts and straps,
And builded parapets and trenches there,
And stretchèd forth the knife to slay his son.
When lo! an angel called him out of heaven,
Saying, Lay not thy hand upon the lad,
Neither do anything to him. Behold,
A ram, caught in a thicket by its horns;
Offer the Ram of Pride instead of him.
But the old man would not so, but slew his son,
And half the seed of Europe, one by one.

ARMS AND THE BOY

Let the boy try along this bayonet-blade
How cold steel is, and keen with hunger of blood;
Blue with all malice, like a madman's flash;
And thinly drawn with famishing for flesh.

Lend him to stroke these blind, blunt bullet-heads
Which long to nuzzle in the hearts of lads,
Or give him cartridges of fine zinc teeth,
Sharp with the sharpness of grief and death.

For his teeth seem for laughing round an apple.
There lurk no claws behind his fingers supple;

And god will grow no talons at his heels,
Nor antlers through the thickness of his curls.

THE SHOW

We have fallen in the dreams the ever-living
Breathe on the tarnished mirror of the world,
And then smooth out with ivory hands and sigh.

W. B. YEATS

My soul looked down from a vague height, with Death,
As unremembering how I rose or why,
And saw a sad land, weak with sweats of dearth,
Gray, cratered like the moon with hollow woe,
And pitted with great pocks and scabs of plagues.

Across its beard, that horror of harsh wire,
There moved thin caterpillars, slowly uncoiled.
It seemed they pushed themselves to be as plugs
Of ditches, where they writhed and shrivelled, killed.

By them had slimy paths been trailed and scraped
Round myriad warts that might be little hills.

From gloom's last dregs these long-strung creatures crept,
And vanished out of dawn down hidden holes.

(And smell came up from those foul openings
As out of mouths, or deep wounds deepening.)

On dithering feet upgathered, more and more,
Brown strings, towards strings of gray, with bristling spines,
All migrants from green fields, intent on mire.

Those that were gray, of more abundant spawns,
Ramped on the rest and ate them and were eaten.

I saw their bitten backs curve, loop, and straighten,
I watched those agonies curl, lift, and flatten.
Whereat, in terror what that sight might mean,
I reeled and shivered earthward like a feather.

And Death fell with me, like a deepening moan.
And He, picking a manner of worm, which half had hid

[291]

Its bruises in the earth, but crawled no further,
Showed me its feet, the feet of many men,
And the fresh-severed head of it, my head.

GREATER LOVE

Red lips are not so red
  As the stained stones kissed by the English dead.
Kindness of wooed and wooer
Seems shame to their love pure.
O Love, your eyes lose lure
  When I behold eyes blinded in my stead!

Your slender attitude
  Trembles not exquisite like limbs knife-skewed,
Rolling and rolling there
Where God seems not to care;
Till the fierce Love they bear
  Cramps them in death's extreme decrepitude.

Your voice sings not so soft,—
  Though even as wind murmuring through raftered loft,—
Your dear voice is not dear,
Gentle, and evening clear,
As theirs whom none now hear,
  Now earth has stopped their piteous mouths that coughed.

Heart, you were never hot,
  Nor large, nor full like hearts made great with shot;
And though your hand be pale,
Paler are all which trail
Your cross through flame and hail:
  Weep, you may weep, for you may touch them not.

SONG OF SONGS

Sing me at morn but only with your laugh;
Even as Spring that laugheth into leaf;
Even as Love that laugheth after Life.

Sing me but only with your speech all day,
As voluble leaflets do; let viols die;
The least word of your lips is melody!

Sing me at eve but only with your sigh!
Like lifting seas it solaceth; breathe so,
Slowly and low, the sense that no songs say.

Sing me at midnight with your murmurous heart!
Let youth's immortal-moaning chords be heard
Throbbing through you, and sobbing, unsubdued.

STRANGE MEETING

It seemed that out of battle I escaped
Down some profound dull tunnel, long since scooped
Through granites which titanic wars had groined.
Yet also there encumbered sleepers groaned,
Too fast in thought or death to be bestirred.
Then, as I probed them, one sprang up, and stared
With piteous recognition in fixed eyes,
Lifting distressful hands as if to bless.
And by his smile, I knew that sullen hall,
By his dead smile I knew we stood in Hell.
With a thousand pains that vision's face was grained;
Yet no blood reached there from the upper ground,
And no guns thumped, or down the flues made moan.
"Strange friend," I said, "here is no cause to mourn."
"None," said the other, "save the undone years,
The hopelessness. Whatever hope is yours,
Was my life also; I went hunting wild
After the wildest beauty in the world,
Which lies not calm in eyes, or braided hair,
But mocks the steady running of the hour,
And if it grieves, grieves richlier than here.
For by my glee might many men have laughed,
And of my weeping something had been left,
Which must die now. I mean the truth untold,
The pity of war, the pity war distilled.
Now men will go content with what we spoiled.
Or, discontent, boil bloody, and be spilled.
They will be swift with swiftness of the tigress,
None will break ranks, though nations trek from progress.
Courage was mine, and I had mystery,
Wisdom was mine, and I had mastery:
To miss the march of this retreating world
Into vain citadels that are not walled.
Then, when much blood had clogged their chariot-wheels,
I would go up and wash them from sweet wells,

Even with truths that lie too deep for taint.
I would have poured my spirit without stint
But not through wounds; not on the cess of war.
Foreheads of men have bled where no wounds were.
I am the enemy you killed, my friend.
I knew you in this dark; for so you frowned
Yesterday through me as you jabbed and killed.
I parried; but my hands were loath and cold.
Let us sleep now. ...."

TO MY FRIEND

(With an Identity Disc)

If ever I had dreamed of my dead name
    High in the heart of London, unsurpassed
By Time for ever, and the Fugitive, Fame,
    There seeking a long sanctuary at last,—

Or if I onetime hoped to hide its shame,
    —Shame of success, and sorrow of defeats,—
Under those holy cypresses, the same
    That shade always the quiet place of Keats,

Now rather thank I God there is no risk
    Of graver scoring it with florid screed.
Let my inscription be this soldier's disc. ...
    Wear it, sweet friend, inscribe no date nor deed.
But may thy heart-beat kiss it, night and day,
Until the name grow blurred and fade away.

1918

Robert Graves (1895–   )

RECALLING WAR

Entrance and exit wounds are silvered clean,
The track aches only when the rain reminds.

The one-legged man forgets his leg of wood,
The one-armed man his jointed wooden arm.
The blinded man sees with his ears and hands
As much or more than once with both his eyes.
Their war was fought these twenty years ago
And now assumes the nature-look of time,
As when the morning traveller turns and views
His wild night-stumbling carved into a hill.

What, then, was war? No mere discord of flags
But an infection of the common sky
That sagged ominously upon the earth
Even when the season was the airiest May.
Down pressed the sky, and we, oppressed, thrust out
For Death was young again: patron alone
Of healthy dying, premature fate-spasm.

Fear made fine bed-fellows. Sick with delight
At life's discovered transitoriness,
Our youth became all-flesh and waived the mind.
Never was such antiqueness of romance,
Such tasty honey oozing from the heart.
And old importances came swimming back—
Wine, meat, log-fires, a roof over the head,
A weapon at the thigh, surgeons at call.
Even there was a use again for God—
A word of rage in lack of meat, wine, fire,
In ache of wounds beyond all surgeoning.

War was return of earth to ugly earth,
War was foundering of sublimities,
Extinction of each happy art and faith
By which the world had still kept head in air,
Protesting logic or protesting love,
Until the unendurable moment struck—
The inward scream, the duty to run mad.

And we recall the merry ways of guns—
Nibbling the walls of factory and church
Like a child, piecrust; felling groves of trees
Like a child, dandelions with a switch.
Machine-guns rattle toy-like from a hill,
Down in a row the brave tin-soldiers fall:
A sight to be recalled in elder days
When learnedly the future we devote
To yet more boastful visions of despair.

[295]

TO JUAN AT THE WINTER SOLSTICE

There is one story and one story only
That will prove worth your telling,
Whether as learned bard or gifted child;
To it all lines or lesser gauds belong
That startle with their shining
Such common stories as they stray into.

Is it of trees you tell, their months and virtues,
Or strange beasts that beset you,
Of birds that croak at you the Triple will?
Or of the Zodiac and how slow it turns
Below the Boreal Crown,
Prison of all true kings that ever reigned?

Water to water, ark again to ark,
From woman back to woman:
So each new victim treads unfalteringly
The never altered circuit of his fate,
Bringing twelve peers as witness
Both to his starry rise and starry fall.

Or is it of the Virgin's silver beauty,
All fish below the thighs?
She in her left hand bears a leafy quince;
When with her right she crooks a finger, smiling,
How may the King hold back?
Royally then he barters life for love.

Or of the undying snake from chaos hatched,
Whose coils contain the ocean,
Into whose chops with naked sword he springs,
Then in black water, tangled by the reeds,
Battles three days and nights,
To be spewed up beside her scalloped shore?

Much snow is falling, winds roar hollowly,
The owl hoots from the elder,
Fear in your heart cries to the loving-cup:
Sorrow to sorrow as the sparks fly upward.
The log groans and confesses:
There is one story and one story only.

Dwell on her graciousness, dwell on her smiling,
Do not forget what flowers
The great boar trampled down in ivy time.
Her brow was creamy as the crested wave,
Her sea-blue eyes were wild
But nothing promised that is not performed.

THE WHITE GODDESS

All saints revile her, and all sober men
Ruled by the God Apollo's golden mean—
In scorn of which we sailed to find her
In distant regions likeliest to hold her
Whom we desired above all things to know,
Sister of the mirage and echo.

It was a virtue not to stay,
To go our headstrong and heroic way
Seeking her out at the volcano's head,
Among pack ice, or where the track had faded
Beyond the cavern of the seven sleepers:
Whose broad high brow was white as any leper's,
Whose eyes were blue, with rowan-berry lips.
With hair curled honey-coloured to white hips.

Green sap of Spring in the young wood a-stir
Will celebrate the Mountain Mother,
And every song-bird shout awhile for her;
But we are gifted, even in November
Rawest of seasons, with so huge a sense
Of her nakedly worn magnificence
We forget cruelty and past betrayal,
Heedless of where the next bright bolt may fall.

THE NAKED AND THE NUDE

For me, the naked and the nude
(By lexicographers construed
As synonyms that should express
The same deficiency of dress
Or shelter) stand as wide apart
As love from lies, or truth from art.

Lovers without reproach will gaze
On bodies naked and ablaze;
The Hippocratic eye will see
In nakedness, anatomy;
And naked shines the Goddess when
She mounts her lion among men.

The nude are bold, the nude are sly
To hold each treasonable eye.
While draping by a showman's trick
Their dishabille in rhetoric,
They grin a mock-religious grin
Of scorn at those of naked skin.

The naked, therefore, who compete
Against the nude may know defeat;
Yet when they both together tread
The briary pastures of the dead,
By Gorgons with long whips pursued,
How naked go the sometime nude!

Basil Bunting (1900–   )

From BRIGGFLATTS

1

Brag, sweet tenor bull,
descant on Rawthey's madrigal,
each pebble its part
for the fells' late spring.
Dance tiptoe, bull,
black against may.
Ridiculous and lovely
chase hurdling shadows
morning into noon.

May on the bull's hide
and through the dale
furrows fill with may,
paving the slowworm's way.

A mason times his mallet
to a lark's twitter,
listening while the marble rests,
lays his rule
at a letter's edge,
fingertips checking,
till the stone spells a name
naming none,
a man abolished.
Painful lark, labouring to rise!
The solemn mallet says:
In the grave's slot
he lies. We rot.

... The mason stirs:
Words!
Pens are too light.
Take a chisel to write.

Every birth a crime,
every sentence life.
Wiped of mould and mites
would the ball run true?
No hope of going back.
Hounds falter and stray,
shame deflects the pen.
Love murdered neither bleeds nor stifles
but jogs the draftsman's elbow.
What can he, changed, tell
her, changed, perhaps dead?
Delight dwindles. Blame
stays the same ...

2

Poet appointed dare not decline
to walk among the bogus, nothing to authenticate
the mission imposed, despised
by toadies, confidence men, kept boys,
shopped and jailed, cleaned out by whores,
touching acquaintance for food and tobacco.

Secret, solitary, a spy, he gauges
lines of a Flemish horse
hauling beer, the angle, obtuse,
a slut's blouse draws on her chest,
counts beat against beat, bus conductor
against engine against wheels against
the pedal, Tottenham Court Road, decodes
thunder, scans
porridge bubbling, pipes clanking, feels
Buddha's basalt cheek
but cannot name the ratio of its curves
to the half-pint
left breast of a girl who bared it in Kleinfeldt's.
He lies with one to long for another,
sick, self-maimed, self-hating,
obstinate, mating
beauty with squalor to beget lines still-born.

4

... As the player's breath warms the fipple the tone clears.
It is time to consider how Domenico Scarlatti
condensed so much music into so few bars
with never a crabbed turn or congested cadence,
never a boast or a see-here; and stars and lakes
echo him and the copse drums out his measure,
snow peaks are lifted up in moonlight and twilight
and the sun rises on an acknowledged land.

My love is young but wise. Oak, applewood,
her fire is banked with ashes till day.
The fells reek of her hearth's scent,
her girdle is greased with lard;
hunger is stayed on her settle, lust in her bed.
Light as spider floss her hair on my cheek which a puff scat-
    ters,
light as a moth her fingers on my thigh.
We have eaten and loved and the sun is up,
we have only to sing before parting:
Goodbye, dear love.

Her scones are greased with fat of fried bacon,
her blanket comforts my belly like the south.
We have eaten and loved and the sun is up.
Goodbye.

Applewood, hard to rive,
its knots smoulder all day.
Cobweb hair on the morning,
a puff would blow it away.
Rime is crisp on the bent,
ruts stone-hard, frost spangles fleece.
What breeze will fill that sleeve limp on the line?
A boy's jet streams from the wall, time from the year,
care from deed and undoing.
Shamble, cold, content with beer and pickles,
towards a taciturn lodging amongst strangers ...

W. H. Auden (1907–1973)

CONSIDER

Consider this and in our time
As the hawk sees it or the helmeted airman:
The clouds rift suddenly—look there
At cigarette-end smouldering on a border
At the first garden party of the year.
Pass on, admire the view of the massif
Through plate-glass windows of the Sport Hotel;
Join there the insufficient units
Dangerous, easy, in furs, in uniform
And constellated at reserved tables
Supplied with feelings by an efficient band
Relayed elsewhere to farmers and their dogs
Sitting in kitchens in the stormy fens.

Long ago, supreme Antagonist,
More powerful than the great northern whale
Ancient and sorry at life's limiting defect,
In Cornwall, Mendip, or the Pennine moor
Your comments on the highborn mining-captains,
Found they no answer, made them wish to die

—Lie since in barrows out of harm.
You talk to your admirers every day
By silted harbours, derelict works,
In strangled orchards, and the silent comb
Where dogs have worried or a bird was shot.

Order the ill that they attack at once:
Visit the ports and, interrupting
The leisurely conversation in the bar
Within a stone's throw of the sunlit water,
Beckon your chosen out. Summon
Those handsome and diseased youngsters, those women
Your solitary agents in the country parishes;
And mobilize the powerful forces latent
In soils that make the farmer brutal
In the infected sinus, and the eyes of stoats.
Then, ready, start your rumour, soft
But horrifying in its capacity to disgust
Which, spreading magnified, shall come to be
A polar peril, a prodigious alarm,
Scattering the people, as torn-up paper
Rags and utensils in a sudden gust,
Seized with immeasurable neurotic dread.

Seekers after happiness, all who follow
The convolutions of your simple wish,
It is later than you think; nearer that day
Far other than that distant afternoon
Amid rustle of frocks and stamping feet
They gave the prizes to the ruined boys.
You cannot be away, then, no
Not though you pack to leave within an hour,
Escaping humming down arterial roads:
The date was yours; the prey to fugues,
Irregular breathing and alternate ascendancies
After some haunted migratory years
To disintegrate on an instant in the explosion of mania
Or lapse for ever into a classic fatigue.

" 'O WHERE ARE YOU GOING?' SAID READER TO RIDER"

'O where are you going?' said reader to rider,
'That valley is fatal when furnaces burn,

Yonder's the midden whose odours will madden,
That gap is the grave where the tall return.'

'O do you imagine,' said fearer to farer,
'That dusk will delay on your path to the pass,
Your diligent looking discover the lacking
Your footsteps feel from granite to grass?'

'O what was that bird,' said horror to hearer,
'Did you see that shape in the twisted trees?
Behind you swiftly the figure comes softly,
The spot on your skin is a shocking disease?'

'Out of this house'—said rider to reader
'Yours never will'—said farer to fearer
'They're looking for you'—said hearer to horror
As he left them there, as he left them there.

MUSÉE DES BEAUX ARTS

About suffering they were never wrong,
The Old Masters: how well they understood
Its human position; how it takes place
While someone else is eating or opening a window or just
    walking dully along;
How, when the aged are reverently, passionately waiting
For the miraculous birth, there always must be
Children who did not specially want it to happen, skating
On a pond at the edge of the wood:

They never forgot
That even the dreadful martyrdom must run its course
Anyhow in a corner, some untidy spot
Where the dogs go on with their doggy life and the torturer's
    horse
Scratches its innocent behind on a tree.

In Brueghel's *Icarus*, for instance: how everything turns
    away
Quite leisurely from the disaster; the ploughman may
Have heard the splash, the forsaken cry,
But for him it was not an important failure; the sun shone
As it had to on the white legs disappearing into the green

Water; and the expensive delicate ship that must have seen
Something amazing, a boy falling out of the sky,
Had somewhere to get to and sailed calmly on.

Stephen Spender (1909–   )

"I THINK CONTINUALLY OF THOSE WHO WERE TRULY GREAT"

I think continually of those who were truly great.
Who, from the womb, remembered the soul's history
Through corridors of light where the hours are suns,
Endless and singing. Whose lovely ambition
Was that their lips, still touched with fire,
Should tell of the Spirit, clothed from head to foot in song.
And who hoarded from the spring branches
The desires falling across their bodies like blossoms.

What is precious is never to forget
The essential delight of the blood drawn from ageless springs
Breaking through rocks in worlds before our earth.
Never to deny its pleasure in the morning simple light
Nor its grave evening demand for love.
Never to allow gradually the traffic to smother
With noise and fog the flowering of the Spirit.

Near the snow, near the sun, in the highest fields
See how these names are fêted by the waving grass
And by the streamers of white cloud,
And whispers of wind in the listening sky.
The names of those who in their lives fought for life,
Who wore at their hearts the fire's centre.
Born of the sun, they travelled a short while toward the sun,
And left the vivid air signed with their honour.

Dylan Thomas (1914–1953)

POEM IN OCTOBER

It was my thirtieth year to heaven
Woke to my hearing from harbour and neighbor wood
    And the mussel pooled and the heron
           Priested shore
        The morning beckon
With water praying and call of seagull and rook
And the knock of sailing boats on the net webbed wall
        Myself to set foot
           That second
In the still sleeping town and set forth.

My birthday began with the water-
Birds and the birds of the winged trees flying my name
    Above the farms and the white horses
           And I rose
        In rainy autumn
And walked abroad in a shower of all my days.
High tide and the heron dived when I took the road
        Over the border
           And the gates
Of the town closed as the town awoke.

A springful of larks in a rolling
Cloud and the roadside bushes brimming with whistling
    Blackbirds and the sun of October
           Summery
        On the hill's shoulder,
Here were fond climates and sweet singers suddenly
Come in the morning where I wandered and listened
        To the rain wringing
           Wind blow cold
    In the wood faraway under me.

Pale rain over the dwindling harbour
And over the sea wet church the size of a snail
With its horns through mist and the castle
Brown as owls
But all the gardens
Of spring and summer were blooming in the tall tales
Beyond the border and under the lark full cloud.
There could I marvel
My birthday
Away but the weather turned around.

It turned away from the blithe country
And down the other air and the blue altered sky
Streamed again a wonder of summer
With apples
Pears and red currants
And I saw in the turning so clearly a child's
Forgotten mornings when he walked with his mother
Through the parables
Of sun light
And the legends of the green chapels

And the twice told fields of infancy
That his tears burned my cheeks and his heart moved in
mine.
These were the woods the river and sea
Where a boy
In the listening
Summertime of the dead whispered the truth of his joy
To the trees and the stones and the fish in the tide.
And the mystery
Sang alive
Still in the water and singingbirds.

And there could I marvel my birthday
Away but the weather turned around. And the true
Joy of the long dead child sang burning
In the sun.
It was my thirtieth
Year to heaven stood there then in the summer noon
Though the town below lay leaved with October blood.
O may my heart's truth
Still be sung
On this high hill in a year's turning.

"IN MY CRAFT OR SULLEN ART"

In my craft or sullen art
Exercised in the still night
When only the moon rages
And the lovers lie abed
With all their griefs in their arms,
I labour by singing light
Not for ambition or bread
Or the strut and trade of charms
On the ivory stages
But for the common wages
Of their most secret heart.

Not for the proud man apart
From the raging moon I write
On these spindrift pages
Not for the towering dead
With their nightingales and psalms
But for the lovers, their arms
Round the griefs of the ages,
Who pay no praise or wages
Nor heed my craft or art.

Philip Larkin (1922–   )

REASONS FOR ATTENDANCE

The trumpet's voice, loud and authoritative,
Draws me for a moment to the lighted glass
To watch the dancers—all under twenty-five—
Shifting intently, face to flushed face,
Solemnly on the beat of happiness.

—Or so I fancy, sensing the smoke and sweat,
The wonderful feel of girls. Why be out here?
But then, why be in there? Sex, yes, but what
Is sex? Surely, to think the lion's share
Of happiness is found by couples—sheer

Inaccuracy, as far as I'm concerned.
What calls me is that lifted, rough-tongued bell
(Art, if you like) whose individual sound
Insists I too am individual.
It speaks; I hear; others may hear as well,

But not for me, nor I for them; and so
With happiness. Therefore I stay outside,
Believing this; and they maul to and fro,
Believing that; and both are satisfied,
If no one has misjudged himself. Or lied.

Thom Gunn (1929–   )

ON THE MOVE

"Man, you gotta Go."

The blue jay scuffling in the bushes follows
Some hidden purpose, and the gust of birds
That spurts across the field, the wheeling swallows,
Have nested in the trees and undergrowth.
Seeking their instinct, or their poise, or both,
One moves with an uncertain violence
Under the dust thrown by a baffled sense
Or the dull thunder of approximate words.

On motorcycles, up the road, they come:
Small, black, as flies hanging in heat, the Boys,
Until the distance throws them forth, their hum

Bulges to thunder held by calf and thigh.
In goggles, donned impersonality,
In gleaming jackets trophied with the dust,
They strap in doubt—by hiding it, robust—
And almost hear a meaning in their noise.

Exact conclusion of their hardiness
Has no shape yet, but from known whereabouts
They ride, direction where the tires press.
They scare a flight of birds across the field:
Much that is natural, to the will must yield.
Men manufacture both machine and soul,
And use what they imperfectly control
To dare a future from the taken routes.

It is a part solution, after all.
One is not necessarily discord
On earth; or damned because, half animal,
One lacks direct instinct, because one wakes
Afloat on movement that divides and breaks.
One joins the movement in a valueless world,
Choosing it, till, both hurler and the hurled,
One moves as well, always toward, toward.

A minute holds them, who have come to go:
The self-defined, astride the created will
They burst away; the towns they travel through
Are home for neither bird nor holiness,
For birds and saints complete their purposes.
At worst, one is in motion; and at best,
Reaching no absolute, in which to rest,
One is always nearer by not keeping still.

Ted Hughes (1930–   )

PIKE

Pike, three inches long, perfect
Pike in all parts, green tigering the gold.
Killers from the egg: the malevolent aged grin.
They dance on the surface among the flies.

Or move, stunned by their own grandeur,
Over a bed of emerald, silhouette
Of submarine delicacy and horror.
A hundred feet long in their world.

In ponds, under the heat-struck lily pads—
Gloom of their stillness:
Logged on last year's black leaves, watching upwards.
Or hung in an amber cavern of weeds

The jaws' hooked clamp and fangs
Not to be changed at this date;
A life subdued to its instrument;
The gills kneading quietly, and the pectorals.

Three we kept behind glass,
Jungled in weed: three inches, four,
And four and a half: fed fry to them—
Suddenly there were two. Finally one.

With a sag belly and the grin it was born with.
And indeed they spare nobody.
Two, six pounds each, over two feet long,
High and dry and dead in the willow-herb—

One jammed past its gills down the other's gullet:
The outside eye stared: as a vice locks—

The same iron in this eye
Though its film shrank in death.

A pond I fished, fifty yards across,
Whose lilies and muscular tench
Had outlasted every visible stone
Of the monastery that planted them—

Stilled legendary depth:
It was as deep as England. It held
Pike too immense to stir, so immense and old
That past nightfall I dared not cast

But silently cast and fished
With the hair frozen on my head
For what might move, for what eye might move.
The still splashes on the dark pond,

Owls hushing the floating woods
Frail on my ear against the dream
Darkness beneath night's darkness had freed,
That rose slowly towards me, watching.

CROW AND THE BIRDS

When the eagle soared clear through a dawn distilling of
    emerald
When the curlew trawled in seadusk through a chime of
    wineglasses
When the swallow swooped through a woman's song in a
    cavern
And the swift flicked through the breath of a violet

When the owl sailed clear of tomorrow's conscience
And the sparrow preened himself of yesterday's promise
And the heron laboured clear of the Bessemer upglare
And the bluetit zipped clear of lace panties
And the woodpecker drummed clear of the rotovator and the
    rose-farm
And the peewit tumbled clear of the laundromat

While the bullfinch plumped in the apple bud
And the goldfinch bulbed in the sun

And the wryneck crooked in the moon
And the dipper peered from the dewball

Crow spraddled head-down in the beach-garbage, guzzling a
dropped ice-cream.

LOVESONG

He loved her and she loved him
His kisses sucked out her whole past and future or tried to
He had no other appetite
She bit him she gnawed him she sucked
She wanted him complete inside her
Safe and sure forever and ever
Their little cries fluttered into the curtains

Her eyes wanted nothing to get away
Her looks nailed down his hands his wrists his elbows
He gripped her hard so that life
Should not drag her from that moment
He wanted all future to cease
He wanted to topple with his arms round her
Off that moment's brink and into nothing
Or everlasting or whatever there was
Her embrace was an immense press
To print him into her bones
His smiles were the garrets of a fairy palace
Where the real world would never come
Her smiles were spider bites
So he would lie still till she felt hungry
His words were occupying armies
Her laughs were an assassin's attempts
His looks were bullets daggers of revenge
Her glances were ghosts in the corner with horrible secrets
His whispers were whips and jackboots
Her kisses were lawyers steadily writing
His caresses were the last hooks of a castaway
Her love-tricks were the grinding of locks
And their deep cries crawled over the floors
Like an animal dragging a great trap
His promises were the surgeon's gag
Her promises took the top off his skull
She would get a brooch made of it
His vows pulled out all her sinews

He showed her how to make a love-knot
Her vows put his eyes in formalin
At the back of her secret drawer
Their screams stuck in the wall

Their heads fell apart into sleep like the two halves
Of a lopped melon, but love is hard to stop

In their entwined sleep they exchanged arms and legs
In their dreams their brains took each other hostage

In the morning they wore each other's face

Derek Walcott (1930–   )

THE POLISH RIDER

The grey horse, Death, in profile bears the young Titus
To dark woods by the dying coal of day;
The father, with worn vision portrays the son
Like Dürer's knight astride a Rozinante;
The horse disturbs more than the youth delights us.
The warrior turns his sure gaze for a second,
Assurance looks its father in the eye,
The inherited, bony hack heads accurately
Towards the symbolic forests that have beckoned
Such knights, squired by the scyther, where to lie.
But skill dispassionately praises the rider,
Despair details the grey, cadaverous steed,
The immortal image holds its murderer
In a clear gaze for the next age to read.

NIGHTS IN THE GARDENS OF PORT OF SPAIN

Night, the black summer, simplifies her smells
into a village; she assumes the impenetrable
musk of the negro, grows secret as sweat,
her alleys odorous with shucked oyster shells,

coals of gold oranges, braziers of melon.
Commerce and tambourines increase her heat.

Hellfire or the whorehouse: crossing Park Street,
a surf of sailors' faces crests, is gone

with the sea's phosphorescence; the boites-de-nuit
tinkle like fireflies in her thick hair.

Blinded by headlamps, deaf to taxi klaxons,
she lifts her face from the cheap, pitch oil flare

towards white stars, like cities, flashing neon,
burning to be the bitch she must become.

As daylight breaks the coolie turns his tumbril
of hacked, beheaded coconuts towards home.

BLUES

Those five or six young guys
hunched on the stoop
that oven-hot summer night
whistled me over. Nice
and friendly. So, I stop.
MacDougal or Christopher
Street in chains of light.

A summer festival. Or some
saint's . . . I wasn't too far from
home, but not too bright
for a nigger, and not too dark.
I figured we were all

[314]

one, wop, nigger, jew,
besides, this wasn't Central Park.
I'm coming on too strong? You figure
right! They beat this yellow nigger
black and blue.

Yeah. During all this, scared
in case one used a knife,
I hung my olive-green, just bought
sports coat on a fire-plug.
I did nothing. They fought
each other, really. Life
gives them a few kicks,
that's all. The spades, the spicks.

My face smashed in, my bloody mug
pouring, my olive-branch jacket saved
from cuts and tears,
I crawled four flights upstairs.
Sprawled in the gutter, I
remember a few watchers waved
loudly, and one kid's mother shouting
like 'Jackie' or 'Terry,'
'Now that's enough!'
It's nothing really.
They don't get enough love.

You know they wouldn't kill
you. Just playing rough,
like young America will.
Still, it taught me something
about love. If it's so tough,
forget it.

ELEGY

Our hammock swung between Americas,
we miss you, Liberty. Che's
bullet-riddled body falls,
and those who cried the Republic must first die
to be reborn are dead,
the freeborn citizen's ballot in the head.
Still, everybody wants to go to bed

with Miss America. And, if there's no bread,
let them eat cherry pie.

But the old choice of running, howling, wounded
wolf-deep in her woods,
while the white papers snow on
genocide is gone;
no face can hide
its public, private pain,
wincing, already statued.

Some splintered arrowhead lodged in her brain
sets the black singer howling in his bear trap,
shines young eyes with the brightness of the mad,
tires the old with her residual sadness;
and yearly lilacs in her dooryard bloom,
and the cherry orchard's surf
blinds Washington and whispers
to the assassin in his furnished room
of an ideal America, whose flickering screens
show, in slow herds, the ghosts of the Cheyennes
scuffling across the staked and wired plains
with whispering, rag-bound feet,

while the farm couple framed in their Gothic door
like Calvin's saints, waspish, pragmatic, poor,
gripping the devil's pitchfork
stare rigidly towards the immortal wheat.

6 June 1968

From ANOTHER LIFE

The Runner at Sauteurs

I am pounding the faces of gods back into the red clay they
leapt from with the mattock of heel after heel as if heel
after heel were my thumbs that once gouged out as sacred
vessels for women the sockets of eyes, the deaf howl
of their mouths and I have wept less for them dead than I
    did
when they leapt from my thumbs into birth, than my
heels which have never hurt horses that now pound them
back into what they should never have sprung from,

staying un-named and un-praised where I found them—
in the god-breeding, god-devouring earth!
We are ground as the hooves of their horses open the wound
of those widening cliffs and the horns of green branches
    come
lowering past me and the sea's crazed horses the foam
of their whinnying mouths and white mane and the pelting
    red
pepper of flowers that make my eyes water, yet who am I,
    under
such thunder, dear gods, under the heels of the thousand
racing towards the exclamation of their single name,
Sauteurs! Their leap into the light? I am no more
than that lithe dreaming runner beside me, my son, the roar
of his heart, and their hearts, I am one with this engine
which is greater than victory, and their pride
with its beauty of pardon, I am one
with the thousand runners who will break on loud sand
at Thermopylae, one wave that now cresting must bear
down the torch of this race, I am all, I am one
who feels with the thousand now his tendons harden
and the wind-god, Hourucan, combing his hair!

PREPARING FOR EXILE

Why do I imagine the death of Mandelstam
among the yellowing cocoanuts,
why does my gift already look over its crouched shoulder
for a shadow to fill the door,
and pass this very stage into eclipse?
Why does the moon increase into an arclamp
and the inkstain on my hand prepare to press my thumb
    downward
before a shrugging sergeant?
What is this new odour in the air,
that was once salt, that smelt like lime at daybreak,
and my cat, I know I imagine it, leap from my path,
and my children's eyes already seem like horizons,
and all of my poems, even this one, wish to hide?

John Lennon (1940–   ) of The Beatles

NORWEGIAN WOOD

I once had a girl,
or I should say
she once had me.
She showed me her room,
isn't it good?
Norwegian wood.
She asked me to stay
and she told me to sit
anywhere,
so I looked around
and I noticed there
wasn't a chair.
I sat on a rug
biding my time,
drinking her wine.
We talked until two,
and then she said,
"It's time for bed."
She told me she worked
in the morning
and started to laugh,
I told her I didn't,
and crawled off
to sleep in the bath.
And when I awoke
I was alone.
This bird had flown,
so I lit a fire,
Isn't it good?
Norwegian wood.

ELEANOR RIGBY

Ah, look at all the lonely people!
Ah, look at all the lonely people!
Eleanor Rigby, picks up the rice in the church
        where a wedding has been,
            lives in a dream.
Waits at the window, wearing the face
        that she keeps in a jar by the door,
            who is it for?

All the lonely people,
        where do they all come from?
All the lonely people,
        where do they all belong?
Father McKenzie, writing the words of a
        sermon that no one will hear,
            no one comes near.
Look at him working, darning his socks in the
        night when there's nobody there,
            what does he care?

All the lonely people,
        where do they all come from?
All the lonely people,
        where do they all belong?
Ah, look at all the lonely people!
Ah, look at all the lonely people!
Eleanor Rigby, died in the church and was
        buried along with her name,
            nobody came.
Father McKenzie, wiping the dirt from his
        hands as he walks from the grave,
            no one was saved.

All the lonely people,
        where do they all come from?
All the lonely people,
        where do they all belong?

Notes

Beowulf. Some of my learned friends object that linguistically *Beowulf* isn't British (much less English), belonging properly in a Scandinavian anthology; to which my answer is that I choose to be a geographical strict-constructionist who refuses to deprive English-language readers of such a great poem—in such a spirited modern equivalent as Burton Raffel's. It's true that the Old English epic has had no influence on English poets thus far. Now it may. . . .

"The poem," Raffel says in the Introduction to his translation, "was composed in England perhaps four centuries before the Norman Conquest. And this England of roughly the eighth century A.D., as reflected in social patterns ascribed to sixth-century Geats and Danes and Swedes, is rigidly feudal, highly civilized and highly violent, and rather newly Christian. Layers of morality and tenderness and piety are intermixed, in *Beowulf*, with the glorification of war, death, and fame; such humdrum occupations as farming, fishing (except for sport . . .) and the care and feeding of both adults and children are all denigrated, casually, when they are mentioned at all. Slavery is taken for granted . . . Swords have personalities, and names; servants of course have neither."

A Woman's Message. This isn't the best known of the shorter poems in Old English, though it is one of the best. As elsewhere in this anthology (selecting from Byron's *Don Juan*, and so on), when absolute excellence didn't dictate the choice, I chose in accordance with our parallel preoccupations of today—in this case Women's Lib.

Piers the Ploughman. Though some (including this anthologist) would place *Piers* for its universality ahead of *Paradise Lost* and on a par with *The Canterbury Tales*, this "epic" has hardly had more influence on the course of English poetry than *Beowulf*. Even in its own time (and Chaucer's) the old-fashioned West English "dialect" in which it was composed was a barrier to its appreciation except among the "lowly clerks" to whom it was addressed by this reformer who scorned fashion. Consequently the poem's "difficulty" has been so great as to require more than glossaries and notes. Nor has there been, to date, any version in modern English that carries over much of the poetry of the original. Another barrier to its appreciation has been the existence of three separate and quite different texts (the "A," "B" and "C" codices in each of which Langland is said to have had a hand, and each of which contains values not present in the other two). In presenting my own translation of two passages from the poem, I have consulted all three texts, not as an exercise in scholarship but to get closer to Langland's voice. My hope is that eventually some poet, with more scholarly qualifications, will put all of *Piers* into a modern English that begins to do it justice.

For his acute observations while engaged in creating an anatomy of man's fall, Langland has been compared to that retarded medievalist of the Renaissance, Hieronymus Bosch. Acid though he can sometimes be, Langland's art could more nicely be compared to that of the more compassionate Peter Brueghel. The poet's humble, godly peasant confronting a corrupt society and church strikes as timely a note as when the poem was written. The form of the verse, the four-stress accentual measure, heavily alliterated, that had served the *Gawain*-poet so well in brocading his courtly tapestry, became with Langland's flexible approximation of colloquial speech, a utilitarian weapon, sometimes revolutionary, sometimes prophetic.

Sir Gawain and the Green Knight. When English verse came to a crossroads in the fourteenth century, luck ran out for those allegorists of the "alliterative revival" like Langland who didn't follow Chaucer, with his continental education, down the main highway. Even the name of the poet of *Sir Gawain* was lost, even the original title of his poem; and it wasn't until 1839 that the work appeared in print. Yet this is, in our translator's words, "a very great poem, equal to the masterworks of Chaucer, or to the best of the Old English poems, including *Beowulf*. It is different from these other masterpieces, but it is different from everything else in English literature. The *Gawain*-poet can do an incredible number of things in brilliant style. His sensibility is both delicate and powerful, as is his language; he can sing like a choirboy or like an angry blacksmith; he can draw characters so vividly that they breathe; he can paint pictures so vitally that one sees them, almost feels them. He can weave a compelling and tightly organized plot out of disparate and sometimes fragile elements; he can be passionately moral; he can be wickedly comic ... His civilized balance, namely his wit, pervades the entire poem, light, dry, and plainly related to things French."

Geoffrey Chaucer. In Chaucer, as in most major poets from Homer and Langland to Whitman and D. H. Lawrence, the "poetry"—as we in our precious way have come to define it—is a by-product of the message. Shakespeare didn't write *Hamlet* as a vehicle for the dozens of passages of "pure poetry" we have discovered in it; any more than Chaucer, two centuries before, had written his tales with any other end in view than to tell a good story, convey an edifying moral, or depict the saints, sensualists, and hypocrites of his time. It is we who comb the narratives for such "magical" lines as

> Up roos the sonne and up roos Emelye

—and having (inescapably) a latter-day romantic's taste for such things myself, I have complied by including the lovely descriptive passage from "The Knight's Tale" and the still more heavily charged envoi to that first of psychological novels, *Troilus and Creseyde.* But more typical of Chaucer, and just as potent with their profound insights into character, are the longer quotations from the Prologue to *The Canterbury Tales* and the "Wif of Bathe's" gutsy confessional.

All of which is not to imply that Chaucer is the simple-minded conveyor belt of facts and morals he sometimes pretends to be—far from it! No poet speaks simultaneously in more voices, so many overlays of personality and meaning. But that is another way of saying that Chaucer—unlike those incapable of clarity, or wilfully complex—is enjoyable on all his levels. Down the ages from Marlowe to Dylan Thomas sound the same ecstasies, the same despairing questions:

> What is this world? What asketh men to have?
> Now with his love, now in his colde grave
> Allone, with outen any compaignye.

William Dunbar is the first of the great triad of Scots poets, and like the two who followed him—Robert Burns and Hugh MacDiarmid—his humor is whimsical and scurrilous. The time he spent in France as a singing friar gave Dunbar a familiarity with contemporary French styles less bookish than Chaucer's. Villon's famous refrain *"Mais ou sont les neiges d'antan!"* echoes in the baleful Latin reiteration of Dunbar's "Lament for the Makaris." I present it here, along with a shorter poem that anticipates Nashe (see p. 23), in versions Andrew Glaze has done for this anthology. (For those who contend that Dunbar's language needs no modernization, I submit a line from the first poem—

> Of qwham all wichtis hes pete

and challenge the reader to find it. Scholars apart, Dunbar's poetry is "modern" enough to deserve wide reading.)

John Skelton. Henry VIII's tutor—in poetry? piety? ribaldry?—Skelton made it at last to Westminster Abbey; but only because Wolsey, the power-mad churchman he'd lampooned so scathingly, forced him to seek sanctuary there. And there he died, not to be enshrined among the laureates, but forgotten for centuries. Now scholars regard him as a missing link between Chaucer, whom he revered, and the Elizabethans, whose opulent exoticism he anticipated:

> The Indy saphire blew
> Her vainés doth ennew;
> The orient pearl so clere,
> The whitnesse of her lere,
> Resemble the rose buddes;
> Her lippes soft and mery
> Embloméd like the cherry,
> It were an hevenly blisse
> Her sugred mouth to kisse.

But Skelton, though lacking the poise to create a complete world of his own, as Chaucer and Shakespeare, seems by his very lack of balance closer to us. Hardy or Hopkins, E. E. Cummings or Marianne Moore, could have written such lines as the following—or wished they had:

> A man would have pity
> To see how she is gummed,
> Fingered and thumbed
> Gently jointed,
> Greased and anointed
> Up to the knuckles;
> The bones of her huckles . . .
> With a whim-wham
> Knit with a trim-tram
> Upon her brain-pan
> Like an Egyptian . . .

Sir Thomas Wyatt. Skelton's younger contemporary—and Anne Boleyn's lover before she married Henry—Wyatt had entered Cambridge at thirteen and at twenty-five been sent to Italy as an ambassador. Bringing back with him Petrarch's sonnets in translation, he gave British poetry at the dawn of the Elizabethan Age a much-needed transfusion. In his skilled hands (and those of his equally gifted friend Henry Howard, Earl of Surrey, who invented blank verse in his bouts with Vergil) the English lyric, hitherto the property of shepherds and street singers, became an art form subtle enough for introspection:

> Forsake me not till I deserve,
> Nor hate me not till I offend;
> Destroy me not till that I swerve;
> But since ye know what I intend,
> Forsake me not ...

Sir Philip Sidney. Sidney's life is more interesting than his poetry. In his thirty-two years he seems to have met everyone of consequence in Europe—and been esteemed by most of them. He witnessed the St. Bartholemew Day's Massacre, sat to Veronese for his portrait and died memorably at the siege of Zutphen. That he had time for poetry at all is remarkable; that the poetry has a dilettantish ring was inevitable. Yet how many professionals have given the world even a handful of sonnets that still are read after five hundred years? or an *Apologie for Poetrie* that is recast every generation?

Sir Walter Ralegh. As complete a Renaissance man as Sidney, Ralegh's personality was less winning. His talent for poetry was greater, but he treated it more cavalierly. The first stanza of the poem I include is worthy of Shakespeare; the second is all clichés. Ralegh—like certain modern poets with life styles as flamboyant—was too busy nurturing his "image" to sustain a poem of even moderate length.

Edmund Spenser. Ever since *The Faerie Queene*'s first three books were published in 1590 (and dedicated to Elizabeth lest she miss the point), Spenser has been considered a major poet. Will the verdict be reversed in our century?—or has this anthologist a blind spot? Perhaps we don't have *time* anymore for this poet's perpetual slow motion. Hazlitt, in the Romantic heyday when Spenser's influence was huge, felt it necessary to reassure readers that even if the ponderous allegorical machinery of Spenser's pastoral epic did indeed exist, it wouldn't bite. Loaded with voluptuous sensuality, but unleavened with an iota of passion or humor, *The Faerie Queene* is consistently dull.

John Lyly. To have given such unlike poets as Shakespeare

and T. S. Eliot two of their famous lines, as Lyly has in the lyric we quote, salvages his reputation from the invidious distinction of having created Euphues, for centuries a synonym for poetic claptrap.

Fulke Greville, Lord Brooke. The poem as puzzle: This particular one with its Oedipal theme seemed to require a Freudian key, until I laid it before Stanley Kunitz who said No. Not wholly convinced, I defer to his better judgement, and present his paraphrase: The child being buried is Merlin's brother. Merlin, being supernatural, disclaims identification with his natural brother. So his unnatural laughter is natural . . . naturally!

Chidiock Tichborne. If ever a poem was written in blood, it was this one, composed in the Tower the night before the poet was disemboweled and then executed, on Elizabeth's orders. Had he been less of a fanatical conspirator for the glory and honor of his Church, Tichborne might have become a famous poet, but he would not have written this immortal poem.

Robert Greene. Had he not written a few deceptively simple and innocent songs like the one selected here, Greene would be known only as the most vindictive pamphleteer of his time, and the man who tried to exorcise Shakespeare's near monopoly of the stage by accusing him of plagiarism. The thinly veiled allusion in one of Greene's pamphlets is to "an upstart crow beautified with our feathers that with his Tygres heart wrapt in a players hyde, supposes he is as well able to bombast out a blanke-verse as the best of you; and being an absolute Iohannes-fac-totum is in his owne conseyt the onely shake-scene in a countrey."

Robert Southwell. Like Tichborne, Southwell was another Elizabethan who found time in a short life (most of it spent preparing to be a Jesuit martyr) to write one memorable poem. Though Southwell was tortured for three years before they finally hung him, the doctrine of guilt by association had not yet been invented: Ben Jonson did not hesitate to say that he would have sacrificed his best lines to have written "The Burning Babe."

Mark Alexander Boyd. My only source for this poem is Sir Arthur Quiller-Couch's *The Oxford Book of English Verse* (1900 edition) and I can find no reference to its author in any other of my books, including *The Encyclopædia Britannica.*

Christopher Marlowe. With the true innovator's arrogance, Marlowe announced his breakthrough in the opening blast of his first play:

From jigging veins of riming mother wits
And such conceits as clownage keeps in pay
We'll lead you to the stately tent of war,
Where you shall hear the Scythian Tamburlaine
Threatening the world with high astounding terms
And scourging kingdoms with his conquering sword.

With six of his twenty-nine years still to live, Marlowe had time for four more plays and a dozen lyrics that fulfilled the promise of his undergraduate translation of Ovid's *Amores*. Cut down in a tavern brawl he himself provoked, Marlowe had done as much as he would probably ever do. Swinburne, for once, wasn't exaggerating when he said: "He is the greatest discoverer, the most daring and inspired pioneer, in all our poetic literature. Before him there was neither genuine blank verse nor a genuine tragedy in our language. After his arrival the way was prepared, the paths were made straight, for Shakespeare."

William Shakespeare. Part of the explanation for Shakespeare's preeminence among the world's poets (see Introduction) lies in the fluid nature of Elizabethan society. As a drinking and wenching companion of the likes of Nashe, Greene and Marlowe, Shakespeare with his middle-class country background could be as intimate with the metropolitan underworld of his time as with the court dandies who were his patrons—and share the enthusiasm of all three classes for the monarchy's aggressive imperialism. Compared with him, major poets like Racine, Milton and Goethe, led sheltered lives. Only Pushkin was to have a remotely comparable experience to draw upon; and Villon—who was too busy evading the police to have time to write much.

It has been said that Shakespeare, unlike his educated contemporaries—all three of the rowdy Elizabethans mentioned above had university educations—worked from the particulars of his experience to generalization. Marlowe, for all his genius, was a windbag. But there have been other self-taught poets, many of whom took refuge in a defiant rusticity or proletarian pride, and none of whom achieved Shakespeare's encompassing humanity. The mystery, like the mystery of life itself, remains. Only another Shakespeare will hold the key to it.

Thomas Nashe. Pamphleteer and polemicist extraordinary, Nashe has been called a journalist born before journalism. His "brilliant and picturesque style," he was careful to explain, "was entirely original." No doubt Nashe would have been mildly surprised (or contemptuously indifferent) to know that his fame rests on a single magical poem—a spin-off, as we'd put it, of the autumn of 1592 spent at Croydon to avoid the plague. I came to it most roundaboutly myself in 1929, an undergraduate electrified by the line "Brightnesse falls from the air" as quoted in a smuggled chapter of Joyce's *Ulysses*.

Sir John Davies. I came upon the author of "Nosce Teipsum" and "Orchestra" as inadvertently in the 1950s, intrigued by the enthusiasm with which Theodore Roethke and Stanley Kunitz spoke of this esoteric poet. They in turn, no doubt, had been alerted by T. S. Eliot who as far back as 1926 had praised Davies for having "that strange gift, so rarely bestowed, for turning thought into feeling" and for converting scientific-philosophical speculation into poetry without ever resorting to "hyperbole or bombast."

Ben Jonson. Jonson was the first substantial poet to be sunk by the sheer weight of his intellect. The plays, for which the seventeenth and eighteenth centuries revered him high above Shakespeare, have become unreadable—and unplayable without monstrous cutting and horseplay. Only when off guard, as in the heartbreaking reaction to his son's death, or in the "blurb" to the folio edition of Shakespeare (whose transcendant genius Jonson alone among Elizabethans sensed) or in a half-dozen occasional lyrics, does this come back to life. Can one help harboring the treasonable suspicion that the great intellectual poet of *our* age may survive for his charming children's verses about cats?

John Donne. As formidable an intellect as Jonson and Eliot, Donne at his best escapes their stuffiness by sheer passion. No matter what labored conceits and games of wit his ecclesiastical schoolman's brain obliges him to indulge in, his basic sensuality overcomes—and in overcoming provides the tension, the counterpoint, and finally (in the matchless religious sonnets of his old age) the mystical resolution that will not be heard so piercingly again until Blake and Yeats give English poetry their terminal commitments.

Cyril Tourneur and *John Webster*. Saintsbury called Webster and Tourneur the "nightshades" of the Elizabethan Age, and Eliot was guilty of understatement when he found Webster "much possessed by death." Like Shakespeare, Webster had no "higher" education, and like him alone could turn from the most exquisite lyricism to dialogues of thunderous invective without breaking step. But tragedy had given way to dramas of horror for its own sake. Kyd's stock villains, discarded by Shakespeare, were reborn in Tourneur and act out their bloody revenges with repulsive singlemindedness—and high poetry.

Francis Beaumont. A child prodigy (he came up to Oxford at twelve), Beaumont found time enough in his thirty years of life to collaborate on at least sixteen plays and (according to Dryden) give Ben Jonson the plots and final touch-ups for most of his. The melancholy admonition of the poem selected here is typical of the epoch the Beaumont–Fletcher dramas rang out.

William Drummond of Hawthornden. Drummond is another one-poem man, his refrain "Repent! Repent!" ringing down the ages to our guilt-ridden time. A rustic solitary who felt no need to make the Elizabethan scene in London, he is justly famous for having entertained the crusty Ben Jonson, during the latter's Scotch junket, and out of that encounter written the first catch-as-catch-can interview with a man of letters.

Robert Herrick. Least complicated and most endearing of the late Elizabethans, Herrick feels no compulsion to lay bare his soul, conceal his motives or anatomize society. Nor is there any reason to suppose that he would have responded with other than a goodhearted laugh to posterity's verdict regarding the price paid for his attitude: superficiality. Like many of his contemporaries, including Donne, he was indifferent to seeing his verses printed in his lifetime. It wasn't until 1810, in fact, that Herrick's lyrical genius became known at all. Time enough, one can hear him saying; and without a smirk. His philosophy—"gather ye rosebuds while ye may"—came back into fashion with our flower children.

William Browne. Another pastoral poet of the transitional Jacobean-Caroline period, Browne of Tavistock is justly renowned for the lines quoted here, the most felicitous of epitaphs.

Henry King, Bishop of Chichester. It was a time when even kings (Henry VIII), statesmen (Sidney, Marvell) and churchmen (Bishop Corbett of Oxford) were accomplished poets, but King was unique among them for making his private grief still touch us.

George Herbert. Had he written only one poem, "The Collar," Herbert would tower among his contemporaries, close to Donne; yet he wrote a dozen, and choosing among them is difficult. His love for God and for the Anglican church and for his flock at Little Gidding and Bemerton was transparent. But had he not felt challenged to express these multiple devotions through the "metaphysical" style of Donne and his other learned friends at the court of his patron, James I, *and to do so with a simplicity mirroring his nature,* he would not have been so fine a poet.

Thomas Carew. Another friend of Jonson and Donne, Carew is one more poet of a century overbrimming with splendid poets (Drayton and Campion among those I arbitrarily excluded). This poem, because its joy gives so much joy, because its style was revivified so engagingly by Richard Eberhart ("Now is the air filled with chiming balls . . .") and because it is so English, I can't exclude.

James Shirley. Still another late Elizabethan? How could any anthologist pass up this three-stanza powerhouse? Carl Sandburg, evidently, couldn't.

"Tom O'Bedlam's Song." Shakespeare himself has been suggested as the author of this mad song, so inspired is its imagery. If a true Bedlamite wrote it, the theory that a thin line separates genius and madness is reinforced.

Edmund Waller. Waller, with Denham and Davenant, is generally credited with having refined and popularized the heroic couplet, soon to be perfected by Dryden. He was as renowned in his time for the speed with which he could change political allegiances. His literary precepts and his lyrical gift, which inspired Henry Lawes' music, are exemplified by the two poems selected here.

William Davenant. England's second poet laureate (Jonson was the first) was by legend Shakespeare's illegitimate son. Another legend has it that the royalist poet was saved from Cromwell's wrath by Milton. If so, Davenant paid the debt quickly, interceding for Milton after the restoration of Charles II. Davenant's once-popular plays, like his rewrites of Shakespeare's, are forgotten, but his innovations in changing scenery and replacing boys with women in women's roles, greatly increased the theater's popularity.

John Milton. A measure of Milton's stature is that he is still a controversial figure after four hundred years. Those who admire his poetry place him second only to Shakespeare; those who detest it (and the man) would hardly dare omit him from the first five. He is controversial because his poetry—austere, inhuman and humorless—"says nothing," at least nothing "relevant" to us; and because its influence has been consistently counterproductive. Those who followed him, like those who followed the other great baroque artist of the time, Michelangelo, were bogged down in his gigantism, mannerisms and religiosity. Centuries later, T. S. Eliot, while conceding Milton's greatness reluctantly, felt obliged to write two essays warning young poets to steer clear of his siren music.

No such reluctance or fear is operative here. Let poets, young or old, steer where they list! Who cares whether Milton's "artificial" and "eccentric" style places the "syntax" and the language itself in peril, as Eliot argues; that it "illustrates no general principles of good writing" and is the antithesis of the colloquial? If our first test of poetry is that it generate pleasure or ecstasy, Milton passes triumphantly; to ask him additionally to be a Blake or a D. H. Lawrence is ridiculous.

"Lycidas," the masterpiece of Milton's first period (his twenties), not only establishes a grand manner out of the accumulated conventions of the period; it establishes a way of describing nature ("What time the Gray-fly winds her sultry horn," and the like) for poets like Collins and Gray still unborn. What is also immediately apparent, however, is that Milton has discovered a way of *sustaining* poetry, over a long paragraph, that no poet until Keats (in the Odes) will ever approach.

It is this long-windedness, perhaps, that makes Milton's best sonnets more tightly structured and compelling than Shakespeare's; and that ennables *Paradise Lost*, by sheer, sustained, verbal hypnosis, to overcome its deficient plot and implausible content. The last successful epic of the western world, *Paradise Lost* is like none of its predecessors. It is, for all its proclaimed intentions and cumbersome machinery, a poem of introspection. All the neuroses generated in Milton by his unhappy childhood, his disastrous marriages, the fifteen years of his prime spent wielding a poison pen for Cromwell and his resultant blindness here body forth unconsciously in the portrait of Satan as individualist, superman, and archrebel against the whole miserable pattern of life and death imposed on Man.

Translators of the King James Bible. No other time but Shakespeare's could have produced such a work of collective genius because no other time produced poets, major and minor, with such profusion. Every attempt to improve on it has been pathetic—so much so that one may be forgiven the suspicion that the original was poorer than what James' scholar poets came up with. I am indebted to an old friend, the late Ernest Sutherland Bates, for his breakdown of the text (*The Bible Designed to be Read as Living Literature*) into something approximating its original wave lengths.

Richard Crashaw. "We learn something about Herbert," Eliot says, "by comparing the typical Anglican devotion which he expresses, with the more continental, and Roman, religious feeling of his contemporary Richard Crashaw." Crashaw's fancy language and uninhibited emotionalism (hysteria, some would call it) are currently the more popular. In deference to A. Alvarez, the best of modern critics, I quote from the second poem.

Abraham Cowley. Who now reads Cowley? The question would have been unthinkable in the mid-seventeenth century when he ruled the poetic roost. But Cowley is worth reading in small draughts. Nor is it desparaging him to suggest that his paraphrase of Anacreon is closer in spirit to FitzGerald's "Omar Khayyam" (see pp. 211–13) than to the Greek poet.

Richard Lovelace. Again I express my indebtedness to A. Alvarez, this time for calling my attention to a poem I was not familiar with, "La Bella Bona Roba." "The impetus behind it," Alvarez writes, "which imparts that extraordinarily disturbed rhythm to the opening stanza, is not a mere preference for fat women; it is instead the shock of being reminded of death, of seeing the skeleton at the moment of sexual attraction. The real poem, in fact, is over by the end of the first stanza when Lovelace counteracts this shock with an almost aggressive attitude of defense ... He uses his wit, in fact, to preserve his balance, not to help him toward some new resolution ... Instead of the drive of Donne's full, difficult, logical honesty, the courtiers seemed to value above all the accomplishment with which their knowledge and ingenuity were used so easily and precisely, the delicacy with which they balanced their arguments and examples" (*The School of Donne*).

Andrew Marvell. The perfection of such a poem as "To His Coy Mistress," with its famous warning of nothingness ahead, has long been appreciated. Less well known is the political poem to Cromwell, though it, too, contains a much-quoted stanza. And less well known still—but too multidimensional to quote from coherently—is "Upon Appleton House," which the American critic Richard Poirier calls "one of the most remarkably neglected masterpieces" in English literature.

Henry Vaughan. Vaughan, and his more philosophical contemporary Thomas Traherne, whose poems lay dormant until this century, anticipated Wordsworth. Only compare "The Retreate" with the more celebrated "Ode" (p. 168–74). The child is father to the man, indeed; Vaughan not only said it sooner but better. In the more mystical poem we select there is a hint of that intimacy with God and the Universe which Emily Dickinson was to express.

John Dryden. In his own time, Dryden's preeminence as poet, dramatist and critic was unquestioned; the Romantics and Victorians ignored him; but in our century interest revived, thanks to a cogent "Homage" by T. S. Eliot. Failing to share Eliot's enthusiasm, I defer to the contemporary consensus, presenting Dryden at his satirical best, and in a stately masque with an ever-prophetic ending—the last a suggestion from Derek Walcott.

John Wilmot, Earl of Rochester. The profligate Restoration found its most outspoken poet in Rochester, whose wit matched his cynicism. It was as gentleman of the bedchamber to Charles II that Rochester prepared his devastating epitaph to his patron—and his pronouncement that "Women, Politics, and Drinking" were "the only important businesses of the age." As late as 1926 his collected poems were banned from the United States by the censor.

George Berkeley, Bishop of Cloyne. These optimistic stanzas by the philosopher, who spent three years in Rhode Island fifty years before the American Revolution, may have an ironical ring today—except to those like Jean-François Revel and this anthologist who see the American Revolution hopefully as a recurrent phenomenon.

Alexander Pope. Pope carried the Rational Enlightenment to heights of balance, wit, refinement and malice undreamed of by even Dryden. Again there was a modern revival, in Pope's case at the hands of Edith Sitwell, but it was as short-lived as Dryden's.

Thomas Gray and *William Collins.* Transitional poets between the Rational and Romantic periods, one, Collins; struck a new note in his slim volume of *Odes* (1746) which must have seemed revolutionary indeed. The one printed here not only dispensed with rhyme entirely, but got back to basics in its quiet, richly melancholy, observation of nature—an astonishing stylistic bridge between *Lycidas* and the *Ode to a Nightingale.*

Whether Gray's "Elegy," which this diffident aristocrat circulated among friends four years later, owed anything to Collins, it was written in the same spirit and with as much genius—differing only in the extraordinary capacity that Gray had for epigrammatic, quotable and unforgettable resolutions, a capacity that has given the poem its deserved reputation as "the most famous in the language."

Christopher Smart. Eliot calls Oliver Goldsmith and Samuel Johnson "major poets," but compared with Christopher Smart, they are journeymen of the trade. Johnson, however incapable he was of recognizing Smart's genius, was an honest enough observer to appreciate his sincerity. Visiting him in the insane asylum to which he was twice confined for his debts, his drinking and his religious nonconformity, the good

Doctor pronounced Smart not "noxious" to society: "He insists on people praying with him—also falling on his knees and praying in the street—but I'd as lief pray with Kit Smart as anyone else." Ever since Browning rediscovered "A Song of David" and incorporated its author in one of his dialogues, Smart has been considered the author of this one poem. I present a shorter one that rises in its concluding stanzas to as dizzying a poetic peak, and a characteristic extract from the rambling, surrealistic *Jubilate Agno* which deserves to be better known than for its charming description of the poet's cat. In all three poems, Smart anticipates (though without his social-psychological insights) Blake, touching the summits of visionary rhetoric and the depths of incoherent nonsense.

Thomas Chatterton. Keats' "marvellous boy" and the Romantic prototype of the unappreciated poet in his teens who starves in a garret and finally commits suicide, Chatterton from his tenth year on, wrote poems which he deliberately "antiqued" in the hope of getting them published as fragments from a manuscript of the reign of Henry VI. This poet's end was tragic indeed, for he was greatly gifted. Though buried in a potter's field, he had written his own epitaph on his deathbed:

> Farewell, Bristolia's dingy piles of brick,
> Lovers of Mammon, worshipers of trick!
> Ye spurned the boy who gave you antique lays,
> And paid for learning with your empty praise.
> Farewell, ye guzzling aldermanic fools,
> By nature fitted for corruption's tools!
> I go to where celestial anthems swell;
> But you, when you depart, will sink to hell.
> Farewell, my mother!—cease, my anguished soul,
> Nor let distraction's billows o'er me roll!
> Have mercy, Heaven! when here I cease to live,
> And this last act of wretchedness forgive.

George Crabbe. The word "crabbed" does not derive from the poet's name, but it might be thought to. He was the last clergyman to write important poetry, and the grim realism with which he described village life was a needful corrective to the saccharine idiocy of Goldsmith's "Sweet Auburn, loveliest village of the plain,/Where health and plenty cheered the labouring swain." Concomitantly, Crabbe could vie with Wordsworth for having written the *worst* lines in English:

> Something had happen'd wrong about a bill
> Which was not drawn with true mercantile skill;
> So, to amend it, I was told to go
> And seek the firm of Clutterbuck and Co.

The best tribute to Crabbe was paid him by the American poet E. A. Robinson:

> ... Whether or not we read him, we can feel
> From time to time the vigor of his name
> Against us like a finger for the shame
> And emptiness of what our souls reveal
> In books that are as altars where we kneel
> To consecrate the flicker, not the flame.

William Blake. So completely is Blake's greatness an axiom among poets of the twentieth century that it is necessary to remind ourselves that most of his contemporaries (if they had heard of the unpublished poet at all) considered him a nut too harmless to confine behind bars. Yet everything we know about Blake in his life of obscure neglect, prodigious industry and passion for revolutionary change—he and his wife Catherine were discovered stark naked in their arbor one day reading *Paradise Lost* to each other—makes him seem the progenitor of our wildest gropings for primordial health. Auden goes so far as to say that "The whole of Freud's teachings may be found in 'The Marriage of Heaven and Hell.'" As painter and engraver (self-taught as in everything), Blake towers above any other English artist and close to Michelangelo, his model. His "pure" lyric poems are not surpassed by the greatest of the Elizabethan singers, and his "impure" ones (like "The Garden of Love") could as easily have been written by John Donne or D. H. Lawrence, and no others. Were this anthologist pressed to isolate the most mysteriously exciting poem in the language and the single *line* he would most wish to have written, he would have to choose "To the Accuser Who is the God of This World" and its final seven words.

Robert Burns. The editor of the particular edition of Burns' collected poems I have does not hesitate to rank him next to Shakespeare among English poets. Perhaps one would have to be a lifelong Burnsian (or Scots nationalist) to make so high a claim. For one thing, the dialect in which most of the best poems are written is a barrier. And for another, a very large proportion of the lyrics are doggerel, or close to it. Yet the claim is not entirely absurd. Burns, in *dozens* of short poems, displays a gift for pure song as spontaneous as any poet's. And in the humanity, compassion and humor of his work as a whole only Shakespeare and Chaucer are his equals. Omitted entirely from all the collected editions are the "pornographic" poems, further evidence of this poet's health and universality. For the text of the one I include I am indebted to Burns' latest and most sympathetic biographer, Robert T. Fitzhugh (*Robert Burns: The Man & the Poet*).

William Wordsworth. Were it not for the sonnets included here, and as many short lyrics, I would be hard pressed to comprehend Wordsworth's immense reputation. His prestige as an innovator of colloquial (?!) nature poetry seems to be based on his own evaluation in the preface to *Lyrical Ballads*. The long poems ("The Excursion" and "The Prelude") are as excruciatingly dull as Byron pronounced the first to be when it fell limply from the presses. Even the famous "Ode"— which I dutifully include, but not without feelings of guilt—is pompously inflated. More than likely I have never gotten over the prejudice instilled in me by the invocation to "Don Juan," which, as a schoolboy, made me howl with delight before I'd read more than a line or two of the hapless victim's verse—nor failed to respond emotionally to Browning's later distaste for the French Revolutionary turned Tory:

> Just for a handful of silver he left us,
> Just for a riband to stick in his coat—

Samuel Taylor Coleridge. Coleridge, for coauthoring the *Lyrical Ballads* manifesto, came in for an equal share of Byron's derision. The shorter "philosophical" poems, sampled in "Limbo" and "Constancy to an Ideal Object," are original enough. But the three "magical" poems included are pure inspiration, raising the question (not successfully answered in a whole library of speculation and detective work) why Coleridge never again let himself go in the thirty remaining years of his life.

Walter Savage Landor. With a long life spanning the entire Romantic period and most of the Victorian as well, Landor was as cantankerous, irascible and disorderly in his private life ("My God!" he exclaimed, throwing his cook out a window, "I forgot about the violets!") as he was cool, classical and restrained in his accomplished verse. I am indebted to Auden for the uncharacteristic but charming one included in this book.

George Gordon, Lord Byron. The spectacular and scandalous nature of Byron's life has always interfered with a just evaluation of his poetry. Adulation received for it during his lifetime—he was by far the best-selling and most publicized poet in history—was for the wrong reasons. People who identified with Byron for his revolutionary rhetoric, for his lack of sexual inhibitions, or simply because he had a handsome face, a twisted foot, an athletic body, a bitchy wife and more lovers (male and female) than he could cope with, read *Childe Harold* and its attendant romances about pirates and incestuous supermen because it gave them a *frisson* to recognize Byron's thinly veiled heroes and thrill vicariously to their persecution by the Establishment. The narratives were put together with great verve but are shoddy; the plays, and most of the occasional lyrics, were no better. But Byron, who had launched his career with a savage attack on the reviewers who had scornfully dismissed his schoolboy verses, rediscovered his *métier* at the end in *Don Juan*. Both as a vehicle for his brilliant wit and social satire, and as an essay in self-portraiture through which he managed at last to laugh at himself, *Don Juan,* in its rambling *ottava rima* stanzas adapted from Pulci, was (and is) inimitable.

Percy Bysshe Shelley. At eighteen, I could not have been convinced that greater lyrics had been written than "Music when soft voices die," "When the lamp is shattered" or "The Indian Serenade." At twenty I gloried in the "difficulties" of "Epipsychidion," "The Sensitive Plant" and "The Triumph of Life." And at twenty-one (with tears in my eyes) I recited whole stanzas from "Adonais" at Keats' grave. Ten years later, I found the lyrics insipid, the intellectual poems pretentious and the elegy frigid. Today I wouldn't be quite so cavalier in dismissal of any of these poems, but discovery of the earlier *political* poems of Shelley (which I found unreadable in adolescence) has convinced me anew of Shelley's stature. Let anyone read these thrilling indictments of heartlessness in high office and the oncoming urban nightmare and still call Shelley (was it Arnold who did?) "an ineffectual angel beating his luminous wings in the void"!

Have we outgrown the "mature" Shelley? Is the loss ours? Or is Shelley a poet for all seasons? I include "Ode to the West Wind" in nostalgia, and because its controlled hurricane of words still surprises me.

John Clare. Clare's tragic life has the sound of an early Marxian text. Child of illiterate parents, he worked in the fields from an early age, educated himself and wrote quiet contemplative verses patterned after Thompson's "Seasons." Discovered and exploited by a miserly publisher, he was a season's sensation in the drawing rooms of the aristocracy. Tiring of his rustic ways, the jaded reading public as quickly dropped him. Overworked and ill, he married, fathered nine children whom he couldn't support, drank heavily and finally became insane. At a performance of *The Merchant of Venice* he attempted to attack Shylock. Escaping from a sanatorium, he described the journey home: "I satisfied my hunger by eating the grass by the roadside which seemed to taste something like bread." Put away for good, he continued to write his gentle poems by the thousands. None of them mirrored his fate or cried out against society. If they had, he might have retained his sanity.

John Keats, whose far shorter life was as tragic as Clare's, was made of sterner stuff. The legend, perpetuated by Byron in "Don Juan," that he was "snuffed out by an article" was not true. No poet, at the age of twenty-five, had ever created such a monument of enduring poems, and when he knew that he was fated to spend his twenty-sixth and last year bedridden, impoverished, and unrecognized, Keats spent none of it in self-pity. The proof that he was conscious of his achievement is in the letters to his friends, which say more about the creative process than any poet has ever said, and are unmatched in the English language. Only in his last poem, the fragment of "Hyperion" from which I quote a passage, is there a hint of bitterness and rebellion against the crowning injustice of mortality itself.

Thomas Lovell Beddoes. Whether Beddoes was a late-Elizabethan, as he tried to be and as some thought he was, born out of his time, or whether he was simply a hopelessly sick human being—incapable of "adjusting" to his time, his country, his sex—no longer matters. The archaic dramas of bloody revenge—for the slighting of which he tried to burn down Drury Lane Theatre—may be anachronistic curiosities with motivations more clinical than human, but the songs they contain are (to borrow Yeats' phrase) barbarous with beauty.

Tennyson, FitzGerald, and the Brownings. Twenty-eight years after his dear wife, the more celebrated poet of the two, had died, Robert Browning opened a book and came upon a just-published letter written in that bygone day by Edward FitzGerald, "translator" of Omar Khayyam's hymn to hedonism. FitzGerald had also (in the Victorian phrase) passed away, but in his private letter he had had the temerity to say "Mrs. Browning's death is rather a relief to me, I must say. No more *Aurora Leighs,* thank God." Whereupon Browning sat down, and in a fury composed one of his last, shortest and simplest poems:

> I chanced upon a new book yesterday;
> I opened it; and where my finger lay
> 'Twixt page and uncut page, these words I read—
> Some six or seven at most—and learned thereby
> That you, FitzGerald, whom by ear and eye
> She never knew, thanked God my wife was dead.
> Ay, dead, and were yourself alive, good Fitz,
> How to return you thanks would task my wits.
> Kicking you seems the common lot of curs,
> While more appropriate greeting lends you grace;
> Surely, to spit there glorifies your face—
> Spitting—from lips once sanctified by hers.

Thomas Hardy would consider it "the greatest mystery of the Nineteenth Century" that Browning, for all the subtlety of his genius, should have "the philosophy of a grocery clerk." Yet is Browning's optimism—his search for some justification or meaning in the lives of the most evil of men— further from Shakespeare's objectivity than Hardy's pessimism?

Tennyson, Victoria's beloved Laureate, when he had plowed through the 5800 lines of the densest of Browning's character studies, made the only witty observation he is credited with: The first line ("Who will, may hear Sordello's story told") and the last ("Who would, has heard Sordello's story told.") were the only two he comprehended—and both were lies.

It was from the high seriousness of Elizabeth Barrett's feminist conscience, Tennyson's melifluous respectability, and Browning's strenuous optimism, that the Victorians turned in relief to FitzGerald's pagan hymn of *dolce far niente*. The poems of FitzGerald and Elizabeth Barrett survive as little more than curiosities and Tennyson's only by virtue of their melancholy music and technical brilliance. Browning, for all his grotesqueries and backslapping, is a major poet whose verse could become influential again. Robert Frost ("Two Tramps in Mud-Time") is not likely to be the last to build creatively on this foundation.

Emily Brontë. The genius of Emily Brontë never bodies forth convincingly in her poetry as it does in *Wuthering Heights*. It may be doubted, in fact, that the poems would be remembered at all were it not for the waves still pulsing out from that depth-charge of a novel. "Remembrance" is memorable mainly for its opening stanza; "Last Lines" for what it tells us of its author's courage.

Arthur Hugh Clough. This troubled Victorian, from whom so much was expected, is remembered best for his "Say not the struggle naught availeth," which Churchill quoted during the Battle of Britain. But Clough was a novelist *manqué* whose rambling *Amours de Voyage*, first printed in the American *Atlantic Monthly* and then forgotten, probed such taboos of the time as married love and patriotism with surgical precision. His genius, as Alvarez writes *(Beyond All This Fiddle)*, "was to see that, whatever pressure to conform his age and friends exerted on him, his unique brand of touchy, choosy sophistication couldn't be expressed in the language of mid-nineteenth-century romanticism." Readers will detect a resemblance to the style Eliot developed out of Laforgue in the passages selected here.

Matthew Arnold. There is a stanza in "Thyrsis," Arnold's memorial poem to Clough, that has been called *(English Poetry: A Short History* by Kenneth Hopkins) a magical glimpse of England's beauty hardly matched "in the whole range of English poetry":

> Too quick despairer, wherefore wilt thou go?
> Soon will the high Midsummer pomps come on,
> Soon will the musk carnations break and swell,
> Soon shall we have gold-dusted snapdragon,
> Sweet-William with its homely cottage smell,
> And stocks in fragrant blow;
> Roses that down the alleys shine afar,
> And open jasmine-muffled lattices,
> And groups, under the dreaming garden-trees,
> And the full moon, and the white evening-star.

The stanza is beautiful, but compared with its models (Keats' "Autumn," and further back Milton's "Lycidas") it sounds like a seed catalogue; it was too late for this kind of voluptuous pastoral. What Arnold did better—and better than anyone—was to anticipate (without desiring it) the breakdown from within of the imperial order with its smug certainties. "Dover Beach" did that unforgettably.

Dante Gabriel Rossetti and *Christina Rossetti.* The best of Rossetti is in his sonnet sequence, "The House of Life," rather than in the more famous "The Blessed Damozel," a typically pre-Raphaelite fantasy; but Rossetti's unhappy sister, Christina, understood better than he did the unsubstantial nature of the love he was celebrating—witness her "In an Artist's Studio."

George Meredith. Meredith's famous sonnet sequence, "Modern Love," hangs on in the Age of Freud more credibly than Rossetti's. If only because loveless and hateful marriages, like Meredith's, have become a staple of our century. The theme holds our interest as the first serious treatment of its kind; yet it is the poetry, in the last analysis, rather than the novelist's insights, that gives "Modern Love" its persistent readability.

Lewis Carroll and *Edward Lear.* Glories of English poetry unmatched, to my knowledge, in any other poetry, are Lear and Carroll—and to an only slightly lesser degree W. S. Gilbert and Hilaire Belloc, who followed them. Nonsense verse, which they took over from nurse- and folk-rhyme, treating it with great sophistication, can be pure invention, like "Jabberwocky" with its portmanteau words that are now common currency, or parody, like "Uncle Arly" which burlesques Wordsworth's sentimental "Leech-Gatherer." Both poets anticipate surrealism, with their patent-medicine signs anchoring dream landscapes. But to read Sophoclean, Shakespearean and Freudian symbolism into Lear, as Robert Graves does, is to turn works of art into case histories.

William Morris. Hopkins, in his history of English poetry already alluded to, points out that the generation of painter poets that included Rossetti and Morris was the same generation that had "discovered" Keats with his richly tapestried "The Eve of St. Agnes" and neomedieval "La Belle Dame Sans Merci." The influence extended into Tennyson and Swinburne (Browning was a Shelleyite), but Morris' narratives of knights and damsels display real people with hangups common to every generation, not puppets in a Victorian morality like Tennyson's. The poetry has a cutting edge.

Algernon Charles Swinburne. In the latest biography of Swinburne (Jean Overton Fuller's) there appear some suppressed lines by the poet on his childhood trips to the flogging block at Eton. What a poet Swinburne might have been had he not felt obliged by Victorian-Edwardian convention to sublimate such scarifying thoughts in classical doubletalk! Miss Fuller also quotes Swinburne's parody of himself—evidence that the poet was all too aware of his weakness for alliterative singsong:

Pallid and pink as the pal of the flag-flower that
flickers with fear of the flies as they float,

Are the looks from our lovers that lustrously lean from
    a marvel of mystic miraculous moonshine,
These that we feel in the blood of our blushes that
    thicken and threaten with throbs through the throat.

Thomas Hardy. Hardy, oddly, admired Swinburne and
wrote a moving elegy upon his death. Oddly, because Hardy's
poetry is everything that Swinburne's was not: crusty,
gnarled, unmellifluous, eccentric, humorous, profound—in a
word, major. They do, however, share one fault in common—
both wrote too much, seeming to have no sense of what to
delete. Of Hardy's 766 collected poems (not including *The
Dynasts* in three volumes) perhaps a hundred are memorable
and ten to twenty first-rate. That's still a larger number of
first-rate poems than most poets ever write—but what a task
to find them! Hardy's grand theme, like that of his novels, the
best of which are major too, is of man lost and afraid in a
hostile universe. Social convention and hypocrisy are this
man's miserable defenses, with God standing off to one side,
indifferent but amused. Hardy speaks sometimes in the voice
of this frigid Creator, but more often with his own brand of
compassion. The poetry derives from the curiosity that im-
pelled the retired novelist in his country cottage to fashion a
new language in which to house the world he alone saw and
understood.

Gerard Manley Hopkins. Hopkins is the only post-Roman-
tic Nineteenth Century poet of Hardy's stature, but the world
of Hopkins (enclosed by a monastery's walls) is narrower,
and the language he invented with so much originality is too
specialized to reach much beyond other poets and religious
mystics. What a language it is, though! Going back to Langland for its alliterative "sprung rhythm" and to Donne for
its "metaphysical" fusion of the sensual and the religious,
Hopkins through this precision instrument of the intellect
truly "unlocks his heart" as he gathers to himself:

All things counter, original, spare, strange;
    Whatever is fickle, freckled (who knows how?)

As a Jesuit priest, Hopkins kept his poetry to himself during
his lifetime. His friend Robert Bridges published some of it in
1919 but it was not until the expanded edition of 1931 that it
began to make an impact. To the Auden generation in England (and the Marianne Moore generation in the United

States) Hopkins became a major influence, and for his refusal to compromise with the Victorian pieties, a god.

Robert Bridges. Hopkins' friend, who became poet laureate in the last year of the Century of Peace (1913), has little of Hopkins' or Hardy's anticipatory rebellion in his poetry. Intellectually he was an indefatigable experimentor. But in the service of the discharged Victorian verities, this complexity of thought and diction pleased mainly the professors of prosody. Housman, though he pronounced Bridges' lyrics "flawless," marched to a different drum.

John Davidson. Among the Georgians like John Drinkwater, James Stephens and Rupert Brooke, who dominated the poetic scene between the turn of the century and World War I, John Davidson found no place. His "proletarian" sensibility had to wait for Hugh MacDiarmid to be matched, but it was Eliot who first called attention to a style as individual as Clough's or Hardy's. Of the poem included in this anthology, Eliot wrote, "Davidson freed himself completely from the poetic diction of English verse of his time," thereby endowing "this thirty-bob-a-week clerk with a dignity that would not have appeared if a more conventional poetic diction had been employed. The personage that Davidson created in this poem," Eliot added, "has haunted me all my life, and the poem to me is a great poem for ever." Davidson, who had long since committed suicide by drowning, was not there to take heart.

A. E. Housman, Housman, who throughout *The Shropshire Lad*, recommends suicide as the only logical response to life's ironies, unlike Davidson made it big—and couldn't have cared less. In effect he had already committed suicide by immuring himself in footnotes to a Roman poet so obscure that even his name and period are uncertain. Yet Housman's lyrics express youth's perennial rejection of adult wisdom with such lilting defiance that they may live as long as the language in which they are written.

Rudyard Kipling. At the time they were published, Kipling's "Barrack Room Ballads" and his more sombre threnodies to British imperialism in its last glory days, were the poetic staple of the English-speaking middle class. Today his reputation as a poet has struck bottom. I submit the three poems included here to back my contention that Kipling is as potent a poet as he is a prose writer (*Kim, Just So Stories,* a dozen short stories equal to any).

W. B. Yeats. It is the virtually unanimous verdict of contemporary poets that Yeats is this century's greatest poet. He will never be a "popular" poet like Chaucer and Shakespeare, or even Keats; but among the "difficult" ones like Milton, Donne and Blake, Yeats will always be an equal—and for his astonishing capacity to *grow* in directness, poignancy and depth through five decades of unflagging creativity, unique.

John Masefield. I am indebted to Auden and John Garrett (*The Poet's Tongue*, 1935) for first bringing to my attention these rollicking, superbly paced and verbally inventive passages from "Reynard the Fox."

Hilaire Belloc. The choice, among Belloc's witty *vers de societé*, has to be between George and his explosive balloon and Lord Lundy's politics. Over the objections of my children, I choose the less well known poem.

James Joyce was as much a major novelist as Hardy and Lawrence, but a minor poet. With few exceptions his poems are sentimental, artful and deliberately "Elizabethan."

D. H. Lawrence. "It is always the lesser artists," says the poet Kenneth Rexroth in his brilliant introduction to Lawrence's *Selected Poems*, "who are artful: they must learn their trade by rote. They must be careful never to make a false step, never to speak out of a carefully synthesized character. The greatest poetry is nobly dishevelled. At least it never shows the scars of taking care. 'Would he have blotted a thousand lines,' said Ben Jonson of Shakespeare. Which thousand? . . . Eliot (who does not write that way), writing of Pound's epigrams, points out that the major poet, unlike the minor, is always writing about everything imaginable, and so, is in good form for the great poem when it comes. Practice makes perfect, and those who wait for the perfect poem before putting pen to paper may wait mute forever."

When Rexroth adds that "Hardy was a major poet. Lawrence was a minor prophet," I disagree only with the implication that Lawrence's poetry is somehow less "major" than Hardy's. The overwhelming conviction, in "tone" as well as in "message," is there even in the early "Georgian" gracenotes of "Cherry Robbers" and "Kisses in the Train."

Edith Sitwell. College undergraduates in the early 'Thirties countered faculty taste by reciting Edith Sitwell, along with Hart Crane, D. H. Lawrence and the early Auden. Sitwell's provocative act at the time was to say nothing with arrogant brilliance. I'm not sure that she was doing otherwise ten years later when she invoked Marlowe to comment on the bombing of London ("Still Falls the Rain") but the performance is still impressive.

Hugh MacDiarmid. First—and perhaps last—of the angry Marxists, this Scots-nationalist poet is at his best in the dialect of his idol, Burns, which he revives with authentic gusto.

Wilfred Owen. Though poets are sometimes poor critics, and tone-deaf to other poets among their contemporaries, none carried this myopia further than Yeats in his *Oxford Book of Modern Verse.* "When I excluded Wilfred Owen, whom I consider unworthy of the poets' corner of a country newspaper," Yeats boasted, "I did not know I was excluding a revered sandwich-board man of the Revolution and that some body has put his worst and most famous poem in a glass-case in the British Museum—however if I had known it I would have excluded him just the same. He is all blood, dirt, and sucked sugar stick . . ."

Greatest of all war poets, Owen was beginning to give promise of even more when killed at the Sambre Canal two days before the end of World War I. He resembles Keats in more than his tragically brief maturity—in nobility of spirit, preoccupation with death and dedication to the *art* of poetry to which he contributed through his use of assonance in rhyme.

Robert Graves. Graves was the only poet to survive being a Georgian and a combat veteran of World War I, and to go on writing good poems well into the seventh decade of this century. Of the moderns, only Yeats—whose poetry Graves' often resembles—combines learning, passion and wit with more mastery.

Basil Bunting. This astonishing late bloomer among twentieth-century English poets missed being a Georgian (and a participant in the Great War) by five years, but has weathered every other poetic influence of the age to emerge, with *Briggflatts* (1970) as an original—quite possibly with his best work still ahead of him.

W. H. Auden. Auden is the last influential *British* poet, almost all of his compelling verse having been written before he left England in 1939 for the United States. Of the three poems included here, in fact, only the last one postdates the shift of scene and citizenship, and that by but a year. Auden long ago repudiated the early poems—some, like the terse "Sir, no man's enemy . . ." and the ineffable "O love the interest itself in thoughtless heaven," he refused even to allow in reprint. But it is the very ingredients which he rejected—the zestful undergraduate nose thumbing, the Marxist-Freudian stance, the mysterious shorthand warnings of some youthful conspiracy about to overthrow the bourgeois establishment—that combined with Auden's wit and resurrection of pre-Elizabethan styles to give his early poems their irresistible impulse.

Stephen Spender wrote many memorable things in the between-Wars period but is cursed (*vis à vis* anthologists) for having created among them one of the noblest poems in the language.

Dylan Thomas. Now that his vogue, cult and hypnotic voice have receded from us by a decade, this poet's undisciplined wordiness can be admitted without detracting from the genius that prevailed over this failing in quite a few poems, including the two included here.

Thom Gunn, like *Philip Larkin,* Norman MacCaig and others, expresses very effectively in his Audenesque poems England's feelings of guilt, humiliation and uncertainty in the post-World War II years.

Ted Hughes. Of England's younger poets in the 'sixties and 'seventies, Ted Hughes is the most gifted and uncompromising.

Derek Walcott. Even before he felt sure enough of himself as a poet to write overtly of the black man's particular élan and hang-ups, Derek Walcott had demonstrated his mastery of English verse. It is revealed in the sonnet on Rembrandt's great picture at the Frick Museum. *Dream on Monkey Mountain,* the most powerful verse drama since Eliot's *Murder in the Cathedral,* rocked the stages of Port of Spain, New York, Toronto and San Francisco in 1970. But it had already been apparent for some time that the English-speaking Caribbean had birthed its first poet. Derek Walcott was born in St. Lucia and lives in Trinidad.

The Beatles. The possibility exists that English poetry, as sampled in this collection, has wound down. If so (and I, for one, hope and pray that it will not be so), the British canon may end as it began with folk poetry. Lyrics, like those of The Beatles, are the first folk poetry of the middle class. Fresh, tart and yet compassionate, these lyrics by John Lennon sing almost as irresistibly as the music with which the Beatles accompanied them.

𝒪

The SIGNET CLASSIC Poetry Series